DISCOVERING THE MEDIEVAL PAST

DISCOVERING THE MEDIEVAL PAST

A LOOK AT THE EVIDENCE

Merry E. Wiesner
University of Wisconsin—Milwaukee

William Bruce Wheeler
University of Tennessee

Kenneth R. Curtis
California State University Long Beach

HOUGHTON MIFFLIN COMPANY **Boston** **New York**

Senior Sponsoring Editor: Nancy Blaine
Editorial Assistant: Annette Fantasia
Associate Project Editor: Reba Libby
Editorial Assistant: Kendra Johnson
Associate Production/Design Coordinator: Christine Gervais
Manufacturing Manager: Florence Cadran
Senior Marketing Manager: Sandra McGuire

Cover image: Players of Castanets and Psalter. Song Book of Nobles. Portugese, 1275. Biblioteca de Ajuda, Lisbon, Portugal. Courtesy Giraudon/Art Resource, NY.

Printed in the U.S.A.

Library of Congress Catalog Card Number: 2002108775

ISBN: 0-618-24668-1

123456789-QUF-06 05 04 03 02

CONTENTS

CHAPTER SIX
The "Commercial Revolution" 115

CHAPTER SEVEN
Medicine and Reproduction in the Middle Ages 132

CHAPTER EIGHT
Facing the Black Death 160

CHAPTER ELEVEN
Lay Piety and Heresy in the Late Middle Ages 240

PREFACE

The title of this book begins with a verb, a choice that reflects our basic philosophy about history. History is not simply something one learns about; it is something one does. One discovers the past, and what makes this pursuit exciting is not only the past that is discovered but also the process of discovery itself. This process can be simultaneously exhilarating and frustrating, enlightening and confusing, but it is always challenging enough to convince those of us who are professional historians to spend our lives at it.

The recognition that history involves discovery as much as physics or astronomy does is often not shared by students, whose classroom experience of history frequently does not extend beyond listening to lectures and reading textbooks. This more passive approach may be particularly strong in courses focusing on eras far removed in time from our own. Providing the background that students need to make historical conclusions and discoveries on their own can be extremely time-consuming, especially in courses on medieval history that may be designed to cover a thousand years in fifteen weeks. *Discovering the Medieval Past: A Look at the Evidence* is thus designed with two goals in mind. The first is to allow students enrolled in medieval history courses to *do* history in the same way we as historians do—to examine a group of original sources in order to answer questions about the past. We feel that contact with original sources is an excellent means of communicating the excitement of doing history, especially for societies that may seem both exotic and familiar, such as the European Middle Ages. The second goal is to provide students with sufficient background in each chapter to allow them to begin the process of interpretation on their own. This book differs from most source collections that cover the Middle Ages in that each chapter includes both sources and background information, and is organized around a question or questions that students can answer from material contained in that chapter. The evidence ranges from the late Roman Empire into the sixteenth century, and the questions cover political, intellectual, social, cultural, and economic issues, but the book does not include sources on every issue normally addressed in medieval history courses.

This book also differs from most medieval source collections in the variety of evidence it presents. We feel that visual material is particularly important in helping students understand an era when the vast majority of people could not read and have included a large number of visual sources, including paintings, cryptograms, tapestries, sculpture, buildings, architectural plans, and maps. In choosing written evidence we again have tried to offer a broad sample—songs, plays, poems, court records, notarial contracts, statistical data, and work regulations all supplement letters, treatises, chronicles, statutes, accounts, and other more traditional sources.

For students to learn history the way we as historians do, they must not only be confronted with the evidence; they must also learn how to use that evidence to arrive at a conclusion. In other words, they must learn historical methodology. Too often methodology (or even the notion that historians *have* a methodology) is reserved for upper-level or graduate methods or historiography courses; students in chronologically—or topically—defined courses are simply presented with historical facts and interpretations without being shown how these were unearthed or formulated. Students may learn that historians hold different interpretations of the significance of an event or individual or different ideas about causation, but they are not informed of how historians come to such conclusions.

Thus, along with evidence and background material, we have provided explicit suggestions about how one might analyze that evidence, guiding students as they reach their own conclusions. As they work through the various chapters, students will discover not only that the sources of historical information are wide-ranging, but also that the methodologies appropriate to understanding and using them are equally diverse. By doing history themselves, students will learn how intellectual historians handle philosophical treatises, economic historians quantitative data, social historians court records, and political and diplomatic historians theoretical treatises and letters. They will also be asked to consider the limitations of their evidence, to explore what historical questions it cannot answer as well as those it can. Instead of passive observers, students become active participants.

Following an approach that we have found successful in many different classroom situations, we have divided each chapter into five parts: The Problem, Sources and Method, The Evidence, Questions to Consider, and Epilogue. The section called "The Problem" presents the general historical background and context for the evidence offered and concludes with the central question or questions explored in the chapter. The section titled "Sources and Method" provides specific information about the sources and suggests ways in which students might best study and analyze this primary evidence. It also discusses how previous historians have evaluated such sources and mentions any major disputes about methodology or interpretation. "The Evidence" forms the core of each chapter, presenting a variety of original sources for students to use in completing the central task. In "Questions to Consider," suggestions are offered about connections among the sources, and students are guided to draw deductions from the evidence. The final section, "Epilogue," traces both the immediate effects of the issue under discussion and its impact on later developments.

Within this framework, we have tried to present a series of historical issues and events from medieval Europe of significance to the instructor as well as of interest to the student. We have also aimed to provide a balance among political, social, diplomatic, intellectual, and cultural history, and among the early-, high-, and late-Middle Ages. In other words, we have attempted to create a kind of historical sampler that we believe will help students learn the methods and skills used by historians. These skills—analyzing arguments, developing hypotheses, comparing evidence, testing conclusions, and reevaluating material—will not only enable students to master historical content; they will also provide the necessary foundation for critical thinking in other college courses and after college as well.

Discovering the Medieval Past is designed to accommodate any format of medieval history course, from the small lecture/discussion class of a liberal arts or community college to the large lecture with discussions led by teaching assistants at a sizable university. The chapters may be used for individual assignments, team projects, class discussions, papers, and exams. Each is self-contained, so that any combination may be assigned. The book is not intended to replace a standard textbook, and it was written to accompany any medieval history text the instructor chooses.

Acknowledgments

In the completion of this book, the authors received assistance from a number of people. Our colleagues and students at the University of Wisconsin–Milwaukee, California State University–Long Beach, and the University of Tennessee, Knoxville, have been generous with their ideas and time. Merry E. Wiesner (-Hanks) wishes especially to thank Katherine French, for suggesting a separate *Discovering the Medieval Past,* and Judith Bennett, Judith Beall, Martha Carlin, Abbas Hamdani, and Marci Sortor for their critiques and suggestions. She also wishes to thank Neil Wiesner-Hanks and Kai and Tyr Wiesner-Hanks for their help in maintaining the author's perspective.

Finally, the authors extend their thanks to the staff of Houghton Mifflin Company for their enthusiastic support.

M.E.W.

W.B.W.

K.R.C.

DISCOVERING THE MEDIEVAL PAST

CHAPTER ONE

SLAVE LAW IN ROMAN AND GERMANIC SOCIETY

THE PROBLEM

In all the cultures of the ancient Mediterranean, some people were slaves, owned as property by other people. In Mesopotamia and Egypt, people became slaves in a variety of ways, and the earliest law codes, such as that of Hammurabi (ca 1780 B.C.E.), include provisions regarding slavery. Many slaves were war captives, brought into the area from outside along with other types of booty. Some were criminals, for whom slavery was the punishment for a crime. Some had been sold into slavery by their parents or had sold themselves into slavery in times of economic hardship. Others became slaves to repay debts, a condition that was often temporary. In these cultures, slaves performed a variety of tasks, from farming to highly skilled professional and administrative work, but the proportion of slaves in the population was not very great and most work was carried out by free persons. Thus, historians describe Mesopotamia and Egypt as slave-using but not slave societies.

By contrast, republican Rome was truly a slave society, in which a significant proportion of the population were slaves—perhaps one-quarter or one-third by the second century B.C.E.—and in which slaves did much of the productive labor. The military conquests of Rome during the second and first centuries B.C.E. provided many new war captives and also increased the wealth of Rome's elite, who invested in huge agricultural estates (termed *latifundia*). These estates were too large to be worked by single peasant families—who were often migrating to the cities in any case—and so an increasing share of agricultural production was carried on by large labor gangs of slaves under the supervision of overseers, who might themselves be slaves. The owners of both the land and the slaves were often absentee, living in Rome or another urban center rather than out on the latifundia themselves. This system of agricultural slavery continued into the Roman Empire, although the influx of new slaves lessened somewhat as military expansion slowed and laws were passed prohibiting the enslavement of subjects of the Empire. In addition, urban slaves who worked as household servants, artisans, teachers, gladiators, or shopkeepers continued to be very common.

The Germanic tribes that gradually migrated into the Roman Empire beginning in the second century were also slave-owning cultures, although the relative number of slaves among them was probably less than that in Rome. When they conquered Roman lands, they generally took a proportion of the slaves and the land for themselves, leaving the rest to the existing Roman proprietors. However, the breakdown in communication and political control that accompanied the disintegration of the Roman Empire in the West made it increasingly difficult for absentee owners to control their estates and to ship their products safely to distant markets. Thus, like many other aspects of life during this period, slavery became increasingly localized and less economically significant than it had been earlier in these areas, although it did not disappear.

Slavery in both Roman and Germanic societies was based not on racial distinctions but on notions of personal freedom that could be very complex. At the heart of this complexity was the issue that a slave was both a person, able to engage in relationships with other persons and to act on his or her own, and a thing, owned by another person. Law codes developed by both Romans and Germans had to balance these two aspects of being a slave, as well as regulate other matters concerning slaves and slavery. They had to establish and protect the boundaries between slave and free, but also establish ways in which those boundaries could be crossed, as slavery was not necessarily a permanent status. Your task in this chapter will be to investigate Roman and Germanic laws regarding slavery during the period 400 to 1000, in order to answer the following questions: How were legal distinctions between slave and free established, structured, and maintained, and how could they be overcome? What similarities and differences are there in Roman and Germanic laws regarding slavery?

SOURCES AND METHOD

When historians investigate legal developments, they often use law codes in conjunction with court records and other documents to examine the actual workings of the law, or to contrast legal theory with reality. For the period we are investigating in this chapter, sources describing actual legal practice in central and western Europe are virtually nonexistent, and so our focus will be strictly on the law codes. (Other sources regarding slavery in the Roman Empire do exist, such as economic treatises, histories of slave revolts, and philosophical discussions of slavery, but there are no parallel sources for early Germanic societies.)

We must thus keep in mind that everything we read is essentially legal theory, describing what is supposed to happen rather than what actually does happen. Law codes are not written in a vacuum, however. They reflect not only the ideals of the legal and political authorities who were their authors, but also these authorities' assumptions about what people—in this case slaves, their owners, and people who came into contact with slaves and their owners—might actually do. In some cases laws also explicitly describe actual conduct, generally as a preamble to a prohibition of this conduct, or a succession of laws implies actual conduct, as prohibitions are made more specific or penalties are made more stringent.

It is important in this chapter, then, to keep in mind the limitations of using law codes as a source, and it is also important to recognize that the law codes we will be using come from two cultures that had very different notions concerning the origin, function, and purpose of law. Roman law began during the republican period as a set of rules governing the private lives of citizens, and was later expanded to include the handling of disputes between Romans and non-Romans and between foreigners under Roman jurisdiction. The first written codification, the Twelve Tables, was made in the middle of the fifth century B.C.E. and posted publicly, giving at least those Romans who could read direct access to it. Legal interpreters called *praetors* and judges called *judices* made decisions based on explicit statutes and also on their own notions of what would be fair and equitable, which gave them a great deal of flexibility. Praetors generally followed the laws set by their predecessors, announcing publicly at the beginning of their terms of office that they would do this, but they also added to the body of law as new issues arose. Thus Roman law was adaptable to new conditions, with jurists in the Empire regarding their work as building on that of earlier centuries rather than negating it. Ultimately all those living within the boundaries of the Roman Empire were regarded as subject to the same law, the *ius gentium,* or "law of peoples."

Roman law regarding slavery—like all Roman law—for most of the republican and imperial periods was a mixture of senatorial statutes, edicts of elected officials, opinions of learned jurists, imperial decrees, and rulings by lesser officials. Under Emperor Theodosius II (r. 408–450), an attempt was made to compile some of the actual imperial decrees, and the resultant Theodosian Code promulgated in 435–438 contained all of the imperial laws issued since the time of the emperor Constantine (r. 311–337) that were still in effect, including those on slavery. Theodosius ruled the eastern half of the Roman Empire (which later came to be called the Byzantine Empire), but his laws were promulgated for both the eastern and western halves. The Theodosian Code was expanded under the direction of the Byzantine Emperor Justinian (r. 527–565), with older and newer laws and the opinions of jurists added. Justinian's Code, promulgated in 529–533 and officially termed the *Corpus Juris Civilis,* became the basis of Byzantine legal procedure for nearly a millennium.

In contrast to Roman written statutory law, Germanic law remained a body of traditions handed down orally for almost a thousand years after the first codification of Roman law. Like all systems of customary law around the world, it was regarded as binding because it represented the immemorial customs of a specific tribe. The ultimate authority in this legal system was not an abstract body of laws or a group of legal interpreters, but the king, whose chief legal function was to "speak the law"—that is, to decide cases based on existing oral tradition; neither the king nor anyone else could (at least in theory) make new laws. This body of custom was regarded as the inalienable possession of all members of a tribe, no matter where they happened to be, and was thus attached to persons rather than to geographic areas the way Roman (and today's) statutory law codes were.

At roughly the same time that codifications of Roman law were promulgated by the emperors Theodosius and Justinian, Germanic kings in western Europe supported the initial written codifications of what had been oral customary law. These codes usually bore the name of the tribe, such as the Lombard Law, the Burgundian Law, or the Salic Law (the law of the Salian Franks). On the continent of Europe, such law codes were written down in Latin, often by Roman jurists employed by Germanic kings, so that they sometimes included Roman legal tradition as well as Germanic customs, particularly in southern Europe, where Roman culture was strongest. In northern Europe and in England—where the laws were initially written in the West Saxon dialect that became Old English—Roman influences were weaker, making the codes of these areas, such as those of the Frisians and the Anglo-Saxons, more purely customary in origin.

When the Germanic tribes came into the Empire, these two notions of the law—statutory and geographic versus customary and personal—came into direct conflict. The problem was solved initially by letting Romans be judged according to written Roman law while non-Romans were judged by their own oral customs. As the Germanic kingdoms became more firmly established, their rulers came to see the merits of a written code, but two legal systems—one for Romans and one for Germanic people—often existed side by side for centuries in these areas. Only in cases that involved a conflict between a Roman and a German was the former expected to follow the new Germanic code. As noted above, however, Roman principles did shape these Germanic codes to some degree. Though the initial codifications claimed to be simply the recording of long-standing customs, in reality the laws often modified customs that no longer fit the needs of the Germanic peoples as they became more settled and adopted some aspects of the more sophisticated Roman culture. Later kings were also not hesitant to make new laws when situations demanded it and to state explicitly that this is what they were doing. Thus Germanic codes gradually evolved from records of tribal customs based on moral sanctions and notions of a common tradition into collections of royal statutes based on the political authority of kings. They remained more closely linked to the ruler than Roman law, and they never included the opinions of legal commentators the way Justinian's Code did, but, like Roman law, they were eventually tied to a geographic area rather than to a group of people.

There were thus significant differences between Roman and Germanic societies in the function and complexity of law, but the legal codes of all these societies included provisions regarding slavery. The sources for this chapter come from seven different law codes, two from Roman tradition—the Theodosian Code and Justinian's Code—and five from Germanic tradition—Burgundian, Salic, Lombard, Alemannic, and Anglo-Saxon. Many of these law codes exist in multiple manuscript versions, with the earliest extant version often dating from centuries after the code was first compiled. This provides much fuel for scholarly disagreement about exactly when they were drawn up, exactly which sections date from the initial codification and which from later revisions, and exactly how certain sections are supposed to read. (Scholars can often trace the path manuscripts followed by noting which errors were recopied by subsequent scribes; often this does not help in determining which versions are more "authentic," however.) For this chapter, we have used the version of these codes most widely accepted by recent scholarship, but you should be aware that any edition or translation of texts like these from manuscript cultures involves a decision on the part of the editor as to which version to use.

To explore the legal definitions of and boundaries between slavery and freedom, we will be examining four basic issues in this chapter: (A) How could a person become a slave, or a slave become free? (B) How were slaves valued, in comparison to other things a person might own, and what limits were placed on the treatment of slaves by their owners? (C) How were personal relationships between slaves and free persons regulated? (D) How were slaves differentiated from free persons in terms of criminal actions committed by them or against them? To assist you in working through the issues in this chapter, provisions in the laws have been grouped according to these four topics rather than being presented in the order in which they appear in the codes. (In many of these codes, particularly the Germanic ones, laws are arranged completely haphazardly in any case, so that the order makes no difference.) Thus, as you are taking notes on the sources, it would be a good idea to draw up a chart for each issue. Other than this, your basic method in this chapter is careful reading.

Source 1 includes selections from the Theodosian Code. According to the selections in Source 1A, what are some of the ways in which one could become a slave in the late Roman Empire? What are some ways in which slaves could become free? According to 1B, what would happen to a master who beat his slaves? According to 1C, what would happen to a woman who had sexual relations with or married one of her slaves? To a man who had sexual relations with one of his slaves? To a decurion (a man who was a member of a local municipal council) who did so? According to 1D, what would happen to rebellious slaves?

Source 2 contains selections from Justinian's Code, which was itself divided into three parts: the *Codex,* actual imperial legislation, including much that was contained in the Theodosian Code; the *Digest,* the opinions of various jurists from throughout the history of Rome; and the *Institutes,* an officially prescribed course for first-year law students, in which some of the opinions found in the *Digest* are repeated. The legal opinions included in the *Digest* sometimes refer to specific imperial statutes, and sometimes simply describe what the commentator saw as Roman tradition in regard to legal categories or procedures. Like legal opinions today, however, the judgments of these jurists shaped the handling of cases, for later judges and lawyers looked to earlier precedents and opinions when making their decisions. They are thus much more important than the opinion of a private person on an issue would be. All the selections included here come from the *Digest.* According to Source 2A, what were some of the ways in which one could become a slave or become free? Would becoming free remove all obligations a slave had toward his master? According to 2C, did slaves have family relationships? According to 2D, what would happen to someone who killed a slave? To slaves whose master was killed while they were within earshot? To runaway slaves and those who protected them?

Putting together the information from Sources 1 and 2, you can begin to develop an idea about the legal status of slaves in the later Roman Empire. What are some of the ways one could cross from slave to free? From free to slave? Is this a hard boundary, as the writers of the *Digest* imply in 2A, or are there intermediate steps? How do restrictions on slave/free sexual relationships help to maintain the boundaries? Why do you think there are gender differences in such restrictions? In what ways do the laws in 1D and 2D regard the slave as a thing? In what ways as a person?

Sources 3 through 7 are selections from Germanic law codes, which were often written down under the reign of one king and then expanded under his successors. Compared with Roman law, Germanic codes were extremely short and consist solely of statements of law, with no juristic opinions such as those contained in the *Digest.* They thus offer a less full picture of slave life than does Roman law, but slaves are mentioned in many of their clauses. In Germanic society, murder, injuries, or insults to honor had once resulted in feuds between individuals and families, but by the time the law codes were written down, a system of monetary compensatory payments—called *wergeld* in the case of murder or *composition* in the case of lesser injuries—was being devised as a substitute. These compensatory payments were set according to the severity of the loss or injury, and also according to the social status of the perpetrator and the victim.

Source 3 comes from one of the earliest Germanic law codes, the Law of Gundobad, drawn up for his Burgundian subjects by King Gundobad (r. 474–516), who ruled the Burgundian kingdom in what is now southeastern France. (Following the principle that customary law applied to persons and not territories, Gundobad also drew up a separate code for his Roman subjects, the *Lex Romana Burgundionem,* at about the same time.) According to the laws in Source 3A, what were some of the ways in which one could become a slave or be freed if one were a slave? According to 3C, what were the penalties for rape of freewomen and slaves? For women who willingly had sexual relations with slaves? According to 3D, what was the relative value of slaves as compared to that of free persons and freedmen (former slaves), at least in regard to their teeth and female honor?

Source 4 comes from the Germanic tribe known as the Franks, who conquered the Burgundian kingdom in 534. The original Frankish code, the *Pactus Legis Salicae,* was issued by King Clovis in about 510 and was amended and revised by many of his successors. (Like all Germanic codes, it did not apply to everyone living under Frankish overlordship; Burgundians living within the Frankish kingdom continued to be judged by Burgundian law for centuries after the conquest.) It includes no laws on how one becomes a slave or is released from slavery, but it does include sections on sexual relations with slaves and on slaves who steal or run away. According to the laws in Source 4C, what would happen to a freeman or freewoman who marries or has sexual intercourse with a slave? To a slave who marries or has sexual intercourse with a free person or another slave? According to 4D, how were the slave's owner's rights balanced against those of the person from whom the slave stole? How were those who encouraged slaves to run away to be punished? How does this punishment compare with that set for slaves who steal?

Source 5 contains selections from the Lombard Laws, written down between 643 and 755 under the direction of various Lombard kings, including King Rothair (issued in 643), King Luitprand (issued 713–735), and King Aistulf (issued 750–755). The Lombards invaded Italy in 568, after the Franks, Burgundians, and other tribes had already established successor kingdoms in parts of the old Roman Empire, and established a kingdom in central and northern Italy that lasted until 774, when it was conquered by the Frankish ruler Charlemagne. Like Burgundian law, Lombard law remained in force for Lombards within Frankish territory for centuries—in fact, until the city-states of Italy began to adopt Roman legal principles and the *Corpus Juris Civilis* in the twelfth century. Lombard law was more comprehensive than the Burgundian and Frankish codes, and included provisions regarding all of the issues we are investigating in this chapter. According to the laws in Source 5A, what were some of the ways in which a person could become a slave in Lombard society? How could a slave be freed? According to 5B, what was the relative value of slaves as compared to horses? According to 5C, how were marriages between slaves, freedpersons, and free people to be handled? According to 5D, how were fugitive slaves and slaves who revolted to be handled?

Source 6 comes from the Germanic

tribe known as the Alamans, who settled in what is now southern Germany and Switzerland in the third century A.D. and wrote their law codes between 613 and 713. Like other Germanic codes, Alamannic law set compensatory payments for various injuries and actions, and also used slavery as a punishment for certain crimes. According to Source 6A, what was one of the ways in which people could become slaves? According to 6B, were there limits on a master's treatment of slaves? According to 6C, what would happen to a free woman who married a slave? According to 6D, what were the relative values placed on men and women from the three basic social groups, free persons, freedpersons, and slaves? How was the rape of slaves to be compensated?

Source 7, the final source for this chapter, contains provisions from Anglo-Saxon law codes from the various kingdoms of England, dating from the sixth through the tenth centuries. These codes were written in Old English, not in Latin, and show no signs of Roman influence, although many of their provisions are similar to those we have seen in other Germanic codes. According to Source 7A, laws issued by Edward the Elder (dated between 901 and 925), what was one way in which a person could become a slave? According to 7B, from the laws of Ine (688–695), what were some of the limitations on a master's treatment of his slaves? According to 7D, laws of Aethelbert of Kent (565–604) and Alfred (890–899), what was the punishment for rape of a slave? How did this differ depending on the status of the slave and the perpetrator?

You now need to put together the Germanic material in the same way that you did the Roman. How could people in Germanic society move from free to slave? From slave to free? Are there intermediate steps between these two, and if so, how do the rights of these people differ from those of free people and slaves? What are the consequences of various types of slave/free sexual relationships? Are there hierarchies of status and value among slaves? On what are these based? Do the laws regarding crimes against slaves and crimes committed by slaves tend to view slaves as things or as persons?

THE EVIDENCE

Source 1 from Clyde Pharr, editor, The Theodosian Code *(Princeton, N.J.: Princeton University Press, 1952), Sections 3.3.1; 4.6.7; 5.6.3; 5.9.1; 7.13.16; 7.18.4; 9.12.1–2; 9.9.1–3, 6; 10.10.33; 14.18.1.*

1. Theodosian Code

A. Slave to Free/Free to Slave

[3.3.1] All those persons whom the piteous fortune of their parents has consigned to slavery while their parents thereby were seeking sustenance shall be restored to their original status of free birth. Certainly no person shall demand repayment of the purchase price, if he has been compensated by the slavery of a freeborn person for a space of time that is not too short.

INTERPRETATION: If a father, forced by need, should sell any freeborn child whatsoever, the child cannot remain in perpetual slavery, but if he has made compensation by his slavery, he shall be restored to his freeborn status without even the repayment of the purchase price.

[4.6.7] We sanction that the name of natural children shall be placed upon those who have been begotten and brought into this world as the result of a lawful union without an honorable performance of the marriage ceremony. But it is established that children born from the womb of a slave woman are slaves, according to the law . . . [I]f natural children have been born from a slave woman and have not been manumitted by their master, they are reckoned among the slaves belonging to his inheritance.

[5.6.3] We have subjected the Scyrae, a barbarian nation, to Our power after We had routed a very great force of Chuni, with whom they had allied themselves. Therefore We grant to all persons the opportunity to supply their own fields with men of the aforesaid race.

[5.9.1] If any person should take up a boy or a girl child that has been cast out of its home with the knowledge and consent of its father or owner, and if he should rear this child to strength with his own sustenance, he shall have the right to keep the said child under the same status as he wished it to have when he took charge of it, that is, as his child or as a slave, whichever he should prefer.

[14.18.1] If there should be any persons who adopt the profession of mendicancy[1] and who are induced to seek their livelihood at public expense, each of them shall be examined. The soundness of body and the vigor of years of each

1. **mendicancy:** begging.

one of them shall be investigated. In the case of those who are able, the necessity shall be placed upon them that the zealous and diligent informer shall obtain the ownership of those beggars who are held bound by their servile status, and such informer shall be supported by the right to the perpetual colonate[2] of those beggars who are attended by only the liberty of their birth rights, provided that the informer should betray and prove such sloth.

[7.13.16] In the matter of defense against hostile attacks,[3] We order that consideration be given not only to the legal status of soldiers, but also to their physical strength. Although We believe that freeborn persons are aroused by love of country, We exhort slaves[4] also, by the authority of this edict, that as soon as possible they shall offer themselves for the labors of war, and if they receive their arms as men fit for military service, they shall obtain the reward of freedom, and they shall also receive two solidi each for travel money. Especially, of course, do We urge this service upon the slaves of those persons who are retained in the armed imperial service, and likewise upon the slaves of federated allies and of conquered peoples, since it is evident that they are making war also along with their masters.

[7.18.4] [In the case of deserters,] if a slave should surrender such deserter, he shall be given freedom. If a freeborn person of moderate status should surrender such deserter, he shall gain immunity.[5]

B. Value and Treatment of Slaves

[9.12.1–2] If a master should beat a slave with light rods or lashes or if he should cast him into chains for the purpose of custody, he shall not endure any fear of criminal charges if the slave should die, for We abolish all consideration of time limitations and legal interpretation.[6] The master shall not, indeed, use his own right immoderately, but he shall be guilty of homicide if he should kill the slave voluntarily by a blow of a club or of a stone, at any rate if he should use a weapon and inflict a lethal wound or should order the slave to be hanged by a noose, or if he should command by a shameful order that he be thrown from a high place or should administer the virus of a poison or should lacerate his body by public punishments,[7] that is, by cutting through his sides with the claws of wild beasts[8] or by applying fire and burning his body, or if with the

2. **colonate:** forced labor on farms.

3. At this time the Roman Empire was gradually crumbling from the attacks of the barbarians.

4. In violation of long-established Roman custom.

5. From compulsory public services, including taxes.

6. The references seem to be to preceding laws, which specified distinctions depending on whether a slave died immediately or after a period of time, and which contained various technicalities.

7. Types of punishment that were inflicted for certain public crimes.

8. Implements of torture, actually made of metal.

savagery of monstrous barbarians he should force bodies and limbs weakening and flowing with dark blood, mingled with gore, to surrender their life almost in the midst of tortures.

Whenever such chance attends the beating of slaves by their masters that the slaves die, the masters shall be free from blame if by the correction of very evil deeds they wished to obtain better conduct on the part of their household slaves. . . .

INTERPRETATION: If a slave should die while his master is punishing a fault, the master shall not be held on the charge of homicide, because he is guilty of homicide only if he is convicted of having intended to kill the slave. For disciplinary correction is not reckoned as a crime.

C. Slave/Free Relations

[9.9.1–6] If any woman is discovered to have a clandestine love affair with her slave, she shall be subject to the capital sentence, and the rascally slave shall be delivered to the flames. All persons shall have the right to bring an accusation of this public crime; office staffs shall have the right to report it; even a slave shall have permission to lodge information, and freedom shall be granted to him if the crime is proved, although punishment threatens him if he makes a false accusation. 1. If a woman has been so married[9] before the issuance of this law, she shall be separated from such an association, shall be deprived not only of her home but also of participation in the life of the province, and shall mourn the absence of her exiled lover. 2. The children also whom she bears from this union shall be stripped of all the insignia of rank. They shall remain in bare freedom, and neither through themselves nor through the interposition of another person shall they receive anything under any title of a will from the property of the woman. 3. Moreover, the inheritance of the woman, in case of intestacy, shall be granted either to her children, if she has legitimate ones, or to the nearest kinsmen and cognates, or to the person whom the rule of law admits, so that whatever of their own property her former lover and the children conceived from him appear by any chance to have had shall be joined to the property of the woman and may be vindicated by the aforesaid successors. . . .

6. For after the issuance of this law We punish by death those persons who commit this crime. But those who have been separated in accordance with this law and secretly come together again and renew the forbidden union and who are convicted by the evidence of slaves or that of the office of the special investigator or also by the information of nearest kinsmen shall sustain a similar penalty.

INTERPRETATION: If any freeborn woman should join herself secretly to her own slave, she shall suffer capital punishment. A slave also who should be con-

9. A loose use of the word *marriage,* as slaves could not enter legally recognized marriages (*conubia*) because those were contracts available only to free persons. Instead they were joined in less formal unions termed *contubernia.*

victed of adultery with his mistress shall be burned by fire. Whoever wishes shall have it in his power to bring accusation of a crime of this kind. Even slaves or maidservants, if they should bring an accusation of this crime, shall be heard, on this condition, however, that they shall obtain their freedom if they prove their accusation; that if they falsify, they shall be punished. The inheritance of a woman who defiles herself with such a crime shall be granted either to her children, if they were conceived from her husband, or to those near kinsmen who succeed according to law.

[12.1.6] Although it appears unworthy for men, even though not endowed with any high rank, to descend to sordid marriages with slave women, nevertheless this practice is not prohibited by law; but a legal marriage cannot exist with servile persons, and from a slave union of this kind, slaves are born. We command, therefore, that decurions shall not be led by their lust to take refuge in the bosom of the most powerful houses. For if a decurion should be secretly united with any slave woman belonging to another man and if the overseers and procurators should not be aware of this, We order that the woman shall be cast into the mines through sentence of the judge, and the decurion himself shall be deported to an island; his movable property and his urban slaves shall be confiscated; his landed estates and rustic slaves shall be delivered to the municipality of which he had been a decurion, if he had been freed from paternal power and has no children or parents, or even close kinsmen, who may be called to his inheritance, according to the order of the law. But if the overseers or procurators of the place in which the disgraceful act was committed were aware of it and were unwilling to divulge this crime of which they were aware, they shall be cast into the mines. But if the master permitted such offense to be committed or afterwards learned of the deed and concealed it, and if indeed, it was perpetrated on his farm, the farm with the slaves and flocks and all other things which are used in rural cultivation shall be [confiscated].

D. Criminal Actions by/toward Slaves

[10.10.33] The lawful distinction between slavery and freedom shall stand firm. We sanction the rights of masters by the restitution of their slaves, who shall not rebel with impunity.

Source 2 from S. P. Scott, translator, Corpus Juris Civilis: The Civil Law *(Cincinnati, Ohio: The Central Trust, 1932), Sections 1.5.4–5; 9.2.2; 11.4.1; 29.5.1; 37.14.1, 19; 38.10.10; 40.1.5.*

2. Selections from the *Digest* of Justinian's Code

A. Slave to Free/Free to Slave

[1.5.4] Liberty is the natural power of doing whatever anyone wishes to do unless he is prevented in some way, by force or by law.

(1) Slavery is an institution of the Law of Nations by means of which anyone may subject one man to the control of another, contrary to nature.

(2) Slaves are so called for the reason that military commanders were accustomed to sell their captives, and in this manner to preserve them, instead of putting them to death.

(3) They are styled *mancipia,* because they are taken by the hands [*manus*] of their enemies.

[1.5.5] One condition is common to all slaves; but of persons who are free some are born such, and others are manumitted.

(1) Slaves are brought under our ownership either by the Civil Law or by that of Nations. This is done by the Civil Law where anyone who is over twenty years of age permits himself to be sold for the sake of sharing in his own price. Slaves become our property by the Law of Nations when they are either taken from the enemy, or are born of our female slaves.

(2) Persons are born free who are born from a free mother, and it is sufficient for her to have been free at the time when her child was born, even though she may have been a slave when she conceived; and, on the other hand, if she was free when she conceived, and was a slave when she brought forth, it has been established that her child is born free, nor does it make any difference whether she conceived in a lawful marriage or through promiscuous intercourse; because the misfortune of the mother should not be a source of injury to her unborn child.

(3) Hence the following question arose, where a female slave who was pregnant, has been manumitted, and is afterwards again made a slave, or, after having been expelled from the city, should bring forth a child, whether that child should be free or a slave? It was very properly established that it was born free; and that it is sufficient for a child who is unborn that its mother should have been free during the intermediate time.

[40.1.5] If a slave should allege that he was purchased with his own money, he can appear in court against his master, whose good faith he impugns, and complain that he has not been manumitted by him; but he must do this at Rome, before the Urban Prefect, or in the provinces before the Governor, in accordance with the Sacred Constitutions of the Divine Brothers; under the penalty, however, of being condemned to the mines, if he should attempt this and not prove his case; unless his master prefers that he be restored to him, and then it should be decided that he will not be liable to a more severe penalty.

(1) Where, however, a slave is ordered to be free after having rendered his accounts, an arbiter between the slave and his master, that is to say, the heir, shall be appointed for the purpose of having the accounts rendered in his presence.

[37.14.1] Governors should hear the complaints of patrons against their freedmen, and their cases should be tried without delay; for if a freedman is ungrateful, he should not go unpunished. Where, however, the freedman fails in the duty which he owes to his patron, his patroness, or their children, he should only be punished lightly, with a warning that a more severe penalty will be imposed if he again gives cause for complaint, and then be dismissed. But if he is guilty of insult or abuse of his patrons, he should be sent into temporary exile. If he offers them personal violence, he must be sentenced to the mines.

[37.14.19] A freedman is ungrateful when he does not show proper respect for his patron, or refuses to manage his property, or undertake the guardianship of his children.

C. Slave/Free Relations

[38.10.10] We make use of this term, that is to say, cognates, even with reference to slaves. Therefore, we speak of the parents, the children, and the brothers of slaves; but cognation is not recognized by servile laws.

D. Criminal Actions by/toward Slaves

[11.4.1] He who conceals a fugitive slave is a thief.

(1) The Senate decreed that fugitive slaves shall not be admitted on land or be protected by the superintendents or agents of the possessors of the same, and prescribed a fine. But, if anyone should, within twenty days, restore fugitive slaves to their owners, or bring them before magistrates, what they had previously done will be pardoned; but it was afterwards stated in the same Decree of the Senate that immunity is granted to anyone who restores fugitive slaves to their masters, or produces them before a magistrate within the prescribed time, when they are found on his premises. . . .

(4) And the magistrates are very properly notified to detain them carefully in custody to prevent their escape. . . .

(7) Careful custody permits the use of irons.

[9.2.2] It is provided by the first section of the *Lex Aquilia* that, "Where anyone unlawfully kills a male or female slave belonging to another, or a quadruped included in the class of cattle, let him be required to pay a sum equal to the greatest value that the same was worth during the past year."

[29.5.1] As no household can be safe unless slaves are compelled, under peril of their lives, to protect their masters, not only from persons belonging to his family, but also from strangers, certain decrees of the Senate were enacted with reference to putting to public torture all the slaves belonging to a household in case of the violent death of their master. . . , for the reason that slaves are punished whenever they do not assist their master against anyone who is guilty of violence towards him, when they are able to do so. . . . Whenever slaves can afford assistance to their master, they should not prefer their own safety to his. Moreover, a female slave who is in the same room with her mistress can give her assistance, if not with her body, certainly by crying out, so that those who are in the house or the neighbors can hear her; and this is evident even if she should allege that the murderer threatened her with death if she cried out. She ought, therefore, to undergo capital punishment, to prevent other slaves from thinking that they should consult their own safety when their master is in danger.

Source 3 from Katherine Fischer Drew, translator, The Burgundian Code *(Philadelphia: University of Pennsylvania Press, 1972), Sections 26, 30, 33, 35, 88, Constitutiones Extravagentes 21.9.*

3. Selections from *The Burgundian Code*

A. Slave to Free/Free to Slave

[Constitutiones Extravagantes, 21.9] If anyone shall buy another's slave from the Franks, let him prove with suitable witnesses how much and what sort of price he paid and when witnesses have been sworn in, they shall make oath in the following manner: "We saw him pay the price in our presence, and he who purchased the slave did not do so through any fraud or connivance with the enemy." And if suitable witnesses shall give oaths in this manner, let him receive back only the price which he paid; and let him not seek back the cost of support and let him return the slave without delay to his former owner.

[88] Since the title of emancipation takes precedence over the law of possession, great care must be exercised in such matters. And therefore it should be observed, that if anyone wishes to manumit a slave, he may do so by giving him his liberty through a legally competent document; or if anyone wishes to give freedom to a bondservant without a written document, let the manumission thus conferred by confirmed with the witness of not less than five or seven native freemen, because it is not fitting to present a smaller number of witnesses than is required when the manumission is in written form.

C. Slave/Free Relations

[30] OF WOMEN VIOLATED.

1. Whatever native freeman does violence to a maidservant, and force can be proved, let him pay twelve solidi to him to whom the maidservant belongs.
2. If a slave does this, let him receive a hundred fifty blows.

[35] OF THE PUNISHMENT OF SLAVES WHO COMMIT A CRIMINAL ASSAULT ON FREEBORN WOMEN.

1. If any slave does violence to a native freewoman, and if she complains and is clearly able to prove this, let the slave be killed for the crime committed.
2. If indeed a native free girl unites voluntarily with a slave, we order both to be killed.
3. But if the relatives of the girl do not wish to punish their own relative, let the girl be deprived of her free status and delivered into servitude to the king.

D. Criminal Actions by/toward Slaves

[26] OF KNOCKING OUT TEETH.

1. If anyone by chance strikes out the teeth of a Burgundian of the highest class, or of a Roman noble, let him be compelled to pay fifteen solidi.
2. For middle-class freeborn people, either Burgundian or Roman, if a tooth is knocked out, let composition be made in the sum of ten solidi.
3. For persons of the lowest class, five solidi.
4. If a slave voluntarily strikes out the tooth of a native freeman, let him be condemned to have a hand cut off; if the loss which has been set forth above has been committed by accident, let him pay the price for the tooth according to the status of the person.
5. If any native freeman strikes out the tooth of a freedman, let him pay him three solidi. If he strikes out the tooth of another's slave, let him pay two solidi to him to whom the slave belongs.

[33] OF INJURIES WHICH ARE SUFFERED BY WOMEN.

1. If any native freewoman has her hair cut off and is humiliated without cause (when innocent) by any native freeman in her home or on the road, and this can be proved with witnesses, let the doer of the deed pay her twelve solidi, and let the amount of the fine be twelve solidi.
2. If this was done to a freedwoman, let him pay her six solidi.
3. If this was done to a maidservant, let him pay her three solidi, and let the amount of the fine be three solidi.
4. If this injury (shame, disgrace) is inflicted by a slave on a native free-

woman, let him receive two hundred blows; if a freedwoman, let him receive a hundred blows; if a maidservant, let him receive seventy-five blows.

5. If indeed the woman whose injury we have ordered to be punished in this manner commits fornication voluntarily (i.e., if she yields), let nothing be sought for the injury suffered.

Source 4 from Katherine Fischer Drew, translator, The Laws of the Salian Franks *(Philadelphia: University of Pennsylvania Press, 1991), Sections 25, 39, 40, 98. Copyright © 1991 University of Pennsylvania Press. Reprinted with permission.*

4. Selections from Salic Law

C. Slave/Free Relations

[25] ON HAVING INTERCOURSE WITH SLAVE GIRLS OR BOYS

1. The freeman who has intercourse with someone else's slave girl, and it is proved against him . . . , shall be liable to pay six hundred denarii (i.e., fifteen solid[i]) to the slave girl's lord.

2. The man who has intercourse with a slave girl belonging to the king and it is proved against him . . . , shall be liable to pay twelve hundred denarii (i.e., thirty solidi).

3. The freeman who publicly joins himself with (i.e., marries) another man's slave girl, shall remain with her in servitude.

4. And likewise the free woman who takes someone else's slave in marriage shall remain in servitude.

5. If a slave has intercourse with the slave girl of another lord and the girl dies as a result of this crime, the slave himself shall pay two hundred forty denarii (i.e., six solidi) to the girl's lord or he shall be castrated; the slave's lord shall pay the value of the girl to her lord.

6. If the slave girl has not died . . . , the slave shall receive three hundred lashes or, to spare his back, he shall pay one hundred twenty denarii (i.e., three solidi) to the girl's lord.

7. If a slave joins another man's slave girl to himself in marriage without the consent of her lord . . . , he shall be lashed or clear himself by paying one hundred twenty denarii (i.e., three solidi) to the girl's lord.

[98] CONCERNING THE WOMAN WHO JOINS HERSELF TO HER SLAVE

1. If a woman joins herself in marriage with her own slave, the fisc[10] shall acquire all her possessions and she herself will be outlawed.

10. **fisc:** king's treasury.

2. If one of her relatives kills her, nothing may be required from that relative or the fisc for her death. The slave shall be placed in the most severe torture, that is, he shall be placed on the wheel. And if one of the relatives of the woman gives her either food or shelter, he shall be liable to pay fifteen solidi.

D. Criminal Actions by/toward Slaves

[40] CONCERNING THE SLAVE ACCUSED OF THEFT

1. In the case where a slave is accused of theft, if [it is a case where] a freeman would pay six hundred denarii (i.e., fifteen solidi) in composition, the slave stretched on a rack shall receive one hundred twenty blows of the lash.

2. If he [the slave] confesses before torture and it is agreeable to the slave's lord, he may pay one hundred twenty denarii (i.e., three solidi) for his back [i.e., to avoid the lashes]; and the slave's lord shall return the value of the property stolen to its owner. . . .

4. . . . If indeed he [the slave] confessed in the earlier torture, i.e., before the one hundred twenty lashes were completed, let him [the slave] be castrated or pay two hundred forty denarii (i.e., six solidi); the lord should restore the value of the property stolen to its owner.

5. If he [the slave] is guilty of a crime for which a freeman or a Frank would be liable to pay eight thousand denarii (i.e., two hundred solidi), let the slave compound fifteen solidi (i.e., six hundred denarii). If indeed the slave is guilty of a more serious offense—one for which a freeman would be liable to pay eighteen hundred denarii (i.e., forty-five solidi)—and the slave confessed during torture, he shall be subjected to capital punishment. . . .

11. If indeed it is a female slave accused of an offense for which a male slave would be castrated, then she should be liable to pay two hundred forty denarii (i.e., six solidi)—if it is agreeable for her lord to pay this—or she should be subjected to two hundred forty lashes.

[39] ON THOSE WHO INSTIGATE SLAVES TO RUN AWAY

1. If a man entices away the bondsmen of another man and this is proved against him . . . , he shall be liable to pay six hundred denarii (i.e., fifteen solidi) [in addition to return of the bondsmen plus a payment for the time their labor was lost].

Source 5 from Katherine Fischer Drew, editor, The Lombard Laws *(Philadelphia: University of Pennsylvania Press, 1973), Sections Rothair 156, 217, 221, 222, 267, 280, 333, 334; Luitprand 55, 63, 80, 140, 152.*

5. Selections from Lombard Laws

A. Slave to Free/Free to Slave

[Rothair 156] In the case of a natural son who is born to another man's woman slave, if the father purchases him and gives him his freedom by the formal procedure . . . , he shall remain free. But if the father does not free him, the natural son shall be a slave to him to whom the mother slave belongs.

[Luitprand 63] He who renders false testimony against anyone else, or sets his hand knowingly to a false charter, and this fraud becomes evident, shall pay his wergeld as composition,[11] half to the king and half to him whose case it is. If the guilty party does not have enough to pay the composition, a public official ought to hand him over as a slave to him who was injured, and he [the offender] shall serve him as a slave.

[Luitprand 80] In connection with thieves, each judge shall make a prison underground in his district. When a thief has been found, he shall pay composition for his theft, and then the judge shall seize him and put him in prison for two or three years, and afterwards shall set him free.

If the thief is such a person that he does not have enough to pay the composition for theft, the judge ought to hand him over to the man who suffered the theft, and that one may do with him as he pleases.

If afterwards the thief is taken again in theft, he [the judge] shall shave . . . and beat him for punishment as befits a thief, and shall put a brand on his forehead and face. If the thief does not correct himself and if after such punishment he has again been taken in theft, then the judge shall sell him outside the province, and the judge shall have his sale price provided, nevertheless, that it be a proved case for the judge ought not to sell the man without certain proof.

[Luitprand 152] If the man who is prodigal or ruined, or who has sold or dissipated his substance, or for other reasons does not have that with which to pay composition, commits theft or adultery or a breach of the peace . . . or injures another man and the composition for this is twenty solidi or more, then a public representative ought to hand him over as a slave to the man who suffered such illegal acts.

11. **composition:** restitution.

[Luitprand 55] If anyone makes his slave folkfree and legally independent . . . or sets him free from himself in any manner by giving him into the hand of the king or by leading him before the altar of a church, and if afterwards that freedman [continues] to serve at the will of his patron, the freedman ought at frequent intervals to make clear his liberty to the judge and to his neighbors and [remind them] of the manner in which he was freed.

Afterward the patron or his heirs may at no time bring complaints against him who was freed by saying that because [he continues to serve] he ought still to obey, for it was only on account of the goodness of his lord that the former slave continued to serve his commands of his own free will. He shall remain permanently free.

[Luitprand 140] If a freeman has a man and woman slave, or aldius and aldia,[12] who are married, and, inspired by hatred of the human race, he has intercourse with that woman whose husband is the slave or with the aldia whose husband is the aldius, he has committed adultery and we decree that he shall lose that slave or aldius with whose wife he committed adultery and the woman as well. They shall go free where they wish and shall be as much folkfree . . . as if they had been released by the formal procedure for alienation . . .—for it is not pleasing to God that any man should have intercourse with the wife of another.

B. Value and Treatment of Slaves

[Rothair 333] On mares in foal. He who strikes a mare in foal and causes a miscarriage shall pay one solidus as composition. If the mare dies, he shall pay as above for it and its young.

[Rothair 334] On pregnant woman slaves. He who strikes a woman slave large with child and causes a miscarriage shall pay three solidi as composition. If, moreover, she dies from the blow, he shall pay composition for her and likewise for the child who died in her womb.

C. Slave/Free Relations

[Rothair 217] On the aldia who marries a slave. The aldia or freedwoman who enters another man's house to a husband and marries a slave shall lose her liberty. But if the husband's lord neglects to reduce her to servitude, then when her husband dies she may go forth together with her children and all the property which she brought with her when she came to her husband. But she shall have no more than this as an indication of her mistake in marrying a slave.

12. **aldius** and **aldia:** freedman and freedwoman.

[Rothair 221] The slave who dares to marry a free woman or girl shall lose his life. With regard to the woman who consented to a slave, her relatives have the right to kill her or to sell her outside the country and to do what they wish with her property. And if her relatives delay in doing this, then the king's gastald or schultheis[13] shall lead her to the king's court and place her there in the women's apartments among the female slaves.

[Rothair 222] On marrying one's own woman slave. If any man wishes to marry his own woman slave, he may do so. Nevertheless he ought to free her, that is, make her worthy born . . . , and he ought to do it legally by the proper formal procedure. . . . She shall then be known as a free and legal wife and her children may become the legal heirs of their father.

D. Criminal Actions by/toward Slaves

[Rothair 267] The boatman who knowingly transports fugitive bondsmen, and it is proved, shall search for them and return them together with any properties taken with them to their proper owner. If the fugitives have gone elsewhere and cannot be found, then the value of those bondsmen together with the sworn value of the property which they carried with them shall be paid by that ferryman who knowingly transported the fugitives. In addition, the ferryman shall pay twenty solidi as composition to the king's fisc.

[Rothair 280] On seditious acts committed by field slaves. If, for any reason, rustics[14] . . . associate together for plotting or committing seditious acts such as, when a lord is trying to take a bondsman or animal from his slave's house, blocking the way or taking the bondsman or animal, then he who was at the head of these rustics shall either be killed or redeem his life by the payment of a composition equal to that amount at which he is valued. And each of those who participated in this evil sedition shall pay twelve solidi as composition, half to the king and half to him who bore the injury or before whom he presumed to place himself. And if that one who was trying to take his property endures blows or suffers violence from these rustics, composition for such blows or violence shall be paid to him just as is stated above, and the rustics shall suffer such punishment as is noted above for this presumption. If one of the rustics is killed no payment shall be required because he who killed him did it while defending himself and in protecting his own property.

13. **gastald** and **schultheis:** royal officials.

14. **rustics:** field slaves.

Source 6 from Theodore John Rivers, translator, Laws of the Alamans and Bavarians *(Philadelphia: University of Pennsylvania Press, 1977), Alamannic Law, Sections 17, 18, 37, 39, 75. Copyright © 1977 University of Pennsylvania Press. Reprinted by permission of the translator.*

6. Laws of the Alamans

A. Slave to Free/Free to Slave

[39] We prohibit incestuous marriages. Accordingly, it is not permitted to have as wife a mother-in-law, daughter-in-law, step-daughter, step-mother, brother's daughter, sister's daughter, brother's wife, or wife's sister. Brother's children and sister's children are under no pretext to be joined together. If anyone acts against this, let them [the married pair] be separated by the judges in that place, and let them lose all their property, which the public treasury shall acquire. If there are lesser persons who pollute themselves through an illicit union, let them lose their freedom; let them be added to the public slaves.

B. Value and Treatment of Slaves

[37] 1. Let no one sell slaves . . . outside the province, whether among pagans or Christians, unless it is done by the order of the duke.

C. Slave/Free Relations

[17] 1. Concerning maidservants.[15] If a freewoman was manumitted by a charter or in a church, and after this she married a slave, let her remain permanently a maidservant of the church.

2. If, however, a free Alamannic woman marries a church slave and refuses the servile work of a maidservant, let her depart. If, however, she gives birth to sons or daughters there, let them remain slaves and maidservants permanently, and let them not have the right of departure.

D. Criminal Actions by/toward Slaves

[18] 1. Concerning waylayers . . . , [if a man blocks the way of a freeman], let him pay six solidi.

2. If it is a freedman [who is blocked], let the perpetrator pay four solidi.

3. If it is a slave, three solidi.

4. If he does this to a free Alamannic woman, let him compensate with twelve solidi.

15. **maidservants:** here, female slaves.

5. If it is a freedwoman, let him compensate with eight solidi.
6. If it is a maidservant, let him pay four solidi.
7. If a man seizes her hair, [let him compensate similarly].

[75] 1. If anyone lies with another's chambermaid against her will, let him compensate with six solidi.

2. And if anyone lies with the first maid of the textile workshop against her will, let him compensate with six solidi.

3. If anyone lies with other maids of the textile workshop against their will, let him compensate with three solidi.

Source 7 from F. L. Attenborough, editor, Laws of the Earliest English Kings, *Laws of Edward the Elder, Section 6; Laws of Ine, Section 3. Laws of Aethelbert, Sections 10, 11, 16; Laws of Alfred, Section 25.*

7. Laws of Anglo-Saxon Kings

A. Slave to Free/Free to Slave

[Edward the Elder 6] If any man, through [being found guilty of] an accusation of stealing, forfeits his freedom and gives up his person to his lord, and his kinsmen forsake him, and he knows no one who will make legal amends for him, he shall do such servile labour as may be required, and his kinsmen shall have no right to his wergeld [if he is slain].

B. Value and Treatment of Slaves

[Ine 3] If a slave works on Sunday by his lord's command, he shall become free, and the lord shall pay a fine of 30 shillings.

§1. If, however, the slave works without the cognisance of his master, he shall undergo the lash or pay the fine in lieu thereof.

§2. If, however, a freeman works on that day, except by his lord's command, he shall be reduced to slavery, or [pay a fine of] 60 shillings. A priest shall pay a double fine.

D. Criminal Actions by/toward Slaves

[Aethelbert 10] If a man lies with a maiden belonging to the king, he shall pay 50 shillings compensation.

[Aethelbert 11] If she is a grinding slave, he shall pay 25 shillings compensation. [If she is of the] third [class], [he shall pay] 12 shillings compensation.

[Aethelbert 16] If a man lies with a commoner's serving maid, he shall pay 6 shillings compensation; [if he lies] with a slave of the second class, [he shall pay] 50 sceattas[16] [compensation]; if with one of the third class, 30 sceattas.

[Alfred 25] If anyone rapes the slave of a commoner, he shall pay 5 shillings to the commoner, and a fine of 60 shillings.[17]

§1. If a slave rapes a slave, castration shall be required as compensation.

16. 20 sceattas = one shilling.

17. The 60 shillings went to the king's treasury.

QUESTIONS TO CONSIDER

The central questions for this chapter ask you to do two things: investigate the boundaries between slave and free in various law codes, and then compare these issues in Roman and Germanic cultures. Your answers to the second question are based, of course, on your answers to the first, and the Sources and Method section suggests some of the questions you might ask yourself about slave law in each of these two cultures.

In addition to these, in the Roman codes, what role does military conquest play in the determination of slave and free? Does conquest simply provide slaves, or does it also offer them opportunities? What limitations were placed on a male owner's treatment of his slaves? On a female owner's treatment of her slaves? What obligations does—or could—the status of freedman or freedwoman entail? Do these obligations make this status appear closer to that of a slave or that of a free person? How are family relationships among slaves regarded legally? The provision in Justinian's Code (Source 2D) that slaves who did not prevent a master's being killed were to be killed themselves may seem very harsh. Why do you think this was part of Roman slave law? What other provisions strike you as especially harsh, and why might these have been enacted? Given the role of slavery in the Roman economy, why were there such strong provisions about runaway slaves? Other than the restrictions on those who aided runaways, what laws discuss actions by those who were neither owners nor slaves? How might these have shaped general attitudes toward slavery and slaves?

Turning now to the Germanic codes, what are the hierarchies you find among slaves based on? Given the nature of Germanic society, in which tribes often moved around a great deal, why do you think there was so much concern about not taking slaves away to other areas, even if it was their owners who were taking them? Historians often point out the importance of personal honor in Germanic societies. Do you find evidence of this? Do slaves have honor? Do any of their actions affect the honor of others in ways that the actions of free people do not? A close examination of the laws indicates that the only nonpunishable sexual relation between slave and free was a man marrying his own slave among the Lombards, mentioned in Source 5C. Why do you think this was allowed? What must a man do before he does this, and why do you think this was important?

You are now ready to investigate some comparative questions: In what ways do the different notions of the law in Roman and Germanic cultures—territorial versus personal, statutory versus traditional—emerge in laws regarding slavery? When comparing Germanic culture to Roman, historians often point to the relative propensity to interpersonal violence and the importance of the family among the Germans. Do the laws from these two cultures regarding slavery provide evidence of these factors? What evidence do you see of the different economic structures in the two cultures, i.e., of the greater complexity of the Roman economic system?

Comparing two cultures involves exploring continuities along with contrasts. One of the issues in slave systems was how to punish slaves without harming their owners. How do the laws handle this? Do you see much difference between Roman and Germanic cultures in this? How do the laws handle the issue that slaves do not own property? How are the actions and obligations of freed slaves toward their former masters handled in both cultures? Why do you think it was important in both cultures to have an intermediate status between slave and free? Do you see much difference with regard to laws concerning sexual relations between slaves and free persons in the two cultures? Why might there have been continuity in this?

After putting all of this material together, you are now ready to answer the central questions for this chapter: How were legal distinctions between slave and free established, structured, and maintained, and how could they be overcome? What similarities and differences are there in Roman and Germanic law regarding slavery?

EPILOGUE

During the Renaissance, scholars and thinkers began to divide the history of Europe into three stages, ancient, medieval, and modern, a division that has persisted until today. They viewed the end of the Roman Empire as a dramatic break in history, and saw the Germanic successor states as being sharply different from Rome. This view is increasingly being modified today as historians point to a number of continuities between late ancient and early medieval society.

As you have discovered in this chapter, the slave system was one of those continuities, for slavery did not disappear from the European scene with the fall of Rome, nor did the spread of Christianity lead to an end of slavery. (Christianity did not oppose slavery on moral grounds, although it did praise those who chose to free their slaves and pushed for slaves being allowed to marry in legally binding ceremonies.) Gradually, however, more people came to occupy the intermediate stage between slave and free that you have seen in these laws, which became known as serfdom. Serfdom was a legal condition in which people were personally free—not owned by another individual as slaves were—but were bound to the land, unable to move and owing labor obligations to their lord. For former slaves, serfdom was a step up; for others, however, it was a step down, and the bulk of the serfs in Europe probably came from families that had originally been free peasants, but had traded their labor and freedom to move in return for protection. In any case, serfdom did not immediately replace slavery; the two continued side by side for centuries, and the laws you have seen here regarding slaves often shaped later laws regarding serfs. Law codes alone, of course, cannot tell us about relative numbers of slaves or serfs, and they sometimes hide major changes. The transformation of slave to serf was so gradual that it occasioned little comment in the codes, which had, as we have seen, long included discussions of intermediate stages between slave and free and of hierarchies among slaves.

The laws you have seen here also had great influence beyond Europe. As you have discovered, Germanic law did not break sharply with Roman on many issues regarding slavery, indicating that Justinian's Code probably influenced some early medieval Germanic codes. Justinian's Code was also rediscovered in western Europe in the eleventh century, and became the basis of legal education at the law schools that were established in southern Europe in the twelfth century. It influenced national and local codes in this era of expanding states and growing cities, and ultimately all of the legal systems of western Europe except for that of England became based on Roman law. When Portugal and Spain set up slave systems extending into the New World, Roman law was the basis of many provisions regarding slavery. Thus, two of the New World's most heavily slave societies—the French Caribbean and Brazil—based their systems on Roman law.

The other slave societies in the New World—the British Caribbean and the southern United States before the Civil War—did not base their laws as directly on those of Rome, but their laws did grow out of Germanic codes such as those you have seen here. Though these systems were different from the Roman and Germanic systems in that slavery came to be based on race, many of the laws—those concerning owners' freedom to treat slaves as they wished, sexual relations between slave and free, and punishment of those who aided runaway slaves—were remarkably similar. Once slavery came to be racially based, however, the permeable boundary between slave and free that you have traced in this chapter, with slavery not necessarily being a permanent status, became much harder to cross. Poverty, begging, theft, debt, capture in war, false testimony, or incest did not make a white person a slave, nor did turning in deserters, marriage to an owner, or—except in rare instances—military service make a black person free.

CHAPTER TWO

THE DOMESDAY BOOK AND MEDIEVAL STATISTICS

THE PROBLEM

In 1066 the Anglo-Saxon king of England, Edward the Confessor, died childless, leaving several claimants to the throne. Later that year the armies of William, Duke of Normandy and one of the contenders, defeated the armies of his Anglo-Saxon rival Harold at the battle of Hastings. William then moved to subdue the rest of the country, quashing all attempts at resistance and replacing Anglo-Saxon officials with Normans. He built many castles at strategic points and stripped the leading Anglo-Saxon nobles of their lands. To keep any of his own nobles from becoming too powerful, he granted them fiefs scattered throughout the country so that they would not be able to unite their forces to oppose the king. William declared himself sole owner of all land and required every feudal lord to swear an oath of allegiance to him.

These were all expensive tactics, and William imposed and collected a variety of taxes throughout his reign to finance them. Increasingly, though, he came to believe that the country could yield still more revenue. He also wanted to sell off royal land, and at the highest possible price. At the meeting of his nobles held at Christmas in 1085, William called for a survey of the entire country that would assess each estate for tax purposes and let him know the extent and value of royal lands. The survey was also intended to count the population and determine the status of every person who lived in England—free, serf, or slave—as a further aid in making tax assessments. The nobles' estates were to be accurately described and valued, which would end disputes among them about land ownership and enable William to judge how many knights each of his nobles should supply for the royal army.

The king's officials set out immediately to take this survey. They acted with a thoroughness that frightened rural residents, who were not used to such extensive royal involvement in their lives. In the words of an Anglo-Saxon chronicler of William's reign:

> Then he sent his men all over England into every shire [county] to ascertain

> how many hundreds of hides[1] of land there were in each shire, and how much land and live-stock the king himself owned in the country, and what annual dues were lawfully his from each shire. He also had it recorded how much . . . each man who was a landholder here in England had in land or in livestock, and how much money it was worth. So very thoroughly did he have the inquiry carried out that there was not a single hide, not one virgate[2] of land, not even—it is shameful to record it, but did not seem shameful to him to do—not even one ox, nor one cow, nor one pig which escaped notice in his survey. And all the surveys were subsequently brought to him.[3]

Earlier medieval kings had also taken surveys, but never in such detail. Reminded of the survey of sinners and saved that God would make at the Last Judgment, a scene depicted in many parish churches, people began to call William's survey the Domesday (i.e., doomsday) Book. To many observers, including the chronicler quoted here, William was seeking details about their lives that only God should know, which is why William's thoroughness is dubbed "shameful."

The detail that so alarmed the English population makes the Domesday Book a unique source of information about everyday life in the Middle Ages. The vast majority of the medieval European population were peasants who lived in villages, and we have very few sources that describe their lives. Most literate people were clerics, who have left us many sources about theology and the church; lay authors of written accounts tended to live in cities and thus also wrote little about rural areas. Chroniclers were interested in the lives of kings and nobles, not in the peasants who farmed the land. The Domesday Book is one of the few primary documents to throw light on the lives of this invisible majority.

The Domesday Book is also unique in another way. It gives us not only qualitative evidence in its descriptions of villages and people, but also quantitative evidence in its measurement of land and enumeration of human and animal populations. Because it is open to statistical interpretation in a way very few medieval sources are, we can use the Domesday Book to identify typical and specific features of medieval rural life. It provides reliable data for one time only, the year 1086, so the Domesday Book does not allow much analysis of change over time; it does, however, permit comparisons between one part of England and another.

Your task in this chapter will be twofold. First, we will evaluate the Domesday survey itself to answer the following question: What patterns of medieval rural life do the Domesday data reveal? We will then use figures drawn from the survey to answer a second question: What factors were important in determining the economic health of a village or area? The first question asks us to make some generalizations; the second asks for comparisons.

1. **hide:** a variable measure of land, 80–120 acres.

2. **virgate:** one-quarter of one hide.

3. *The Anglo-Saxon Chronicle,* translated by G. N. Garmonsway (London: J. M. Dent, 1953), p. 216.

SOURCES AND METHOD

The way in which surveys are constructed can reveal a great deal about a society. To begin with, survey takers generally divide whatever they are counting into those categories they rate as important. For example, modern census takers divide people by sex, race, occupation, age, income level, and place of residence because these categories are judged interesting or important in understanding economic, social, and geographic patterns. They also count certain material possessions, like televisions, telephones, and bathtubs, because these are held to be good indicators of economic status.

William's survey takers similarly counted specific objects as measures of economic status and divided people into categories they believed were meaningful. Though not every category appears on each page of the Domesday Book, certain categories appear over and over, enabling us to make generalizations. (It is important to keep in mind throughout this chapter that the categories in the Domesday Book were determined by William's officials, not by rural residents themselves. Domesday provides us with a perspective of rural society as seen from the top, which may not always correspond with the way rural people viewed themselves.)

The best place to begin your assessment of the Domesday Book is with the actual text. Source 1 consists of three parallel versions of the same text, part of the survey of the king's land in the county of Yorkshire. The first version is the original Domesday Book manuscript; the second is a printed transcription of the first two paragraphs. As you can see, the first challenge for anyone using the Domesday survey is to read and understand the actual document. The third version, an English translation of the entire page shown in Version 1, is the sample we will use to analyze the survey itself.

Even though this sample is in English, you will need to know a few more facts before you can make any generalizations. Like the entire Domesday Book, this extract is organized by *manor,* which generally meant a village and its surrounding lands. Easingwold is one manor, North Atherton a second, and so on. Most manors also controlled some land that was not directly adjacent and was either designated by a name (e.g., HUBY) or identified as an "outlier" (e.g., BIRKBY).

As you read the sample entries, make a list of what is being described and counted. As you would expect, the amount of taxable land appears first in each entry; the next figure is a note: "which *x* ploughs can plough." This figure is not a count of actual plows but an estimate of how many plows could possibly be used on the land if all the arable land were farmed. William wanted this figure, usually called the "ploughlands," to determine how well each manor was fulfilling its potential. The survey then notes who held the land before the Norman Conquest and who currently holds it. Following this are the actual counts of people, plows, and plow teams as well as other information the surveyors felt was important to note, and in some cases an assessment of the worth of the land before 1066 along with its worth at the time of the survey. After this comes a description and measure of the various uses to which the manor's land could be put and a count of people and plow teams in the outliers.

As you read the entries, note that the people are divided into categories: This sample includes *freemen* (free peasants), *villagers* (serfs with some land), *smallholders* (serfs with little or no land), and *priests*. (Other categories, such as slaves, swineherds, and fishermen, appear elsewhere in the Domesday Book, but not for Yorkshire.) What do these categories indicate about the social structure of rural eleventh-century England? These numbers do not count every individual, only adult males. Though in actuality a free woman could be married to a serf, and vice versa, the officials chose to regard the status of a wife as identical to that of her husband. Note that the land is also divided into categories: arable, meadow, woodland and pasture, waste. Why did William's surveyors feel it important to measure meadows and pastures along with arable land? What does this indicate about medieval agriculture?

From just this small sample of seven manors, you can already make some generalizations about rural life, or at least about rural life on the king's land in Yorkshire. What types of people resided on the manors? What types of land did most manors contain? What had happened to the value of most manors after 1066? Judging by the change in value, what was the economic impact of the conquest? Besides houses, what other types of buildings could be found in villages?

The Domesday Book contains similar entries for a total of 13,418 manors. Historians, economists, and geographers have compiled these figures to arrive at generalizations of the sort you have just made that apply to all of England. In so doing, they came to realize that such generalizations may be highly misleading, that a typical manor could vary enormously from one part of England to another. Because the Domesday Book is arranged according to manors, however, and these manors are listed by county, comparisons between one part of England and another are possible; such comparisons are ultimately more meaningful than generalized statistics. We will now turn to the second question, which involves statistical comparisons of several English counties.

Analysis by county is appropriate historically because each county had its own administration and its own identity, in the same way that each state in the United States does. Thirty-three counties were surveyed in the Domesday Book, a relatively large number, so the statistics you will be working with come from five different counties. This reduction in the number of cases, called *sampling*, is frequently done by anyone taking a survey; political polls, the Nielsen ratings for television, and the full U.S. census are all done today by sampling. Because we are comparing counties, it is not important which ones are included in the sample, so the five—Cornwall, Norfolk, Shropshire, Wiltshire, and Yorkshire—were chosen somewhat at random to represent a wide range of geographic areas. (If we were using our conclusions to make generalizations about all of England, we would need a more representative sample, like those modern political pollsters attempt to gather.) Before you turn to the statistics, look at the map showing the counties' locations; keep referring to this map as you come up with explanations for the differences you find.

Modern governments and private industry both generate huge amounts of statistics measuring every conceivable aspect of life. Economists and other social scientists have developed sophisticated quantitative techniques for making comparisons and evaluating how various factors and changes are related. They often use these measurements to predict the future, advising political leaders about the probable results of this or that policy. Quantitative techniques can also be used to understand the past, however, and historians are employing them increasingly to describe societies accurately and to assess the relationships among various types of change. For instance, census data are now used to chart the ways in which immigrants become acculturated into American society; import and export statistics, to assess changes in trade patterns. The amount of statistical evidence available decreases the further back in time we go, however, and the problems of interpretation increase. For a period as early as the eleventh century, sophisticated techniques are not appropriate, and their results can be very misleading. Thus, to evaluate the evidence in this chapter, you will not need extensive knowledge of statistics, simply some basic understanding of math and a calculator.

The Five Sample Counties

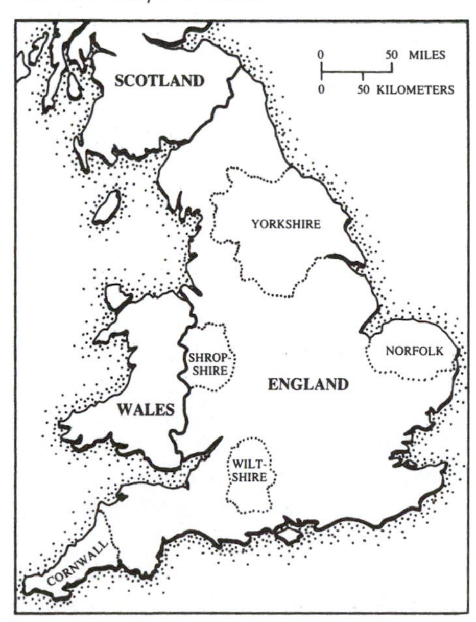

The first stage in quantitative analysis—gathering and compiling the raw data—has already been done for you. The next stage is to transform the data into figures that will allow useful and significant comparisons. To do this, you will need to expand on the tables given here. To help you in this task, the work sheet that follows the sources allows you to gather all your calculations in one place. You should complete these calculations before you begin to draw up your explanation for the numbers you have generated, but you also need to keep in mind why certain measurements are important. Why, for instance, might population density be more significant than total population?

The statistical tables probably look familiar enough, but you need some additional information to understand the numbers and make your own calculations. Table 1 gives you the area of each county and the number of inhabitants as recorded in the Domesday Book. The first column needs no explanation, but remember that the second is not a count of all individuals, but only of adult males. To arrive at a total population, historians have to speculate about the size of the average household, taking into account what can be known about average age at marriage, fertility rates, likelihood of live-in servants, life expectancy, and so on. As you can imagine, little is known about many of these factors for the eleventh century, so household size remains an educated guess. Though there is disagreement, many historians use 4.5 persons as a rough estimate of average household size. For your first calculation—the total rural population in each county—you will thus need to multiply the number of inhabitants listed by 4.5.

This population figure is only preliminary, for several historians have pointed out that in some counties one factor may render population figures arrived at by simply multiplying by household size especially inaccurate—namely, the presence of slaves. Adult male slaves are included in the Domesday count, but they would not have had their own households; they should be counted simply as one person and not multiplied. Table 2 gives you the number of slaves in each county. To arrive at a more accurate total population than your first figure, you need to subtract this number from the original count, multiply the resulting number by 4.5, and then add the number of slaves. Your second calculation will thus be a more accurate reflection of total population. (In this and in all calculations, be sure you understand exactly how you are arriving at the numbers you are, and why. Calculators and computers do the work for you, but they do not think.) Now you can make a third calculation—population density expressed in persons per square mile.

Table 3 gives you the number of manors in each county, so you can make a fourth calculation—the average size of the settlement expressed in persons per settlement. Table 4 provides the number of plow teams, which in Norman England consisted of eight oxen. With these figures you can make two more calculations—the population per plow team and the number of plow teams per square mile.

So far we have been using only what was physically counted by William's officials—people, oxen, settlements. This count may be somewhat inaccurate because officials may have missed things or counted them twice, or because the records themselves are unclear. It did not, however, require a value judgment from the officials, which was the case with the next two tables. William wanted to know not only how much of everything he had, but also what everything was worth and what it might possibly be worth if it were worked to its fullest capacity. He therefore ordered his officials to assess the value of all land; in other words, to give an estimate of how much the grain, sheep, or other products of the land were worth in a year.

Table 5 gives you these figures and also breaks them down in terms of value per square mile, adult male, and plow team.

Table 6 offers an even more subjective figure, the number of "ploughlands." As we saw in the sample from Yorkshire, this figure is more or less an estimate of the total amount of arable land in each county, usually expressed in a phrase like "there are *x* carucates, which *y* teams can plow." By dividing the number of plow teams by the number of plowlands, you arrive at a measure of how well each county was working up to its theoretical capacity. Such a figure is best expressed as a percentage, so you should multiply this fraction by 100. No plowlands are mentioned for Norfolk in the Domesday Book, so you will have to leave this county out of these calculations.

As you can see, William's officials judged some counties to be producing much less than they could, and others to be nearer optimum production levels. You can arrive at a further estimate—the highest annual value theoretically possible in each county—by dividing the annual value by the percentage of theoretical capacity each county is currently producing. (As an example, here are the calculations for Cornwall: 1,221 plow teams/2,557 plowlands = 0.48 or 48% capacity. If £670—the annual value for Cornwall given in Table 5—= 48%, 100% of Cornwall's possible annual value = 670/0.48, or 1,396. You can then perform these calculations per square mile and per adult male. Again using Cornwall as an example: 10 shillings/sq mi/0.48 = 21 shillings/sq mi possible annual value; 3 shillings/man/0.48 = 6.3 shillings/man possible annual value.)

On your work sheet you now have ten columns of figures: (1) total rural population unadjusted for slaves, (2) total rural population adjusted for slaves, (3) population density, (4) average manor size, (5) population per plow team, (6) plow teams per square mile, (7) percent of its theoretical capacity each county was currently producing, (8) highest annual value theoretically possible, (9) highest annual value possible per square mile, and (10) highest annual value possible per adult male.

You have completed the second stage of quantitative analysis—arriving at a series of figures that will make comparison possible—and are now ready to begin evaluating your numbers. Many different comparisons are possible, but here are a few suggestions: Look first at your figures for population density and size of manor. Which counties are heavily populated, and which have the largest settlements? Based on these figures alone, which counties have larger villages close together? Smaller villages close together? Larger villages far apart? Smaller villages far apart?

Now look at the columns for population per plow team and plow teams per square mile of area. What do these figures indicate about the fertility of the land in each county? Yorkshire and Wiltshire have roughly equal populations per team yet vastly different numbers of plow teams per square mile. What does this circumstance indicate about agriculture and the condition of the land in these two counties? (It is important to keep in mind that a plow team could plow only about 100 acres, or ⅙ of a square mile, per year; therefore a county with fewer plow teams per square mile would have more untilled land, not plow teams that worked much larger areas.) Does this help explain why the villages in Yorkshire are smaller and farther apart from one another than those elsewhere?

Look at Table 5, showing annual values, and your own calculations for possible annual values. Which county is the most productive? The least? How are annual value and population density related? Does the presence of slaves affect the annual value? Cornwall and Yorkshire are about even in annual value per man yet very different in annual value per square mile. Why might this be? In which counties did William's officials see the greatest possibility for improvement in annual value? What suggestions might they have made to effect this (e.g., an increase in the number of plow teams working, an increase in the population)?

Population density, number of plows, and average manor size all help to explain some of the differences in agricultural production levels and economic well-being in these counties, but other factors also recorded in the Domesday Book might also help to explain the patterns you have discovered. As you remember from the sample, mills were always noted; Table 7 gives you the number of grain mills in each county, both total and broken down per 1,000 teams and 1,000 men. How do these figures relate to the figures for annual value? Might building mills have helped some counties increase their productivity? As you also remember, the Domesday Book classifies the rural population according to social status (free, villager, smallholder, slave) and, in some cases, occupation. Table 8 gives you these figures for the five counties. We have already considered the relationship between the presence of slaves and the annual value for each county. Do you see any relationship between the percentage of free peasants and the annual value? Between the presence of smallholders, who were not much better off than slaves? Does either the presence of mills or a rough understanding of the social structure help explain any anomalies in your earlier comparisons?

You are now ready to answer both questions: What does the Domesday survey reveal about medieval rural life? What factors were important in determining the economic health of a village or county?

THE EVIDENCE

Source 1 from the Public Records Office E 31/2, f. 299, London (version 1); Margaret L. Faull and Marie Stinson, editors, Domesday Book, *Vol. 30,* Yorkshire, *Part 1 (Chichester, England: Phillimore, 1986), 299a (versions 2 and 3).*

1. From the Domesday Book

VERSION 1

EVRVICSCIRE.

TERRA REGIS IN EVRVIC SCIRE.
In [illegible] sunt ad geldu. xii. carucate
terre. q's. vii. caruce possunt arare. Hanc tenuit Morcar
p uno manerio. T.R.E. modo. e in manu regis. 7 sunt
ibi. x. uitti habentes. iiii. carucas. Eccla cu pbro.
Silua pastilis. ii. lev long. 7 ii. lat. Int totu. iii. leug
long. 7 ii. lat. Te ual. xxx ii. lib. m. xx. solidos.
Ad hoc man ptinet soca haru terraru. In hobi.
iiii. car. In Molebi. iii. car. In Mortune. ii. car 7 di
mid. In Torp Sudtune Chelesterd. 7 Carebi. xvii. car.
In Tormozbi. i. car 7 dim. In hotune. vi. car. In So
rebi. iii. car. 7 due alie ad halla ptinentes. cu molen
dino. qd redd. xx. sol. Int totu sunt ad gld. xxx ix.
carucate. q's. xx. caruce possunt arare. Non sunt
ibi nisi. ii. uitti 7 iiii. bord. hntes. i. car 7 dimidia.
Reliq tra wasta. e. Silua tam pastilis. e in aliqb.
In long. i. leug 7 dim. 7 in lat similit.

In Aluertune sunt ad gld. xl iiii. carucate tre.
q's xxx. car poss arare. Hanc tenuit Eduin com p uno
manerio. T.R.E. 7 habeb. lx vi. uillos cu xxx v. car.
Huic m appendest. xi. bereuuite. Bretebi. Smide
tune. Sourebi. Smitune. Kirkebi. Corketune. Lan
demot. Bergebi. Griftorentun. Romundebi. Iaforbe.
Modo. e in manu regis. 7 wast. e. Te ual quat. xx.
lib. Ibi. e pti. xl. ac. Silua 7 plan. v. leug lg
7 latu similit.
Ad hoc man ptinet soca haru traru. Neuhuse. West
huse. Mannebi. Werlegesbi. Emarebi. Iaforde. Leisen
chi. Bigneshale. Runtune. Irebi. Herelsaie. Sighestun.
Colebi. Timbelbi. Leche. Chennieton. Rauenestorp.
Torentun. Craxebi. Otrinctun. Romundebi. Brimton.
Cheluintun. Keneuetun. Int totu sunt ad gld
quat xx. 7 v. carucate. quas possunt arare. xl v. car.
Ibi sunt. lx. ac pti. Ibi fuer. c. 7 xvi. sochemans.
Om wast est.

In Walesgrif [nordfeld. e] sunt ad gld xv. carucate terre.
q's poss arare. viii. caruce. Hanc tenuit Tosti p uno
manerio. Nc. e regis. Sunt ibi. v. uitti hntes. ii. car.
Silua past. iii. leug lg. 7 ii. leug lat. Int totu
vi. leug lg. 7 iiii. lat. T.R.E. ual. l vi. libras
m. xxx. sol.
Ad hoc man ptinet soca haru traru. Asgozbi. Ledbe
stun. Gristorp. Scagetorp. Euerstorp. Rodebestorp.
Fiuelac Bertune. Depedale. Atune. Neuuetun. Pre
stetune. Hotune. Martune. Wicha. Rostune. Tornelai.

Steintun. Brinnistun. Scallebi. Cloctune.
Int totu sunt ad gld quat xx. 7 iiii. carucate. q's possun
arare. xl. ii. caruce. In his fuer. c 7 viii. sochem. cu
xl. vi. car. Modo sun vii. sochm. 7 xv. uitti. 7 xiii.
bord. hntes. vii. car 7 dimid. Cetra sun wasta.

In Pichering sun ad gld. xxx vii. carucate tre. q's
possun arare. xx. caruce. Hanc tenuit Morcar p uno
manerio cu bereuuitis suis. Bartune. Neuuetune.
Blandebi. 7 Estorp. m ht rex. Ibi. e. i. car. 7 xx. uitti
cu. vi. car. Pratu. dimid. lev lg. 7 tant lat. Omis u
silua q ptinet ad man. ht. xvi. lev lg. 7 iiii. lat.
H man ual T.R.E. quat xx 7 viii. lib. m. xx sol. 7 iiii. den.
Ad h man ptinet soca haru traru. Bruntun. Odul
fesmare. Edbriztune. Aluestune. Wituune. Farma
nesbi. Rozebi. Chinetorp. Chiluesmares. Aschilesmares.
Maxudesmares. Snechintune. Chigogemers. Elre
burne. Torentune. Leuecen. Middeltun. Bartune.
Int totu sunt ad gld. l. carucate. q's poss arare
xx vii. caruce. Non sunt m ibi nisi. x. uitti. hntes
ii. car. Cetra wasta. Se tam pti ac. xx. Int totu
xvi. lev lg. 7 iiii. lat.

In Haanburg. sunt ad gld. iii. carucate. q's possun
arare ii. caruce. Hanc tenuit Tosti p. i. manerio. m ht rex ibi
v. uillos 7 iii. bord. cu. ii. car. pbr 7 eccla ibi. e.
prati ac. vii. Silua past dim lev lg. 7 tant lat.
Int totu. i. lev lg. 7 dim lat. T.R.E. ual. xl. sol.
m. xvi. sol.

In Wiestun. cu bereuuita Epton sun ad gld. xxx.
carucate. in qb possun. e. xxx. caruce. Hanc tenuit
Morcar p uno manerio. Modo ht rex ibi. i. car.
7 viii. uillos cu. iiii. car. 7 v. bord. pti. i. lev lg.
7 dim lat. Totu. iiii. leug lg. 7 iii. lat. T.R.E. ual
xxx. lib. m lx. sol.
Ad h man ptinet soca In Cliue uni carucate. q. una
caruca potest arare. In Gudmundha. i. car 7 dim ad gld. soca.
In houeton. iii. car 7 dim ad gld soca.

In Walchingas cu. iii. bereuuitis Ersceuelle Torp
Brunha. sun ad gld. xx ix. carucate. quas poss
arare. xv. caruce. Hanc tenuit Morcar p uno manio.
Nc ht rex ibi. x. uitt cu. ii. car. pbr 7 eccla ibi. e.
Molendinu. ii. solid reddes. pti ac. xx. Totu. ii. lev
lg. 7 dimid lat. T.R.E. ual. xl. lib. m xxx. sol.
Ad h man ptinet soca viii. carucataru. in Dighelibi
7 Turodebi. ubi poss. e. iiii. caruce. Wasta sun.

In hase [illegible]
In Sua [illegible]

VERSION 2

TERRA REGIS *IN EVRVIC SCIRE.*

IN EISICEWALT sunt ad geldū. XII. carucatæ terræ. q̃s. VII. carucæ possunt arare. H̄ tenuit Morcar p uno manerio. T.R.E. Modo. ē in manu regis. 7 sunt ibi. X. uilli habentes. IIII. carucas. Æccła cū pbro. Silua pastilis. II. lev long. 7 II. laĩ. Int totū. III. leug long. 7 II. lat. Tc ual. XXXII. lib. m̄. XX. solidos.

Ad hoc Man ptinet soca harū terrarū. In hobi. IIII. car. In Molzbi. III. car. In Mortune. II. car 7 dimid. In Torp Sudtune Chelesterd. 7 Carebi. XVII. car. In Tormozbi. I. car 7 dim. In Hottune. VI. car. In Sorebi. III. car. 7 duæ aliæ ad hallā ptinentes. cū Molendino. qđ redđ. XX. sol. Int totū sunt ad glđ. XXXIX. carucatæ. q̃s. XX. carucæ possunt arare. Non sunt ibi nisi. II. uilli 7 IIII. borđ. hn̄tes. I. car 7 dimidiā. Reliq tra wasta. ē. Silua tam̄ pastilis. ē in aliqb3. in long. I. leug & dim. 7 in lat similit.

In Aluertune sunt ad glđ. XLIIII. carucatæ træ. q̃s XXX. car poss arare. H̄ tenuit Eduin com p uno manerio. T.R.E. 7 habeb. LXVI. uillos cū XXX.V. car. Huic Ꝯ appendent. XI. bereuuitæ. Bretebi. Smidetune. Sourebi. Smitune. Kirkebi. Corketune. Landemot. Bergebi. Gristorentun. Romundebi. Jaforbe. Modo. ē in manu regis. 7 wast. ē. Tc ual quat. XX. lib. Ibi. ē p̃tū. XL. ac. Silua 7 plan. V. leug lḡ 7 latū similit.

VERSION 3

LAND OF THE KING

In YORKSHIRE

[NORTH RIDING]

1 In EASINGWOLD there are 12 carucates[4] of land taxable, which 7 ploughs can plough. Morcar held this as one manor before 1066. Now it is in the King's hands; and

there are there 10 villagers who have 4 ploughs.

A church with a priest.

Woodland and pasture, 2 leagues long and 2 wide.

In all, 3 leagues long and 2 wide.

Value then £32;[5] now 20s.

To this manor belongs the jurisdiction of these lands: in HUBY, 4 carucates; in MOXBY (Hall), 3 carucates; in MURTON (Farm), 2½ carucates; in THORPE (Hill), SUTTON (on the Forest), KELSIT (Grange) and (Cold) KIRBY, 17 carucates; in THORMANBY, 1½ carucates; in (Sand) HUTTON, 6 carucates; In SOWERBY, 3 carucates and 2 others belonging to the hall, with a mill which pays 20s.

In all there are 39 carucates taxable, which 20 ploughs can plough.

There are there only 2 villagers and 4 smallholders who have 1½ ploughs.

The rest of the land is waste.

There is, however, woodland, pasturable in some parts, 1½ leagues in length and the same in width.

2 In (North) ALLERTON there are 44 carucates of land taxable, which 30 ploughs can plough. Earl Edwin held this as one manor before 1066, and he had

66 villagers with 35 ploughs.

To this manor are attached 11 outliers: BIRKBY; (Great) SMEATON; SOWERBY (under Cotcliffe); (Little) SMEATON; KIRBY (Wiske); (East) COWTON; LANDMOTH; BORROWBY; THORNTON (le Beans); ROMANBY; YAFFORTH. Now it is in the King's hands. Waste. Value then £80.

There is there, meadow, 40 acres; wood and open land, 5 leagues long and as wide.

To this manor belongs the jurisdiction of these lands: NEWSHAM (Grange); 'WESTHOUSE'; MAUNBY; WARLABY; AINDERBY (Steeple); YAFFORTH; LAZENBY (Hall); (Over) DINSDALE (Grange); (West) ROUNTON; IRBY (Manor); (West) HARLSEY; (Kirby) SIGSTON; COWESBY; THIMBLEBY; LEAKE; KNAYTON;

4. **carucate:** approximately 140 acres.

5. 1 pound (£) = 20 shillings (s) = 240 pence (d).

RAVENSTHORPE (Manor); THORNTON (le Street); CROSBY (Grange); (North) OTTERINGTON; ROMANBY; BROMPTON; (North) KILVINGTON; KNAYTON. In all there are 85 carucates taxable which 45 ploughs can plough.

There is there, meadow, 60 acres.

There were there 116 Freemen.

Now waste.

3 In FALSGRAVE and NORTHFIELD (Farm), its outlier, there are 15 carucates of land taxable, which 8 ploughs can plough. Tosti held this as one manor. Now it is the King's.

There are there 5 villagers who have 2 ploughs.

Woodland pasture, 3 leagues long and 2 leagues wide.

In all, 6 leagues long and 4 wide.

Value before 1066 £56; now 30s.

To this manor belongs the jurisdiction of these lands: OSGODBY, 4 C.; LEBBERSTON; GRISTHORPE; 'SCAWTHORPE'; *ETERSTORP; RODEBESTORP;* FILEY; 'BURTON (Dale)'; (High, Middle and Low) DEEPDALE; (West) AYTON; 'NEWTON'; PRESTON (Hill); HUTTON (Buscel); MARTIN (Garth); WYKEHAM; RUSTON; THIRLEY (Cotes); STAINTON (Dale); 299 b BURNISTON; SCALBY; CLOUGHTON. In all, there are 84 carucates taxable, which 42 ploughs can plough.

In these there were 108 Freemen with 46 ploughs; now there are 7 Freemen, 15 villagers and 14 smallholders who have 7½ ploughs. The rest waste.

4 In PICKERING there are 37 carucates of land taxable, which 20 ploughs can plough. Morcar held this as one manor with its outliers: BARTON (le Street), NEWTON, (High) BLANDSBY and EASTHORPE (House). Now the King has it. There is there 1 plough; and

20 villagers with 6 ploughs.

Meadow, ½ league long and as wide; nevertheless all the wood which belongs to the manor is 16 leagues long and 4 wide.

Value of this manor before 1066 £88; now 20s 4d.

To this manor belongs the jurisdiction of these lands: BROMPTON, 3 carucates; *ODULFESMARE;* EBBERSTON; ALLERSTON; WILTON; *FARMANBY;* ROXBY (Hill); KINGTHORPE (House); *CHILUESMARES; ASCHILESMARES; MAXUDESMARES;* SNAINTON; *CHIGOGEMERS;* ELLERBURN; THORNTON (Dale); LEVISHAM; MIDDLETON; BARTON (le Street). In all there are 50 carucates taxable which 27 ploughs can plough. Now there are there only 10 villagers who have 2 ploughs. The rest waste.

However, there are 20 acres of meadow.

In all, 16 leagues long and 4 wide.

[EAST RIDING]

5 In HEMINGBROUGH there are 3 carucates taxable which 2 ploughs can plough. Tosti held this as one manor. Now the King has there

5 villagers and 3 smallholders with 2 ploughs.
A priest is there and a church.
Meadow, 7 acres; woodland pasture, ½ league long and as wide.
In all, 1 league long and ½ wide.
Value before 1066, 40s; now 16s.

6 In (Market) WEIGHTON with SHIPTON (Thorpe), its outlier, there are 30 carucates taxable, on which 30 ploughs possible. Morcar held this as one manor. Now the King has there 1 plough; and
8 villagers with 4 ploughs; and 5 smallholders.
Meadow 1 league long and ½ wide.
The whole, 4 leagues long and 3 wide.
Value before 1066 £30; now 60s.
To this manor belongs jurisdiction in (North) CLIFFE of 1 carucate, which 1 plough can plough; in GOODMANHAM, 1½ carucates taxable, jurisdiction; in HOUGHTON, 4½ carucates taxable, jurisdiction.

7 In WARTER with its 3 outliers, HARSWELL, *TORP* and (Nun)-BURNHOLME, there are 29 carucates taxable, which 15 ploughs can plough. Morcar held this as one manor. Now the King has there
10 villagers with 2 ploughs.
A priest is there and a church.
A mill paying 2s; meadow, 20 acres;
The whole, 2 leagues long and as wide.
Value before 1066 £40; now 30s.
To this manor belongs the jurisdiction of 8 carucates in DUGGLEBY and *TURODEBI*, where 4 ploughs possible. In HOTHAM, 1 carucate of land; in SEATON (Ross), 4 carucates of land.
They are waste.

Source 2 from H. C. Darby, Domesday England *(New York: Cambridge University Press, 1977), appendices 1, 3, 13, 14.*

2. Statistical Tables

TABLE 1

County	Area (sq mi)	Population (adult males)
Cornwall	1,348	5,368
Norfolk	2,037	26,309
Shropshire	1,353	4,757
Wiltshire	1,379	9,944
Yorkshire	7,024	7,566

TABLE 2

County	Slaves
Cornwall	1,149
Norfolk	973
Shropshire	928
Wiltshire	1,588
Yorkshire	0

TABLE 3

County	Settlements
Cornwall	332
Norfolk	730
Shropshire	459
Wiltshire	344
Yorkshire	1,993

TABLE 4

County	Plow teams[a]
Cornwall	1,221
Norfolk	5,006
Shropshire	1,999
Wiltshire	3,003
Yorkshire	2,927

a. 1 plow team = 8 oxen.

TABLE 5

	Annual Value			
County	*Total* *(£)*[a]	*Per sq mi* *(s.)*	*Per man* *(s.)*	*Per plow team* *(s.)*
Cornwall	670	10	3	11
Norfolk	2,037	40	3	16
Shropshire	852	13	4	10
Wiltshire	4,470	69	11	32
Yorkshire	1,084	3	3	7

a. £1 = 20s.

TABLE 6

County	Plowlands
Cornwall	2,557
Norfolk	?
Shropshire	3,130
Wiltshire	3,475
Yorkshire	5,710

TABLE 7

	Mills		
County	*Total*	*Per 1,000 teams*	*Per 1,000 men*
Cornwall	6	50	1
Norfolk	538	107	21
Shropshire	94	53	34
Wiltshire	433	144	50
Yorkshire	120	41	16

TABLE 8

	Population by Social Category					
County	*Freemen*	*Villagers*	*Smallholders*	*Slaves*	*Others*	*Total*
Cornwall	0	1,704 (31%)	2,426 (45%)	1,149 (21%)	89	5,368
Norfolk	10,637 (40%)	4,607 (18%)	9,886 (38%)	973 (9%)	217	26,309
Shropshire	20 (0.4%)	1,833 (39%)	1,179 (25%)	928 (20%)	767	4,757
Wiltshire	0	3,497 (35%)	4,479 (45%)	1,588 (16%)	380	9,944
Yorkshire	450 (6%)	5,030 (66%)	1,822 (24%)	0	264	7,566

WORK SHEET

County	Unadjusted Total Rural Population	Total Rural Population Adjusted for Slaves	Population Density	Average Manor Size	Population per Plow Team	Plow Teams per Sq Mi	Percent of Theoretical Capacity Currently Producing	Highest Theoretical Annual Value	Highest Theoretical Annual Value per Sq Mi	Highest Theoretical Annual Value per Adult Male
Cornwall										
Norfolk										
Shropshire										
Wiltshire										
Yorkshire										

QUESTIONS TO CONSIDER

Information that can be quantified is extremely persuasive in assessing historical trends or making comparisons, but researchers using statistics must always be careful to ask several questions in weighing any conclusions drawn from the numbers. The first is the most basic: Do the conclusions make sense? It is easy to be led astray by numbers that seem to correlate if you do not step back and try to figure out why they do. As statisticians are fond of pointing out, all kinds of correlations can be discovered between entities that could in no way be causally related to each other, such as the price of wheat and the number of blue-eyed babies born in a certain year. Put the conclusions you have drawn about medieval rural life to this test. Do your findings pass the test of common sense?

Once you have satisfied yourself that your explanations are logical, you then need to examine the limitations of your data and think about what sorts of hidden assumptions are contained in the statistics that might influence the results. Is the survey large enough to be meaningful? Are the categories clearly defined, so that no room for ambiguity exists? Do the figures involve value judgments, with the result that two people gathering information might arrive at different figures? (A good example here is such categories as lower class, middle class, and upper class, which observers might define very differently.) What biases might have influenced those gathering information? What was the original intent of the survey, and how might this have affected the results? What does a government survey like Domesday leave out? What aspects of rural life does it reveal nothing about? How might a similar survey designed by villagers themselves differ from the Domesday Book? These are all questions you can ask of the Domesday Book.

A third line of questioning in any statistical study involves nonquantifiable factors that may have influenced the results. All statistical studies, even the most sophisticated computer-assisted ones that take dozens of different factors into account, possess some variance that cannot be explained by quantifiable factors. What sorts of nonquantifiable factors might have influenced the economic health of a village? How might productivity have been affected by people's attitudes about work? What about traditions of land use? How might the fact that the survey was taken by officials of a conquering ruler have affected the outcome? You can doubtless come up with many other factors that might have affected productivity.

Now that you have thought about the limitations of your statistics, you can also consider how your conclusions can be expanded. The way in which surveys are constructed can reveal a great deal about a society in addition to the information the survey gathers. Think about the Domesday survey. What does the fact that only adult males were counted for Domesday tell you about the status of women in medieval society? What does the presence of slaves as late as the eleventh century indicate about the power of the Christian church, whose leaders encouraged the freeing of slaves? What does the fact that this survey counted only rural residents indicate about the importance of towns in eleventh-century England? From the Domesday Book, what can we learn about the personality of William the Conqueror? The monarchs of France and Germany never instituted similar surveys or even attempted to do so. What does this circumstance indicate about the power of the English kings as compared to those on the Continent? As you can see, quantitative studies can also reveal many qualitative aspects of life.

EPILOGUE

The Domesday survey was immediately put to use by William, who began to sell his "royal land" at the highest possible price. He died the following year, but the survey remained one of the most important acts of his reign. Throughout the rest of the Middle Ages, individual landholders turned to the Domesday Book to answer all sorts of questions about land ownership and boundaries and the extent of royal forests. The Church used it in disagreements with the crown over who held the rights to certain pieces of land. The most important of these questions was whether certain land was "ancient demesne," that is, former royal land. Peasants on this land, such as the manors we examined in Yorkshire, were free of many labor services and were entitled to special legal privileges well into the nineteenth century. Copies of parts of the survey were often made, and the parchment on which it was written became yellowed and glossy from the oil of many human hands. The original document, kept with the records of the royal treasury, was one of the most carefully guarded treasures in all of England.

The Domesday Book gradually achieved a mythic status in the minds of many, who felt that it contained the answers to all conceivable questions about land ownership. Later writers assumed that its name came not from the thoroughness of the survey but from the fact that its word was regarded as final, just as God's word would be final at the Last Judgment. The document's reputation was greater than the information it contained, however, and by the eighteenth century a growing disappointment in its limitations combined with the increasing problems of interpretation to limit its use as a legal source.

Domesday remained extremely important as a historical source, however, and efforts were begun to make the document easier to use. It was first printed in 1783; the original was copied directly by photozincography, an early photographic process, in 1861. These procedures made the work accessible to a much wider audience, but using it still demanded knowledge of Latin as well as medieval handwriting and terminology. Scattered translations and indexes were made for individual counties, but not until the 1980s did a full translation with new indexes appear; the sample from Yorkshire reprinted here was only published in 1986. In that same year, work was begun on a computer-based, multimedia version supported by a £2.5 million grant from the BBC. Unfortunately the videodisks on which it was recorded could only be read by special computers, which were too expensive for libraries or other institutions to buy. Thus by 2002, the project director declared the project "unreadable and obsolete." Similar problems plague data recorded in many other types of digital formats—floppy disks, cassettes, videos—and experts in preservation note there is no easy solution to this problem. Luckily the original Domesday Book, on parchment, needs nothing other than a trained eye to read it.

CHAPTER THREE

THE DEVELOPMENT OF THE MEDIEVAL STATE

THE PROBLEM

The governments of medieval Europe are generally described as *feudal,* a word that perhaps confuses more than it clarifies. The term *feudalism* was unknown in the Middle Ages; it was invented only later to describe the medieval system of landholding and government. Used correctly, feudalism denotes a system of reciprocal rights and obligations, in which individuals who fight (knights) promise their loyalty, aid, and assistance to a king or other powerful noble, becoming what were termed *vassals* of that lord. The lord in turn promises his vassals protection and material support, which in the Early Middle Ages was often board and room in the lord's own household. As their vassals became more numerous or lived farther away, lords increasingly gave them grants of land as recompense for their allegiance. This piece of land, termed a *fief* (*feudum* in Latin), theoretically still belonged to the lord, with the vassal obtaining only the use of it. Thus feudalism involved a mixture of personal and property ties. Unlike the systems of property ownership in the Roman Empire or most modern governments, it did not involve any ties to an abstract state or governmental system, but was simply a personal agreement between individuals.

This promise of allegiance and support could be made only by free individuals, so that the slaves we examined in Chapter 1 and serfs who were tied to the land were not actually part of the feudal system. In the economic structure of medieval Europe, estates or *manors* of various sizes were worked by slaves, serfs, and free peasants. The whole economic system is termed *manorialism.* Fiefs were generally made up of manors and included the peasants who lived on them, but manorialism and feudalism are not synonymous.

Though serfs were not included in the feudal system, church officials were. Rulers rewarded church officials with fiefs for their spiritual services or promises of allegiance. In addition, the Church held pieces of land on its own, and granted fiefs in return for promises of assistance from knightly vassals. Abbots and abbesses of monasteries, bishops, and archbishops were either lords[1] or vassals in many feudal arrangements. In addition, both secular and clerical vassals further subdivided their fiefs, granting land to people who became their vassals, a process known as *subinfeudation*. Thus the same person could be a lord in one relationship and a vassal in another.

This system could easily become chaotic, particularly as it was easy to forget, once a family had held a piece of land for several generations, that the land actually belonged to the lord. This is more or less what happened from 700 until 1050, with political power becoming completely decentralized and vassals ruling their fiefs quite independently. About 1050 this began to change, however, and rulers started to manipulate feudal institutions to build up rather than diminish their power.

The rulers of England after the Norman Conquest in 1066 were particularly successful at manipulating feudal institutions to build up their own power. William the Conqueror (1066–1087) and Henry II (1154–1189) dramatically increased royal authority, as did later rulers of France, especially Philip II Augustus (1180–1223), and of Germany, especially Frederick Barbarossa (1152–1190). Gradually the feudal system was transformed into a system that is sometimes termed *feudal monarchy*. Because monarchs in the High Middle Ages had so much more power than they had had in the Early Middle Ages, however, some historians no longer term such governments feudal at all, but simply call them monarchies, and see in them the origins of the modern state.

In asserting their power, the rulers of western Europe had to suppress or limit the independent powers of two groups in medieval society—their noble vassals and church officials. The challenge provided by each group was somewhat different. Noble vassals often had their own armies, and the people living on their fiefs were generally more loyal to—or afraid of—them than to any faraway ruler. During the period before the mid-eleventh century, vassals often supervised courts, which heard cases and punished crimes, and regarded themselves as the supreme legal authority in their fief. Though they were vassals of the ruler, Church officials also owed allegiance to an independent, international power—the papacy in Rome. Throughout the Middle Ages, the pope and higher church officials claimed that all church personnel, down to village priests and monks, were not subject to any secular legal jurisdiction, including that of a ruler. They also argued that the spiritual hierarchy of Western Christianity, headed by the pope, was elevated by God over all secular hierarchies, so that every ruler was subject to papal authority.

In this chapter we will be exploring the ways in which medieval monarchs asserted their authority over their vassals and the Church. We will use both visual and written evidence in answering the question, How did the rulers of the High Middle Ages overcome challenges to their power and begin the process of recentralization of power?

1. Because abbesses and, in some parts of Europe, noblewomen who inherited land could grant fiefs and have vassals, the word *lord* in the context of feudalism did not always mean a man. It simply means "the person who holds the rights of lordship."

SOURCES AND METHOD

Traditionally, political history has been seen as the history of politics, and has used as its sources laws, decrees, parliamentary debates, and other written documents that give information about political changes. These are still important, but recently political history has been seen more broadly as the history not only of politics but of all relations involving power, and a wider range of sources is now used to understand the power relationships in past societies. Picking up techniques from anthropologists, political historians now use objects as well as written documents to explore the ways in which power is externally expressed and symbolized as well as the ways in which it is manipulated in relationships. The rulers of medieval western Europe were aware of the power of symbols, and along with actual military and legal moves to increase their authority, they also demonstrated that authority symbolically.

A symbol is basically something that stands for something else, that has a meaning beyond the actual object or words. Symbols can be used consciously or unconsciously, and can be interpreted differently by different observers or readers. Anthropologists have pointed out that symbols can often be read at many different levels, so understanding them in all their meanings can be very complicated. The symbols we will be looking at here are less complicated than many, however, because they were consciously employed by rulers and officials who wanted to be very sure that their correct meaning was understood. Since many of the observers were not highly educated or even literate, rulers chose simple symbols and repeated them so that their meaning would certainly be grasped. Because many of these symbols have much the same meaning to us today, you will find them easier to analyze than the symbols from unfamiliar cultures that are often the focus of anthropologists' studies. As we explore the ways in which rulers asserted their authority, then, we must keep in mind both the tactical and the symbolic impact of their actions.

The first four sources all provide evidence of one of the ways in which William the Conqueror and his successors gained power over the English nobility. Source 1 is from a history of England written in the early twelfth century by Ordericus Vitalis, a monk who was half Anglo-Saxon and half Norman. The author provides a relatively unbiased account of William's reign, and here describes how William subdued one of the many rebellions against him. Read the selection carefully. Rather than simply sending out armies, what does William do to establish royal power? Why does Ordericus feel this was effective in ending the rebellion?

Visual depictions of Norman castles may help you judge whether Ordericus's opinion about their importance was valid, so turn to the next three sources. Sources 2 and 3 are photographs of castles built by English kings. The first was begun at Richmond in 1089, and the second was built at Harlech between 1283 and 1290. Source 4 is a map of all the castles built in England by William the Conqueror during his reign, from 1066 to 1087. Many of these were wooden fortifications rather than the enormous stone castles shown in Sources 2 and 3, but William's successors expanded these simpler castles into larger stone ones as quickly as time and resources permitted. As you look at these, try to imagine yourself as a vassal or subject confronted by castles that looked like these in all the places you see on the map. What message would you get about the power of the king? What strategic value is gained by placing a castle on a hill? How would this also increase the castle's symbolic value? What other features of the castles depicted increase either their strategic value as fortresses or their symbolic value? The map indicates that the castles built by William were not evenly distributed. Given what your text tells you about the Norman Conquest and the problems that William faced, why might he have built his castles where he did? Does this pattern of castle building surprise you? (A clue here is to keep in mind that castles are both symbols of power and a means to enforce that power, and that these castles may not all have been built for the same reason.)

Source 5 provides evidence of another way in which William and his successors both gained and demonstrated authority over their vassals. It is an excerpt from *The Anglo-Saxon Chronicle* describing William's requirement in 1086 that all vassals swear loyalty to him in what became known as the Salisbury Oath. Rulers such as William recognized that people regarded oaths as very serious expressions of their duties as Christians, and so they required their vassals to swear allegiance regularly in person in ceremonies of *homage* (allegiance) and *fealty* (loyalty). They expanded the ceremonies of knighthood, impressing on young knights their duties of obedience and loyalty. After you read this short selection, think about how the fact that the vassals had to leave their fiefs to swear the Oath might have also helped to increase royal power.

After William, Henry II was the most innovative fashioner of royal power in medieval England. In 1166, he issued the Assize[2] of Clarendon (the location of the king's hunting lodge), which set up inquest juries to report to the king's sheriff or traveling judges the name of anyone suspected of having committed a major crime. Source 6 gives you some of the clauses from the Assize of Clarendon. As you read it, note the ways in which the independent powers of the vassals in their territories are restricted. Who does it state is the ultimate legal authority? Who gains financially from these provisions?

Henry II directly limited not only the legal power of his vassals, but also that of the Church in England. Two years before the Assize of Clarendon, he issued the Constitutions of Clarendon, which purported to be a codification of existing practices governing relations between the Church and the state. Source 7 is an extract from this document. Read it carefully, noting first under whose authority Henry issues it. Who does he say has agreed to its provisions? How do these provisions limit the legal power of the

2. **assize:** a decree made by an assembly.

Church over its own clergy? Over lay-people? What role is the king to play in the naming of church officials? In hearing cases involving clergy? How are church officials to be reminded of their duties as the king's vassals?

The Constitutions of Clarendon are perhaps the strongest statement of the power of a secular ruler over the Church to emerge from the Middle Ages, and, as we will see in the epilogue to this chapter, they were quickly opposed by the Church. This was not the only time a ruler asserted his power over the Church, however, for on the Continent German kings and emperors also claimed extensive powers over all aspects of Church life up to and including the papacy. Source 8 gives an example of this assertion of power. It is a selection from the biography of the German emperor Frederick Barbarossa (1152–1190), begun by Bishop Otto of Freising. Otto was Frederick's uncle, so though he is a bishop of the Church, he is quite favorably inclined toward the emperor. In this selection, Otto describes Frederick's coronation and some later responses by the emperor to papal ambassadors. What roles do church officials play in Frederick's coronation? What does Otto view as a further symbol of Frederick's right to rule? What role does Otto report that the pope claimed to have played in granting Frederick power? What, in contrast to this, does Frederick view as the source of his authority? What does he see to be his religious duties as emperor?

Along with actions such as constructing castles or requiring oaths of loyalty, both of which combined tactical with symbolic assertions of power, medieval rulers also demonstrated their power over vassals and the Church in purely symbolic ways. The final sources in this chapter provide examples of some of these. Source 9 is a description of the coronation ceremony of Richard the Lionhearted, Henry II's son, in 1189. More than the much shorter description of Frederick Barbarossa's coronation, which you have already read, it gives evidence of the way in which kings and other territorial rulers expanded their coronation ceremonies, turning them into long, spectacular celebrations of royal wealth and power. As you read it, look first for things that symbolize power relationships. What titles are used to describe the participants? What objects are used in the ceremonies? Who is in attendance, and what roles do they play? What actions are required of the various participants, either during the ceremony or as part of their later duties?

Living in the media age as we do, we are certainly used to the manipulation of symbols to promote loyalty and allegiance. Indeed, given the barrage of symbols accompanying the celebrations of the anniversaries of the Constitution, the Statue of Liberty, and the Bill of Rights, we may even be a bit jaded by flag-waving and military bands. Medieval people did not live in a world as full of visual stimulation as ours, so the ceremonies surrounding a monarch were truly extraordinary.

Coronation ceremonies were rare events, and rulers also used symbols in more permanent visual demonstrations of their power, such as paintings and statuary, which they commissioned or which were designed in a way that would gain their approval. The next three sources all depict rulers. Source 10 is a manuscript-illumination portrait of the German emperor Otto III (983–1002) seated on his throne. Source 11 is a section of the Bayeux tapestry showing on the left King Harold of England (1053–1066) seated on the throne. In the center, Englishmen acclaim him as king and point up to Halley's Comet (identified in the tapestry as a star). Source 12 is a tomb sculpture of Duke Henry of Brunswick in Germany and his wife, Matilda, dating from about 1240, shortly after they died. The Church that Henry holds in his right hand is Brunswick Cathedral, which he completed and which houses his tomb. Because we no longer live in a world of royal authority, you may need some assistance in interpreting the meaning of the objects shown with the rulers, although medieval people would have understood them immediately. Many of these objects had both a secular and a religious meaning: The crown represented royal authority (the points symbolized the rays of the sun) and the crown of thorns worn by Jesus before the Crucifixion; the orb (the ball surmounted by a cross) represented the ruler's domination of the land and protection of the Church; the scepter also represented Church and state power by being ornamented with both religious and secular designs. Seeing a monarch in full regalia or a portrait of a monarch would impress on anyone that this was not just the greatest of the nobles, but also someone who was considered sacred, whose authority was supported by Scripture. Monarchs also demonstrated the sacred aspects of their rule with purely religious symbols, such as crosses and chalices.

Now look carefully at the pictures. What symbols are used to depict the sources of royal authority? How do these communicate the ruler's secular and religious authority? What types of individuals are shown with the ruler? What does this indicate about the relationship between lord and vassal, and between Church and state? Why might the appearance of the heavenly body that came to be known as Halley's Comet have been viewed as an appropriate symbol of monarchy?

You have now examined evidence of a number of ways in which rulers increased their own authority, decreased that of their noble vassals and church officials, and expressed their greater power symbolically. As you assess how all of these helped rulers overcome challenges to their authority, it will be useful to recognize that symbols are not just passive reflections of existing power relationships, but are actively manipulated to build up or decrease power. Therefore it is often difficult to separate what we might term the real or tactical effect of an action or legal change from the symbolic. As you answer the central question in this chapter, then, think about the ways in which symbols and real change are interwoven.

THE EVIDENCE

Source 1 from Ordericus Vitalis, The Ecclesiastical History of England and Normandy, *trans. Thomas Forester (London: Henry G. Bohn, 1854). This source is taken from a reprint of this edition (New York: AMS Press, 1968), vol. 2, pp. 17–20.*

1. From Ordericus Vitalis's *Ecclesiastical History of England and Normandy*

The same year [1068], Edwin and Morcar, sons of Earl Algar, and young men of great promise, broke into open rebellion, and induced many others to fly to arms, which violently disturbed the realm of Albion.[3] King William, however, came to terms with Edwin, who assured him of the submission of his brother and of nearly a third of the kingdom, upon which the king promised to give him his daughter in marriage. Afterwards, however, by a fraudulent decision of the Normans, and through their envy and covetousness, the king refused to give him the princess who was the object of his desire, and for whom he had long waited. Being, therefore, much incensed, he and his brother again broke into rebellion, and the greatest part of the English and Welsh followed their standard. The two brothers were zealous in the worship of God, and respected good men. They were remarkably handsome, their relations were of high birth and very numerous, their estates were vast and gave them immense power, and their popularity great. The clergy and monks offered continual prayers on their behalf, and crowds of poor daily supplications. . . .

At the time when the Normans had crushed the English, and were overwhelming them with intolerable oppressions Blethyn, king of Wales, came to the aid of his uncles, at the head of a large body of Britons. A general assembly was now held of the chief men of the English and Welsh, at which universal complaints were made of the outrages and tyranny to which the English were subjected by the Normans and their adherents, and messengers were dispatched into all parts of Albion to rouse the natives against their enemies, either secretly or openly. All joined in a determined league and bold conspiracy against the Normans for the recovery of their ancient liberties. The rebellion broke out with great violence in the provinces beyond the Humber. The insurgents fortified themselves in the woods and marshes, on the estuaries, and in some cities. York was in a state of the highest excitement, which the holiness of its bishop was unable to calm. Numbers lived in tents, disdaining to dwell in houses lest they should become enervated; from which some of them were called savages by the Normans.

3. **Albion:** England.

In consequence of these commotions, the king carefully surveyed the most inaccessible points in the country, and, selecting suitable spots, fortified them against the enemy's excursions. In the English districts there were very few fortresses, which the Normans call castles; so that, though the English were warlike and brave, they were little able to make a determined resistance. One castle the king built at Warwick, and gave it into the custody of Henry, son of Roger de Beaumont.[4] Edwin and Morcar, now considering the doubtful issue of the contest, and not unwisely preferring peace to war, sought the king's favour, which they obtained, at least, in appearance. The king then built a castle at Nottingham, which he committed to the custody of William Peverell.

When the inhabitants of York heard the state of affairs, they became so alarmed that they made hasty submission, in order to avoid being compelled by force; delivering the keys of the city to the king, and offering him hostages. But, suspecting their faith, he strengthened the fortress within the city walls, and placed in it a garrison of picked men. At this time, Archill, the most powerful chief of the Northumbrians, made a treaty of peace with the king, and gave him his son as a hostage. The bishop of Durham, also being reconciled to King William, became the mediator for peace with the king of the Scots, and was the bearer into Scotland of the terms offered by William. Though the aid of Malcolm had been solicited by the English, and he had prepared to come to their succour with a strong force, yet when he heard what the envoy had to propose with respect to a peace, he remained quiet, and joyfully sent back ambassadors in company with the bishop of Durham, who in his name swore fealty to King William. In thus preferring peace to war, he best consulted his own welfare, and the inclinations of his subjects; for the people of Scotland, though fierce in war, love ease and quiet, and are not disposed to disturb themselves about their neighbours' affairs, loving rather religious exercises than those of arms. On his return from this expedition, the king erected castles at Lincoln, Huntingdon, and Cambridge, placing in each of them garrisons composed of his bravest soldiers.

4. **Roger de Beaumont:** a Norman noble.

Source 2 courtesy of *The British Tourist Authority.*

2. Richmond Castle, Begun in 1089

Source 3: Photograph courtesy of the British Tourist Authority. Ground plan courtesy of the Ministry of Public Building and Works.

3. View and Ground Plan of Harlech Castle, Built by Edward I Between 1283 and 1290

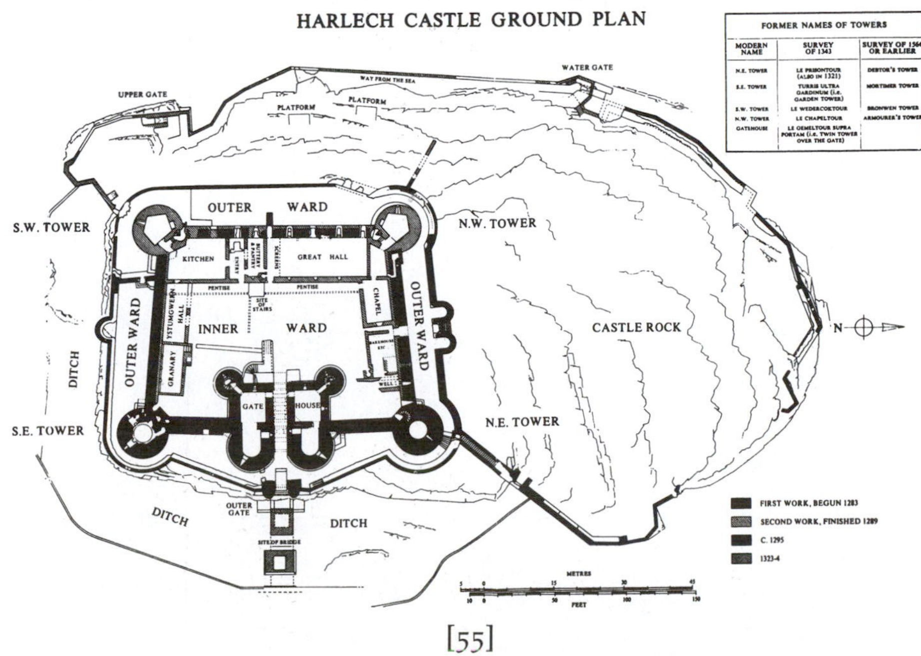

FORMER NAMES OF TOWERS

MODERN NAME	SURVEY OF 1343	SURVEY OF 1564 OR EARLIER
N.E. TOWER	LE PRISONTOUR (ALSO IN 1321)	DEBTOR'S TOWER
S.E. TOWER	TURRIS ULTRA GARDINUM (i.e. GARDEN TOWER)	MORTIMER TOWER
S.W. TOWER	LE WEDERCOKTOUR	BRONWEN TOWER
N.W. TOWER	LE CHAPELTOUR	ARMOURER'S TOWER
GATEHOUSE	LE GEMELTOUR SUPRA PORTAM (i.e. TWIN TOWER OVER THE GATE)	

Source 4 adapted from map in H. C. Darby, Domesday England *(Cambridge: Cambridge University Press, 1977), p. 316.*

4. Major Royal Castles Built During the Reign of William the Conqueror, 1066–1087

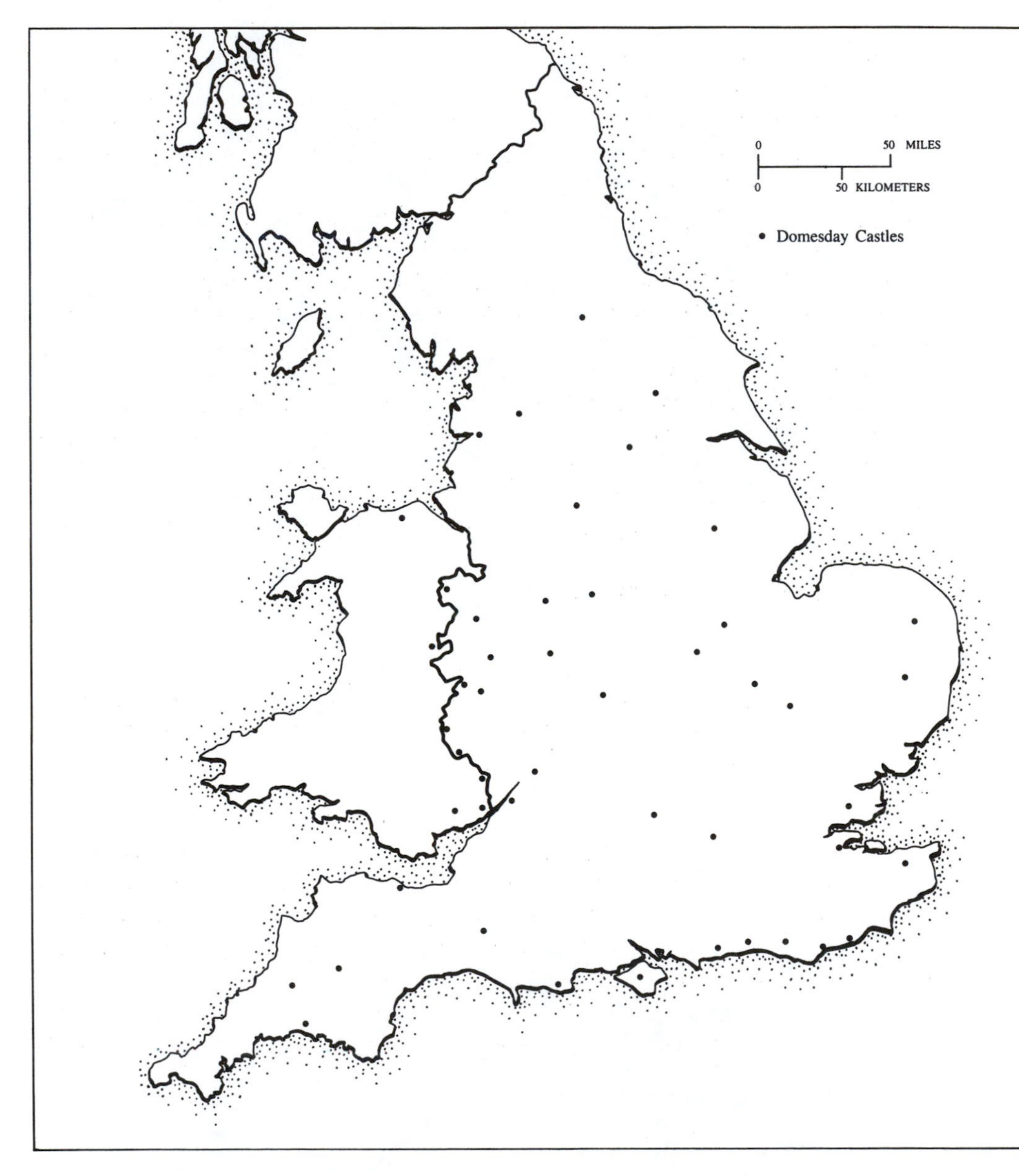

Source 5 from The Anglo-Saxon Chronicle *(London: Eyre and Spottiswoode, 1961, and New Brunswick, N.J.: Rutgers University Press), p. 162.*

5. From *The Anglo-Saxon Chronicle*

1086—In this year the king wore his crown and held his court at Winchester for Easter, and travelled so as to be at Westminster for Whitsuntide, and there dubbed his son, Henry, a knight. Then he travelled about so as to come to Salisbury at Lammas,[5] and there his councillors came to him, and all the people occupying land who were of any account all over England, no matter whose vassals they might be; and they all submitted to him and became his vassals, and swore oaths of allegiance to him, that they would be loyal to him against all other men. . . .

Sources 6 and 7 from Edward P. Cheyney, editor, "English Constitutional Documents," Translations and Reprints from the Original Sources of European History *(Philadelphia: University of Pennsylvania, 1900), vol. I, no. 6, pp. 22–25; pp. 26–30.*

6. Assize of Clarendon

Here begins the Assize of Clarendon, made by King Henry II, with the assent of the archbishops, bishops, abbots, earls and barons of all England.

1. In the first place, the aforesaid King Henry, with the consent of all his barons, for the preservation of the peace and the keeping of justice, has enacted that inquiry should be made through the several counties and through the several hundreds,[6] by twelve of the most legal men of the hundred and by four of the most legal men of each manor, upon their oath that they will tell the truth, whether there is in their hundred or in their manor, any man who has been accused or publicly suspected of himself being a robber, or murderer, or thief, or of being a receiver of robbers, or murderers, or thieves, since the lord king has been king. And let the justices make this inquiry before themselves, and the sheriffs before themselves.

2. And let any one who has been found by the oath of the aforesaid to have been accused or publicly suspected of having been a robber, or murderer, or thief, or a receiver of them, since the lord king has been king, be arrested and go to the ordeal of water and let him swear that he has not been a robber, or

5. **Lammas:** the wheat-harvest festival, August 1.

6. **hundred:** a division of a county.

murderer, or thief, or receiver of them since the lord king has been king, to the value of five shillings, so far as he knows. . . .

4. And when a robber, or murderer, or thief, or receiver of them shall have been seized through the above-mentioned oath, if the justices are not to come very soon into that country where they have been arrested, let the sheriffs send word to the nearest justice by some intelligent man that they have arrested such men, and the justices will send back word to the sheriffs where they wish that these should be brought before them; and the sheriffs shall bring them before the justices; and along with these they shall bring from the hundred and the manor where they have been arrested, two legal men to carry the record of the county and of the hundred as to why they were seized, and there before the justice let them make their law.

5. And in the case of those who have been arrested through the aforesaid oath of this assize, no one shall have court, or judgment, or chattels,[7] except the lord king in his court before his justices, and the lord king shall have all their chattels. In the case of those, however, who have been arrested, otherwise than through this oath, let it be as it has been accustomed and ought to be. . . .

17. And if any sheriff shall have sent word to any other sheriff that men have fled from his county into another county, on account of robbery or murder or theft, or the reception of them, or for outlawry or for a charge concerning the forest of the king, let him arrest them. And even if he knows of himself or through others that such men have fled into his county, let him arrest them and hold them until he shall have secured pledges from them.

18. And let all sheriffs cause a list to be made of all fugitives who had fled from their counties; and let them do this in the presence of their county courts, and they will carry the written names of these before the justices when they come first before these, so that they may be sought through all England, and their chattels may be seized for the use of the king. . . .

7. Constitutions of Clarendon

In the year of the incarnation of the Lord, 1164, of the papacy of Alexander, the fourth year, of the most illustrious king of the English, Henry II, the tenth year, in the presence of the same king, has been made this memorial or acknowledgment of a certain part of the customs and franchises and dignities of his predecessors, that is to say of King Henry, his grandfather, and of other kings, which ought to be observed and held in the kingdom. And on account of the discussions and disputes which have arisen between the clergy and the justices of our lord and king and the barons of the kingdom concerning the customs and dignities, this acknowledgment is made in the presence of the archbishops and bishops and clergy and earls and barons and principal men of the kingdom.

7. **chattels:** all items of property and goods except land.

And these customs, acknowledged by the archbishops and bishops and earls and barons, and by the most noble and ancient of the kingdom, Thomas, archbishop of Canterbury, and Roger, archbishop of York, . . . [plus 12 bishops and 38 named barons] and many others of the principal men and nobles of the kingdom, as well clergy as laity.

Of these acknowledged customs and dignities of the realm, a certain part is contained in the present writing. Of this part the heads are as follows:

1. If any controversy has arisen concerning the advowson[8] and presentation of churches between laymen and ecclesiastics, or between ecclesiastics, it is to be considered or settled in the courts of the lord king.

2. Churches of the fee of the lord king cannot be given perpetually without his assent and grant.

3. Clergymen charged and accused of anything, when they have been summoned by a justice of the king shall come into his court, to respond there to that which it shall seem good to the court of the king for them to respond to, and in the ecclesiastical court to what it shall seem good should be responded to there; so that the justice of the king shall send into the court of holy church to see how the matter shall be treated there. And if a clergyman shall have been convicted or has confessed, the church ought not to protect him otherwise.

4. It is not lawful for archbishops, bishops, and persons of the realm to go out of the realm without the permission of the lord king. And if they go out, if it please the lord king, they shall give security that neither in going nor in making a stay nor in returning will they seek evil or loss to the king or the kingdom. . . .

7. No one who holds from the king in chief, nor any one of the officers of his demesnes shall be excommunicated, nor the lands of any one of them placed under an interdict, unless the lord king, if he is in the land, first agrees, or his justice, if he is out of the realm, in order that he may do right concerning him; . . .

8. Concerning appeals, if they should occur, they ought to proceed from the archdeacon to the bishop, from the bishop to the archbishop. And if the archbishop should fail to show justice, it must come to the lord king last, in order that by his command the controversy should be finally terminated in the court of the archbishop, so that it ought not to proceed further without the assent of the lord king. . . .

10. If any one who is of a city or a castle or a borough or a demesne manor of the lord king has been summoned by the archdeacon or the bishop for any offence for which he ought to respond to them, and is unwilling to make answer to their summons, it is fully lawful to place him under an interdict, but he ought not to be excommunicated before the principal officer of the lord king for that place agrees, in order that he may adjudge him to come to the answer. And if the officer of the king is negligent in this, he himself will be at the mercy of the lord king, and afterward the bishop shall be able to coerce the accused man by ecclesiastical justice.

8. **advowson:** the right to recommend candidates for vacant church positions that carried with them capital assets.

11. Archbishops, bishops, and all persons of the realm, who hold from the king in chief, have their possessions from the lord king as a barony, and are responsible for them to the justices and officers of the king, and follow and perform all royal rules and customs; and just as the rest of the barons ought to be present at the judgment of the court of the lord king along with the barons, at least till the judgment reaches to loss of limbs or to death.

12. When an archbishopric or bishopric or abbacy or priorate of the demesne of the king has become vacant, it ought to be in his hands, and he shall take thence all its rights and products just as demesnes. And when it has come to providing for the church, the lord king ought to summon the more powerful persons of the church, and the election ought to be made in the chapel of the lord king himself, with the assent of the lord king and with the agreement of the persons of the realm whom he has called to do this. And there the person elected shall do homage and fealty to the lord king as to his liege lord, concerning his life and his limbs and his earthly honor, saving his order, before he shall be consecrated. . . .

This acknowledgment of the aforesaid royal customs and dignities has been made by the aforesaid archbishops, and bishops, and earls, and barons, and the more noble and ancient of the realm, at Clarendon, on the fourth day before the Purification of the Blessed Mary, perpetual Virgin, Lord Henry being there present with his father, the lord king. There are, however, many other and great customs and dignities of holy mother church and of the lord king, and of the barons of the realm, which are not contained in this writing. These are preserved to holy church and to the lord king and to his heirs and to the barons of the realm, and shall be observed inviolably forever.

8. Coronation of Emperor Frederick Barbarossa, 1152

[*From* Gesta Friderici]

In the year . . . 1152, after the most pious King Conrad had died in the spring . . . in the city of Bamberg . . . there assembled in the city of Frankfort from the vast expanse of the transalpine kingdom [Germany], marvellous to tell, the whole strength of the princes, not without certain of the barons from Italy, in one body, so to speak. Here, when the primates were taking counsel about the prince to be elected—for the highest honour of the Roman Empire claims this point of law for itself, as if by special prerogative, namely, that the kings do not succeed by heredity but are created by the election of the princes—finally Frederick, duke of Swabia, son of Duke Frederick, was desired by all, and with the approval of all, was raised up as king. . . .

When the king had bound all the princes who had assembled there in fealty and homage, he, together with a few whom he had chosen as suitable, having dismissed the others in peace, took ship with great joy on the fifth day and, going by the Main and Rhine, he landed at the royal palace of Sinzig. There, taking horse, he came to Aachen on the next Saturday; on the following day, Sunday [March 9th] . . . led by the bishops from the palace to the church of the blessed Virgin Mary, and with the applause of all present, crowned by Arnold, archbishop of Cologne, assisted by the other bishops, he was set on the throne of the Franks, which was placed in the same church by Charles the Great. Many were amazed that in such a short space of time not only so many of the princes and nobles of the kingdom had assembled but also that not a few had come even from western Gaul, where, it was thought, the rumour of this event could not yet have penetrated. . . .

Nor should I pass over in silence that on the same day in the same church the bishop-elect of Münster, also called Frederick, was consecrated as bishop by the same bishops who had consecrated the king; so that in truth the highest king and the priest believed this to be a sort of prognostication[9] in the present joyfulness that, in one church, one day saw the unction[10] of two persons, who alone are anointed sacramentally with the institution of the old and new dispensations and are rightly called the anointed of Christ. . . .

[From *"The Deeds of Frederick Barbarossa"*]

In the middle of the month of October (1157) the emperor set out for Burgundy to hold a diet at Besançon. . . . We must speak of the ambassadors of the Roman pontiff, Hadrian. . . . The personnel of the embassy consisted of Roland, cardinal priest of the title of St. Mark and chancellor of the Holy Roman Church, and Bernard, cardinal priest of the title of St. Clement, both distinguished for their wealth, their maturity of view, and their influence, and surpassing in prestige almost all others in the Roman Church. . . . When this letter had been read and carefully set forth by Chancellor Rainald in a faithful interpretation, the princes who were present were moved to great indignation, because the entire content of the letter appeared to have no little sharpness and to offer even at the very

9. **prognostication:** prophecy.

10. **unction:** anointing.

outset an occasion for future trouble. But what had particularly aroused them all was the fact that in the aforesaid letter it had been stated, among other things, that the fullness of dignity and honor had been bestowed upon the emperor by the Roman pontiff, that the emperor had received from his hand the imperial crown, and that he would not have regretted conferring even greater benefits (*beneficia*) upon him. . . . And the hearers were led to accept the literal meaning of these words and to put credence in the aforesaid explanation because they knew that the assertion was rashly made by some Romans that hitherto our kings had possessed the imperial power over the City, and the kingdom of Italy, by gift of the popes, and that they made such representations and handed them down to posterity not only orally but also in writing and in pictures. . . .

They returned without having accomplished their purpose, and what had been done by the emperor was published throughout the realm in the following letter (October, 1157):

"Whereas the Divine Sovereignty, from which is derived all power in heaven and on earth, has entrusted unto us, His anointed, the kingdom and the empire to rule over, and has ordained that the peace of the churches is to be maintained by the imperial arms, not without the greatest distress of heart are we compelled to complain to Your Benevolence that from the head of the Holy Church, on which Christ has set the imprint of his peace and love, there seem to be emanating causes of dissentions and evils, like a poison, by which, unless God avert it, we fear the body of the Church will be stained, its unity shattered, and a schism created between the temporal and spiritual realms. . . . And since, through election by the princes, the kingdom and the empire are ours from God alone, Who at the time of the passion of His Son Christ subjected the world to dominion by the two swords, and since the apostle Peter taught the world this doctrine: 'Fear God, honor the king,' whosoever says that we received the imperial crown as a benefice (*pro beneficio*) from the lord pope contradicts the divine ordinance and the doctrine of Peter and is guilty of a lie. . . ."

Source 9 from J. A. Giles, translator and editor, Roger of Wendover's Flowers of History *(London: H. G. Bohn, 1849), vol. II, pp. 79–81.*

9. Coronation of Richard the Lionhearted, 1189

Duke Richard, when all the preparations for his coronation were complete, came to London, where were assembled the archbishops of Canterbury, Rouen, and Treves, by whom he had been absolved for having carried arms against his father after he had taken the cross. The archbishop of Dublin was also there, with all the bishops, earls, barons, and nobles of the kingdom. When all were assembled, he received the crown of the kingdom in the order following: First came the archbishops, bishops, abbots, and clerks, wearing their caps, preceded by the cross, the holy water, and the censers, as far as the door of the inner chamber, where they received the duke, and conducted him to the church of Westminster, as far as the high altar, in a solemn procession. In the midst of the bishops and clerks went four barons carrying candlesticks with wax candles, after whom came two earls, the first of whom carried the royal sceptre, having on its top a golden cross; the other carried the royal sceptre, having a dove on its top. Next to these came two earls with a third between them, carrying three swords with golden sheaths, taken out of the king's treasury. Behind these came six earls and barons carrying a chequer,[11] over which were placed the royal arms and robes, whilst another earl followed them carrying aloft a golden crown. Last of all came Duke Richard, having a bishop on the right hand, and a bishop on the left, and over them was held a silk awning. Proceeding to the altar, as we have said, the holy Gospels were placed before him together with the relics of some of the saints, and he swore, in presence of the clergy and people, that he would observe peace, honour, and reverence, all his life, towards God, the holy Church and its ordinances: he swore also that he would exercise true justice towards the people committed to his charge, and abrogating all bad laws and unjust customs, if any such might be found in his dominions, would steadily observe those which were good. After this they stripped him of all his clothes except his breeches and shirt, which had been ripped apart over his shoulders to receive the unction. He was then shod with sandals interwoven with gold thread, and Baldwin archbishop of Canterbury anointed him king in three places, namely, on his head, his shoulders, and his right arm, using prayers composed for the occasion: then a consecrated linen cloth was placed on his head, over which was put a hat, and when they had again clothed him in his royal robes with the tunic and gown, the archbishop gave into his hand a sword wherewith to crush all the enemies of the Church; this done, two earls placed his shoes upon his feet, and when he had received the mantle, he was adjured by the archbishop, in the name of God, not to presume to accept these honours unless his mind was steadily purposed to observe the oaths which he had made: and he answered that, with God's assistance, he would faithfully observe everything which he had promised. Then the king taking the crown from the altar gave it to the archbishop, who placed it upon the king's head, with the sceptre in his right hand and the royal wand in his left; and so, with his crown on, he was led away by the bishops and barons, preceded by the candles, the cross and the three swords aforesaid. When they came to the offertory of the mass, the two bishops aforesaid led him forwards and again led him back. At length, when the mass was chanted, and everything finished in the proper manner, the two bishops aforesaid led him away with his crown on, and bearing in his right hand the sceptre, in his left the royal wand, and so they returned in procession into the choir, where the king put off his royal robes, and taking others of less

11. **chequer:** a small table.

weight, and a lighter crown also, he proceeded to the dinner-table, at which the archbishops, bishops, earls, and barons, with the clergy and people, were placed, each according to his rank and dignity, and feasted splendidly, so that the wine flowed along the pavement and walls of the palace.

Source 10 from Hirmer Fotoarchiv.

10. Portrait of Emperor Otto III

11. Portion of the Bayeux Tapestry Showing King Harold Seated on the Throne of England, with Halley's Comet Above

Source 11 with special authorization of the City of Bayeux. Musée de la Tapisserie, Bayeux, France. Giraudon/Art Resource, NY.

Source 12 from Erwin Panofsky, Tomb Sculpture *(New York: Harry N. Abrams), fig. 222. Photograph copyright Foto Marburg/Art Resource, NY.*

12. Tomb Sculpture of Duke Henry of Brunswick and His Wife, Matilda

QUESTIONS TO CONSIDER

The power relationships we have been investigating involve three main groups in medieval society: the nobles, the Church, and the rulers. To understand changes in the balance of power among them, you will need to extract information about them, from each of the sources, and then compare your findings.

Take the nobles first. How would you compare the role of the nobles in the ceremonies of homage such as the Salisbury Oath with their role in the coronation ceremonies? How is their relationship to the ruler expressed in the pictures of Otto III and Harold? How does this compare with the way this relationship is expressed in the Assize of Clarendon? What differences do you see in the role of the nobles in Germany and those in England, as expressed in the coronation accounts?

Turning to the Church, what types of religious objects appear in the ceremonies and depictions of rulers? Do they serve to express the power of the Church as an institution or of someone else? What do they reveal to you about medieval religious beliefs and practices? What do the pictures of Otto III and Harold indicate about the relationship between the ruler and church officials? How does this compare with the expression of this relationship in the Constitutions of Clarendon?

The most prominent group in the sources are rulers. How would you compare the three visual depictions of rulers? Might any of the differences you see be explained by differences in the function of these depictions, that is, the fact that the last one is a tomb sculpture? Why might rulers wish to express certain aspects of their rule while they are still living, and make sure that others are stressed for posterity after they are dead?

The claim of rulers such as Henry II and Frederick Barbarossa to religious authority was accompanied in the High Middle Ages by changes in the theory underlying kingship. In the Early Middle Ages, the king was viewed as simply the greatest of the nobles, whose power derived from the agreements he had made with his vassals. This idea continued into the High Middle Ages, but alongside it developed the idea that the king got his power from God as well. Rulers were increasingly viewed not only as the apex of a pyramid of vassals, but also as the representative to God for their entire kingdom. They were not regarded as divine in the way that ancient rulers such as the Egyptian pharaohs and Roman emperors had been, for Christianity would not allow this, but they were considered sacred in some ways. What evidence of this new idea of kingship can you find in either the Constitutions of Clarendon or the statements of Frederick Barbarossa? The two coronation ceremonies, Sources 8 and 9, are from the period of the building up of the monarchy. What evidence do you see in them of both the older idea of the king as the greatest of the nobles and the newer idea of the king as ordained by God?

Remember that most literate people in the Middle Ages were clerics, so that all of the documents included here were probably written by priests or monks. How might this have affected their account of the events? Given what you have read and looked at here, what actions would you now regard as most significant in the creation of the medieval state?

EPILOGUE

The moves undertaken by rulers to increase their power during the High Middle Ages did not go unchallenged. The Constitutions of Clarendon were immediately opposed by church officials, including Henry II's friend Thomas Becket, whom Henry had made the Archbishop of Canterbury. The controversy between them grew very bitter, and ended with Becket's murder by several of Henry's nobles. After this the Constitutions were officially withdrawn, but Henry continued to enforce many of their provisions anyway.

In the area ruled by the German emperors, the Church was better able to assert its independent power; in fact, constant disputes with the pope were one of the reasons that the German emperors were not successful at establishing a unified country. Church officials patterned themselves after secular rulers and began in the twelfth century to demand regular oaths of homage and loyalty. They made sure that Church power was clearly symbolized in any royal ceremony and in all ceremonies of knighthood. As rulers built castles, they built cathedrals, permanent monuments in stone to both the glory of God and the authority of the Church. The consecrations of churches and cathedrals rivaled the coronations of monarchs in splendor and pomp. The Church was fortunate in this regard, for opportunities for special ceremonies and celebrations were much more frequent than they were for secular rulers. Even the regular mass could be used to convey the Church's might to all who observed it. The king may have had sacred authority, but church officials wanted to make sure that everyone knew that they did as well.

Nobles in England also opposed the growth of royal power, and were more effective than the Church in enforcing limits to royal authority. The most famous of these was the Magna Carta in 1215, which King John was forced to sign at a meeting in Runnymede, giving the higher nobles of England the right to participate in government. This document said nothing about the rights of the vast majority of English people, but it is still unusual in its limitation of the power of the king, though John immediately refuted it once he left Runnymede.

Despite opposition, however, the expansion of royal power at the expense of the nobles and the Church continued, for this expansion had only begun during the High Middle Ages. Monarchs in the later Middle Ages, the Renaissance, and the early modern period continued to build up their power, devising new methods of taxation to raise revenue, creating a centralized legal system under firm royal control, reducing the role of or doing away with feudal assemblies of nobles, hiring middle-class lawyers and bureaucrats as their advisers and officials, and forbidding the nobles to maintain their own armies while building up royal armies led by generals whom they chose for loyalty.

This expansion of royal power was made easier in many countries in the sixteenth century because of the Protestant Reformation. Many rulers, such as Henry VIII of England, resented any independent power of the Church; they thus found Protestant theology, which declared the papacy to be evil and the ruler the proper source of all religious authority, very attractive. Some rulers became Protestant out of sincere religious conviction, but for others the chance to take over church property and appoint church officials was the strongest motivation.

The growth of actual royal power was accompanied, as you would expect after working through this chapter, by changes in the theory underlying kingship and in the symbols used to portray the king. Political theorists developed the idea of the divine right of kings, whereby kings got their power directly and pretty much only from God, and so were not answerable to their subjects for their behavior. You can see this idea beginning in the documents you have just read, and it was to be developed to its furthest extent in seventeenth-century absolutism.

Centralized monarchy did not develop in all parts of Europe, however. Germany and Italy remained divided, and in fact did not become unified nations until the late nineteenth century, just a little over a hundred years ago. From the description of Frederick Barbarossa's coronation, you can see one reason for this, the fact that the emperorship was elected rather than hereditary. The lack of strong central governments in Germany and Italy was one reason for their decreasing political importance in the early modern period. The rulers of western Europe had much greater financial resources, and so could field larger armies and encourage economic development. After the voyages of the Portuguese and Spanish revealed new lands and new ways to the East, these rulers also supported exploration and colonization, which further increased royal and national power. Some type of feudal structure existed in most parts of western Europe in the High Middle Ages, but it was the rulers of France, England, and Spain who were most successful at manipulating both actual power and the symbols of that power to build up their own authority and end the feudal system.

CHAPTER FOUR

LIFE AT A MEDIEVAL UNIVERSITY

THE PROBLEM

Centers of learning grew up in several European cities—particularly Paris and Bologna, Italy—during the twelfth and thirteenth centuries. In Paris, scholars, drawn by excellent teachers such as Peter Abelard, gathered at the bishop's cathedral school. Because only an official of the bishop, called the *scholasticus* or chancellor, had the authority to issue licenses to teach, students and teachers clustered around the cathedral of Notre Dame, located on an island in the Seine. This educational community soon grew so large that it required additional housing on the left bank of the river, which came to be known as the "Latin Quarter" after the official academic language. Special residence halls for students, called *colleges,* were opened, though the teachers themselves had no classrooms and simply rented rooms on their own for lecturing.

As the number of students in Paris increased, the teachers joined together into a "universal society of teachers," or *university* for short. Believing that the chancellor often either granted the right to teach to unqualified parties or simply sold licenses outright, they began to require that prospective teachers pass an examination set by the university besides getting the chancellor's approval. This certificate to teach was the earliest form of academic degree, granting the holder one of the titles, *master* or *doctor,* that we still use today. (Bachelor's degrees were to come later.) Most of the students studied theology, and Paris became the model for later universities such as Oxford and Cambridge in England and Heidelberg in Germany.

Colleges at many universities changed their character over the centuries. Originally no more than residence halls, the colleges gradually began to sponsor lectures and arrange for courses, and the university became simply the institution that granted degrees. This process was especially noticeable at the English universities of Oxford and Cambridge. When colleges were first established in the United States, they generally modeled themselves on the colleges of Oxford and Cambridge; because they were not part of larger universities, the colleges also granted degrees themselves. Thus modern U.S. colleges may be either completely independent institutions or part of a university, such as the College of Engineering or the College of Letters and Science found at many universities. In most cases, colleges that are part of modern universities have completely lost their original function as residences.

The University of Bologna had somewhat different roots and a different emphasis. Professional schools for the training of notaries and lawyers had grown up in Bologna in the twelfth century because the city, located at the crossing of the main trade routes in northern Italy, was a center of commerce. The university developed from these professional schools, and consequently the students were older and more sophisticated than those at Paris. Here, the students themselves banded into a university; they determined the fees that teachers would be paid, the hours of classes, and the content of lectures. The most important course of study at Bologna was law. Bologna became the model for European universities such as Orleans or Padua, where students have retained their traditional power through modern times.

Because all those associated with the universities were literate, a great many records survive detailing every aspect of university life, both inside and outside the classroom. We can observe the process by which universities were established, read the rules students were required to live by, and learn what they were supposed to be studying (as well as what they actually spent time doing!). Much of medieval university life will seem familiar to us, for modern colleges and universities have inherited a great deal from their medieval predecessors. Indeed, most of the universities that had their beginning in the Middle Ages are still thriving today, making universities one of the few medieval institutions that we can evaluate to some extent as insiders, rather than the outsiders we are when we look at such vanished social forms as serfdom or feudalism.

Because of the many parallels between medieval and modern universities, your task in this chapter will be twofold. First, you will be asked to use a variety of records to answer this question: What was life like for students at a medieval university? You can then use this description and your own experiences as a student to answer the second question: How would you compare medieval with modern student life, and what factors might account for the differences?

SOURCES AND METHOD

You will be using four types of sources in this chapter. The first type (Sources 1 through 4) consists of rules for university or college life issued by the founders. These are prescriptive documents, setting forth standards of functioning and behavior. The second type (Sources 5 through 8), written by teachers at medieval universities, describes the teacher's methods of teaching or presents the area on which he concentrated. The third type (Source 9) is a critique of university teaching by an individual outside the university structure. These two types of sources provide us with information about how and what students studied or were supposed to study and so have both prescriptive and descriptive qualities. Selections of the fourth type (Sources 10 through 13) describe actual student life or were written by students themselves. These sources are thus fully descriptive, recounting real events or the problems and desires of real students.

As you read each selection, keep in mind the identity of its author and his position in the university. (No women were allowed to attend medieval universities in any capacity, so we can be sure that all authors, even anonymous students, were male.) Then as now, the perspective of administrators, those who established and ran the universities, was very different from that of students and faculty. It is also important to identify the source as prescriptive or descriptive. Prescriptive rules were often written in response to real problems, but the standards they laid down should never be mistaken for reality.

Begin your analysis of medieval university life with a careful reading of Sources 1 through 4. Source 1 describes privileges granted to the students at the University of Paris by the king of France in 1200. Though the University of Paris was originally started by the teachers themselves, the king took the scholars under his special protection and guaranteed them certain extraordinary rights. What privileges are they granted in this document?

Source 2 consists of the statutes issued for the University of Paris by Cardinal Robert Courçon in 1215. Courçon, a representative of Pope Innocent III, took a special interest in the university and approved rules governing academic life. Innocent had been a student at Paris himself and wanted to ensure the continuation of the university's tradition of theological orthodoxy and high levels of scholarship and behavior. As you read the selection, note the restrictions placed on those allowed to teach the arts. What restrictions are placed on teachers of theology? Why would Innocent be stricter about theology? What other areas did he believe important to regulate? What matters were the masters and students allowed to decide for themselves?

Source 3 contains further statutes issued for the University of Paris by Pope Gregory XI in 1231. What rules did he set for the chancellor's granting of teaching licenses? What issues was the university permitted to decide for itself? What special legal protections did students and teachers have? As pope, Gregory was particularly concerned with the manner in which theology was taught. What special restrictions did he lay down for students and teachers of theology? How would you compare these rules with the earlier ones established by Innocent III?

Source 4 is a series of rules governing life in one of the residential colleges, not the university as a whole. They were issued by Robert de Sorbon, the chaplain of King Louis IX, who established the college in the thirteenth century. This college was originally a residence hall for students of theology. By the sixteenth century, however, the word *Sorbonne* was used to describe the faculty of theology; since the nineteenth century, the entire University of Paris has been called the Sorbonne.

As you can see from Source 4, Sorbon's establishment was simply a residence hall, with none of the broader functions that colleges later assumed. What aspects of student life did he regulate? What qualities did he attempt to encourage in the students living at his college?

By reading these four prescriptive sources, you have gained some information about the structure of one university (Paris), the hierarchy of authority, special student privileges, daily life in a residential college, and the handling of rule infractions. You have also learned something about the ideals held by authorities and patrons, for the popes and Sorbon established these rules because they held certain beliefs about how students should behave. What qualities would their ideal student exhibit? What did they see as the ultimate aim of the university? You can also use these sources to assess how church and secular leaders reacted to scholars, students, and the university in general. How would you describe their attitude—patronizing, respectful, hostile? How might their opinions about members of the university community have influenced other citizens of these university towns?

Besides informing us of standards, rules can also expose real-life problems because those who set the regulations were often responding to events in their environment. Which rules were specifically aimed at halting acts that were already taking place? Which rules seem most likely to have been a response to actual behavior? What kinds of acts did the authorities appear most upset about? Why do you think they believed these acts were important? Judging by the information in these sources, how would you describe relations between university students and the other residents of Paris? Before you go on to the next selections, write a brief description of medieval university life as you now see it. What types of sources would help you test whether your assumptions at this point are correct?

You have probably realized that so far you do not know very much about what or how students actually studied, other than those writings that the popes recommended or forbade. The next four selections provide specific academic information. Sources 5 and 6 were written by teachers of theology and philosophy at Paris; Sources 7 and 8, by teachers of law at Bologna. Source 5 is the introduction to Peter Abelard's *Sic et Non,* a philosophical treatise introducing students and other readers to the *scholastic method* of inquiry, which applied logic to Christian theology. Source 6 is a demonstration of the scholastic method by one philosopher, Anselm of Canterbury, to prove the existence of God. If you are not familiar with philosophical works, you will need to read these excerpts very carefully, with special attention to the author's main points and the way in which logic is used to advance arguments. Because scholastic philosophers regarded logic as the most important aid to human understanding, it is fair for you to be critical if you see any flaws in their own logic. In making this analysis, you will be engaging in an activity that students in medieval universities both did themselves and were encouraged to do.

Begin with Abelard's introduction. How did he suggest to students that they read the works of the church fathers? How were they to handle seeming contradictions? Was all literature to be treated in this way? What, for Abelard, was the most important quality a student could possess? How was education supposed to strengthen this quality? Proceed to Anselm's proof, which you may need to read a number of times. Do you see any flaws in the logic? If you were a student disputing his proof, where would you begin?

Source 7 is an announcement of lectures in law by Odofredus, a teacher at the University of Bologna, written about 1250. Although later in the thirteenth century the city of Bologna began to pay teachers in order to control the university faculty more closely, at this point teachers were still paid directly by their students, and so Odofredus did not simply announce his course, he advertised it in a way that would make it attractive. What did he see as the positive qualities of his teaching method? How did he propose to handle a text? What specific skills was he trying to teach his students?

Source 8 is the introduction to the *Digest*, the main part of the collection of laws and commentaries made by the Emperor Justinian in the sixth century and one of the basic legal texts taught by Odofredus and his colleagues at Bologna. Like many textbooks, it opens with definitions of what is to be taught. What distinctions among types of law does it present? What is the ultimate aim of legal education to be? Return to the description of university life you wrote after reading the first group of sources. What can you now add about the way in which teachers approached their subjects or the way in which material was taught? What do you now know about the content of courses in medieval universities?

Though teachers of theology and law used both logic and reason as means of analysis, there were some thinkers in the Middle Ages who questioned their value, particularly in matters of theology. Source 9 is an excerpt from two letters of St. Bernard of Clairvaux (1090–1153), a very influential French abbot, mystic, and adviser to the papacy. What does Bernard object to in Abelard's teaching? Why does he view Abelard's ideas as dangerous? What is his opinion of the scholastic method being developed at that time in the universities?

Students did not spend all their time studying, nor did they always behave in the ways popes or patrons hoped they would. The final group of sources come from students themselves or describe what might be termed their extracurricular activities. Source 10 is an anonymous account of a riot in Oxford in 1298, and Source 11 is a description of student life at Paris written by Jacques de Vitry, a high-minded scholar and historian who had studied at Paris himself. Source 12 consists of two letters, one from a student at Oxford to his father and the other from a father to his son, a student at Orleans; Source 13 contains three anonymous short poems written originally in Latin by twelfth-century students.

The account of the riot is relatively straightforward and objective, like a story you might read in a newspaper today. What does this incident indicate about the relations between university scholars and townspeople? Whom did the two sets of disputants ask to decide the matter?

The other selections are more subjective than this account, so you must keep the point of view and the intent of the authors in mind as you read them. What kind of language does de Vitry use to describe students? With what authority did he criticize their actions? How would you describe his general opinion of university life? How would you compare his critique of logic and the philosophers who used it with Bernard's? What tactics did the student use to convince his father to send money? How would you compare the father's attitude with de Vitry's?

Most medieval student poetry was written by young scholars who wandered from university to university and took much longer at their studies than normal, if they ever finished at all. When reading from this genre, it is important to remember that the authors were not describing the daily grind but celebrating their wild escapades, in the same way that you might talk about an academic year in terms of homecoming parties, weekend bashes, and early morning cramming for exams. This does not mean that we should reject their poetry as a valid historical source; rather, we must simply be aware of its intent and limitations. Keeping this in mind, how do the poets describe themselves and their problems? How does this description of student life reinforce or change what you have learned so far?

Return to your original description of university life. What would you add now?

THE EVIDENCE

Sources 1 through 3 from Dana Carleton Munro, editor and translator, Translations and Reprints from the Original Sources of European History, *vol. 2, no. 3 (Philadelphia: University of Pennsylvania Press, no date), pp. 4–5; pp. 12–15; pp. 7–11.*

1. Royal Privileges Granted to the University of Paris by the King of France, 1200

In the Name of the sacred and indivisible Trinity, amen. Philip, by the grace of God, King of the French. . . .

Concerning the safety of the students at Paris in the future, by the advice of our subjects we have ordained as follows: we will cause all the citizens of Paris to swear that if any one sees an injury done to any student by any layman, he will testify truthfully to this, nor will any one withdraw in order not to see [the act]. And if it shall happen that any one strikes a student, except in self-defense, especially if he strikes the student with a weapon, a club or a stone, all laymen who see [the act] shall in good faith seize the malefactor or malefactors and deliver them to our judge; nor shall they withdraw in order not to see the act, or seize the malefactor, or testify to the truth. Also, whether the malefactor is seized in open crime or not, we will make a legal and full examination through clerks or laymen or certain lawful persons; and our count and our judges shall do the same. And if by a full examination we or our judges are able to learn that he who is accused, is guilty of the crime, then we or our judges shall immediately inflict a penalty, according to the quality and nature of the crime; notwithstanding the fact that the criminal may deny the deed and say that he is ready to defend himself in single combat, or to purge himself by the ordeal by water.

Also, neither our provost nor our judges shall lay hands on a student for any offence whatever; nor shall they place him in our prison, unless such a crime has been committed by the student, that he ought to be arrested. And in that case, our judge shall arrest him on the spot, without striking him at all, unless he resists, and shall hand him over to the ecclesiastical judge, who ought to guard him in order to satisfy us and the one suffering the injury. And if a serious crime has been committed, our judge shall go or shall send to see what is done with the student.

2. Statutes for the University of Paris Issued by Robert Courçon, 1215

R., servant of the cross of Christ, by the divine mercy cardinal priest of the title of St. Stephen in Monte Celio and legate of the apostolic seat, to all the masters and scholars at Paris—eternal safety in the Lord.

Let all know, that having been especially commanded by the lord pope to devote our energy effectively to the betterment of the condition of the students at Paris, and wishing by the advice of good men to provide for the tranquillity of the students in the future, we have ordered and prescribed the following rules:

No one is to lecture at Paris in arts before he is twenty-one years old. He is to listen in arts at least six years, before he begins to lecture. He is to promise that he will lecture for at least two years, unless he is prevented by some good reason, which he ought to prove either in public or before the examiners. He must not be smirched by any infamy. When he is ready to lecture, each one is to be examined according to the form contained in the letter of lord P. bishop of Paris (in which is contained the peace established between the chancellor and the students by the judges appointed by the lord pope, approved and confirmed namely by the bishop and deacon of Troyes and by P., the bishop, and J., the chancellor of Paris).

The treatises of Aristotle on logic, both the old and the new, are to be read in the schools in the regular and not in the extraordinary courses. The two Priscians,[1] or at least the second, are also to be read in the schools in the regular courses. On the feast-days nothing is to be read except philosophy, rhetoric, *quadrivialia*,[2] the Barbarism, the Ethics, if they like, and the fourth book of the Topics. The books of Aristotle on Metaphysics or Natural Philosophy, or the abridgements of these works, are not to be read, nor the writings of Master David of Dinant, the heretic Amauri, or the Spaniard Mauricius.[3]

In the promotions and meetings of the masters and in the confutations or arguments of the boys or youths there are to be no festivities. But they may call in some friends or associates, but only a few. We also advise that donations of garments and other things be made, as is customary or even to a greater extent, and especially to the poor. No master lecturing in arts is to wear anything except a cope,[4] round and black and reaching to the heels—at least, when it is new. But he may well wear a pallium.[5] He is not to wear under the round cope embroidered shoes and never any with long bands.

If anyone of the students in arts or theology dies, half of the masters of arts are to go to the funeral one time, and the other half to the next funeral. They are not to withdraw until the burial is completed, unless they have some good reason. If any master of arts or theology dies, all the masters are to be present at the vigils, each one is to read the psalter or have it read. Each one is to remain in the church, where the vigils are celebrated, until midnight or later, unless prevented by some good reason. On the day when the master is buried, no one is to lecture or dispute.

We fully confirm to them the meadow of St. Germain in the condition in which it was adjudged to them.

Each master is to have jurisdiction over his scholars. No one is to receive either schools or a house without the consent of the occupant, if he is able to obtain it. No one is to receive a license from the chancellor or any one else through a gift of money, or furnishing a pledge or making an agreement. Also, the masters and students can make among themselves or with others agreements and regulations, confirmed by a pledge, penalty or oath, about the following

1. **Priscian:** a Roman grammarian whose two works presented models of correct letters and legal documents.
2. **quadrivialia:** the four more advanced fields of study within the seven liberal arts: arithmetic, geometry, astronomy, and music.
3. Aristotle's treatises on metaphysics and natural philosophy were forbidden by the pope because they stated that the world was eternal (rather than created by God) and that the human soul was not immortal. The last three authors the Church regarded as heretics.
4. **cope:** a long cloak or cape.
5. **pallium:** a white stole usually worn by popes and archbishops as a symbol of their authority. In this case, a master teacher was allowed to wear one as an indication of his level of academic achievement and its corresponding institutional authority; the pallium thus served a function similar to the master's or doctoral hood.

matters: namely, if a student is killed, mutilated or receives some outrageous injury—if justice is not done; for fixing the prices of lodgings; concerning the dress, burial, lectures and disputations; in such a manner, however, that the university is not scattered or destroyed on this account.

We decide concerning the theologians, that no one shall lecture at Paris before he is thirty-five years old, and not unless he has studied at least eight years, and has heard the books faithfully and in the schools. He is to listen in theology for five years, before he reads his own lectures in public. No one of them is to lecture before the third hour on the days when the masters lecture. No one is to be received at Paris for the important lectures or sermons unless he is of approved character and learning. There is to be no student at Paris who does not have a regular master.

3. Statutes for the University of Paris Issued by Pope Gregory XI, 1231

Gregory, the bishop, servant of the servants of God, to his beloved sons, all the masters and students of Paris—greeting and apostolic benediction. . . .

Concerning the condition of the students and schools, we have decided that the following should be observed: each chancellor, appointed hereafter at Paris, at the time of his installation, in the presence of the bishop, or at the command of the latter in the chapter at Paris—two masters of the students having been summoned for this purpose and present in behalf of the university—shall swear that, in good faith, according to his conscience, he will not receive as professors of theology and canon law any but suitable men, at a suitable place and time, according to the condition of the city and the honor and glory of those branches of learning; and he will reject all who are unworthy without respect to persons or nations. Before licensing anyone, during three months, dating from the time when the license is requested, the chancellor shall make diligent inquiries of all the masters of theology present in the city, and of all other honest and learned men through whom the truth can be ascertained, concerning the life, knowledge, capacity, purpose, prospects and other qualities needful in such persons; and after the inquiries, in good faith and according to his conscience, he shall grant or deny the license to the candidate, as shall seem fitting and expedient. The masters of theology and canon law, when they begin to lecture, shall take a public oath that they will give true testimony on the above points. The chancellor shall also swear, that he will in no way reveal the advice of the masters, to their injury; the liberty and privileges being maintained in their full vigor for the canons at Paris, as they were in the beginning. Moreover, the chancellor shall promise to examine in good faith the masters in medicine and arts and in the other branches, to admit only the worthy and to reject the unworthy.

In other matters, because confusion easily creeps in where there is no order, we grant to you the right of making constitutions and ordinances regulating the manner and time of lectures and disputations, the costume to be worn, the burial of the dead; and also concerning the bachelors,[6] who are to lecture and at what hours, and on what they are to lecture; and concerning the prices of the lodgings or the interdiction of the same; and concerning a fit punishment for those who violate your constitutions or ordinances, by exclusion from your society. And if, perchance, the assessment of the lodgings is taken from you, or anything else is lacking, or an injury or outrageous damage, such as death or the mutilation of a limb, is inflicted on one of you; unless through a suitable admonition satisfaction is rendered within fifteen days, you may suspend your lectures until you have received full satisfaction. And if it happens that any one of you is unlawfully imprisoned, unless the injury ceases on a remonstrance from you, you may, if you judge it expedient, suspend your lectures immediately.

We command, moreover, that the bishop of Paris shall so chastise the excesses of the guilty, that the honor of the students shall be preserved and evil deeds shall not remain unpunished. But in no way shall the innocent be seized on account of the guilty; nay rather, if a probable suspicion arises against anyone, he shall be detained honorably and on giving suitable bail he shall be freed, without any exactions from the jailors. But if, perchance, such a crime has been committed that imprisonment is necessary, the bishop shall detain the criminal in his prison. The chancellor is forbidden to keep him in his prison. We also forbid holding a student for a debt contracted by another, since this is interdicted by canonical and legitimate sanctions. Neither the bishop, nor his official, nor the chancellor shall exact a pecuniary penalty for removing an excommunication or any other censure of any kind. Nor shall the chancellor demand from the masters who are licensed an oath, or obedience, or any pledge; nor shall he receive any emolument[7] or promise for granting a license, but be content with the above-mentioned oath.

Also, the vacation in summer is not to exceed one month, and the bachelors, if they wish, can continue their lectures in vacation time. Moreover, we prohibit more expressly the students from carrying weapons in the city, and the university from protecting those who disturb the peace and study. And those who call themselves students but do not frequent the schools, or acknowledge any master, are in no way to enjoy the liberties of the students.

Moreover, we order that the masters in arts shall always read one lecture on Priscian, and one book after the other in the regular courses. Those books on natural philosophy which for a certain reason were prohibited in a provincial council, are not to be used at Paris until they have been examined and purged of all suspicion of error. The masters and students in theology shall strive to exercise themselves laudably in the branch which they profess; they shall not show themselves philosophers, but they shall strive to become God's learned. And they

6. **bachelor:** a student who had his first degree and could teach beginning-level subjects.

7. **emolument:** fee.

shall not speak in the language of the people, confounding the sacred language with the profane. In the schools they shall dispute only on such questions as can be determined by theological books and the writings of the holy fathers.

It is not lawful for any man whatever to infringe this deed of our provision, constitution, concession, prohibition and inhibition or to act contrary to it, from rash presumption. If anyone, however, should dare to attempt this, let him know that he incurs the wrath of almighty God and of the blessed Peter and Paul, his apostles.

Given at the Lateran, on the Ides of April [April 13], in the fifth year of our pontificate.

Source 4 from Lynn Thorndike, editor and translator, University Records and Life in the Middle Ages *(New York: Columbia University Press, 1944), pp. 88–98.*

4. Robert de Sorbon's Regulations for His College, Before 1274

I wish that the custom which was instituted from the beginning in this house by the counsel of good men may be kept, and if anyone ever has transgressed it, that henceforth he shall not presume to do so.

No one therefore shall eat meat in the house on Advent, nor on Monday or Tuesday of Lent, nor from Ascension Day to Pentecost.

Also, I will that the community be not charged for meals taken in rooms. If there cannot be equality, it is better that the fellow eating in his room be charged than the entire community.

Also, no one shall eat in his room except for cause. If anyone has a guest, he shall eat in hall. If, morever, it shall not seem expedient to the fellow to bring that guest to hall, let him eat in his room and he shall have the usual portion for himself, not for the guest. If, moreover, he wants more for himself or his guest, he should pay for it himself. . . .

Also, the fellows should be warned by the bearer of the roll that those eating in private rooms conduct themselves quietly and abstain from too much noise, lest those passing through the court and street be scandalized and lest the fellows in rooms adjoining be hindered in their studies. . . .

Also, the rule does not apply to the sick. If anyone eats in a private room because of sickness, he may have a fellow with him, if he wishes, to entertain and wait on him, who also shall have his due portion. What shall be the portion of a fellow shall be left to the discretion of the dispenser. If a fellow shall come late to lunch, if he comes from classes or a sermon or business of the community, he shall have his full portion, but if from his own affairs, he shall have bread only. . . .

Also, all shall wear closed outer garments, nor shall they have trimmings of vair or grise[8] or of red or green silk on the outer garment or hood.

Also, no one shall have loud shoes or clothing by which scandal might be generated in any way.

Also, no one shall be received in the house unless he shall be willing to leave off such and to observe the aforesaid rules.

Also, no one shall be received in the house unless he pledges faith that, if he happens to receive books from the common store, he will treat them carefully as if his own and on no condition remove or lend them out of the house, and return them in good condition whenever required or whenever he leaves town.

Also, let every fellow have his own mark on his clothes and one only and different from the others. And let all the marks be written on a schedule and over each mark the name of whose it is. And let that schedule be given to the servant so that he may learn to recognize the mark of each one. And the servant shall not receive clothes from any fellow unless he sees the mark. And then the servant can return his clothes to each fellow. . . .

Also, for peace and utility we propound that no secular person living in town—scribe, corrector, or anyone else—unless for great cause eat, sleep in a room, or remain with the fellows when they eat, or have frequent conversation in the gardens or hall or other parts of the house, lest the secrets of the house and the remarks of the fellows be spread abroad.

Also, no outsider shall come to accountings or the special meetings of the fellows, and he whose guest he is shall see to this.

Also, no fellow shall bring in outsiders frequently to drink at commons, and if he does, he shall pay according to the estimate of the dispenser.

Also, no fellow shall have a key to the kitchen.

Also, no fellow shall presume to sleep outside the house in town, and if he did so for reason, he shall take pains to submit his excuse to the bearer of the roll. . . .

Also, no women of any sort shall eat in the private rooms. If anyone violates this rule, he shall pay the assessed penalty, namely, sixpence.[9] . . .

Also, no one shall form the habit of talking too loudly at table. Whoever after he has been warned about this by the prior shall have offended by speaking too loudly, provided this is established afterwards by testimony of several fellows to the prior, shall be held to the usual house penalty, namely two quarts of wine.

The penalty for transgression of statutes which do not fall under an oath is twopence, if the offenders are not reported by someone, or if they were, the penalty becomes sixpence in the case of fines. I understand "not reported" to mean that, if before the matter has come to the attention of the prior, the offender accuses

8. **vair:** squirrel fur. **grise:** any type of gray fur.

9. This was a substantial amount for most students to pay.

himself to the prior or has told the clerk to write down twopence against him for such an offence, for it is not enough to say to the fellows, "I accuse myself."

Source 5 from James Harvey Robinson, editor and translator, Readings in European History, *vol. 1 (Boston: Ginn, 1904), pp. 450–452.*

5. Introduction to Peter Abelard's *Sic et Non,* ca 1122

There are many seeming contradictions and even obscurities in the innumerable writings of the church fathers. Our respect for their authority should not stand in the way of an effort on our part to come at the truth. The obscurity and contradictions in ancient writings may be explained upon many grounds, and may be discussed without impugning the good faith and insight of the fathers. A writer may use different terms to mean the same thing, in order to avoid a monotonous repetition of the same word. Common, vague words may be employed in order that the common people may understand; and sometimes a writer sacrifices perfect accuracy in the interest of a clear general statement. Poetical, figurative language is often obscure and vague.

Not infrequently apocryphal works are attributed to the saints. Then, even the best authors often introduce the erroneous views of others and leave the reader to distinguish between the true and the false. Sometime, as Augustine confesses in his own case, the fathers ventured to rely upon the opinions of others.

Doubtless the fathers might err; even Peter, the prince of the apostles, fell into error; what wonder that the saints do not always show themselves inspired? The fathers did not themselves believe that they, or their companions, were always right. Augustine found himself mistaken in some cases and did not hesitate to retract his errors. He warns his admirers not to look upon his letters as they would upon the Scriptures, but to accept only those things which, upon examination, they find to be true.

All writings belonging to this class are to be read with full freedom to criticise, and with no obligation to accept unquestioningly; otherwise the way would be blocked to all discussion, and posterity be deprived of the excellent intellectual exercise of debating difficult questions of language and presentation. But an explicit exception must be made in the case of the Old and New Testaments. In the Scriptures, when anything strikes us as absurd, we may not say that the writer erred, but that the scribe made a blunder in copying the manuscripts, or that there is an error in interpretation, or that the passage is not understood. The fathers make a very careful distinction between the Scriptures and later works. They advocate a discriminating, not to say suspicious, use of the writings of their own contemporaries.

In view of these considerations, I have ventured to bring together various dicta of the holy fathers, as they came to mind, and to formulate certain questions which were suggested by the seeming contradictions in the statements. These questions ought to serve to excite tender readers to a zealous inquiry into truth and so sharpen their wits. The master key of knowledge is, indeed, a persistent and frequent questioning. Aristotle, the most clear-sighted of all the philosophers, was desirous above all things else to arouse this questioning spirit, for in his *Categories* he exhorts a student as follows: "It may well be difficult to reach a positive conclusion in these matters unless they be frequently discussed. It is by no means fruitless to be doubtful on particular points." By doubting we come to examine, and by examining we reach the truth.

[*Abelard provides arguments for and against 158 different philosophical or theological propositions. The following are a few of the questions he discusses.*]

Should human faith be based upon reason, or no?
Is God one, or no?
Is God a substance, or no?
Does the first Psalm refer to Christ, or no?
Is sin pleasing to God, or no?
Is God the author of evil, or no?
Is God all-powerful, or no?
Can God be resisted, or no?
Has God free will, or no?
Was the first man persuaded to sin by the devil, or no?
Was Adam saved, or no?
Did all the apostles have wives except John, or no?
Are the flesh and blood of Christ in very truth and essence present in the sacrament of the altar, or no?
Do we sometimes sin unwillingly, or no?
Does God punish the same sin both here and in the future, or no?
Is it worse to sin openly than secretly, or no?

Source 6 from Roland H. Bainton, The Medieval Church *(Princeton, N.J.: D. VanNostrand, 1962), pp. 128–129.*

6. St. Anselm's Proof of the Existence of God, from His *Monologium*, ca 1070

I sought if I might find a single argument which would alone suffice to demonstrate that God exists. This I did in the spirit of faith seeking understanding. . . .

Come now, O Lord my God, teach my heart where and how it may seek Thee. O Lord, if Thou art not here where shall I seek Thee absent, and if Thou art everywhere why do I not see Thee present? Surely Thou dwellest in light inaccessible. When wilt Thou enlighten our eyes? I do not presume to penetrate Thy profundity but only in some measure to understand Thy truth, which my heart believes and loves, for I seek not to understand that I may believe, but I believe in order that I may understand.

Now the fool will admit that there can be in the mind something than which nothing greater can be conceived. This, being understood, is in the mind, but it cannot be only in the mind, because it is possible to think of something which exists also in reality and that would be greater. If, therefore, that than which nothing greater can be conceived is only in the mind, that than which a greater cannot be conceived is that than which a greater can be conceived and this certainly cannot be. Consequently, without doubt, that than which nothing greater can be conceived exists both in the mind and in reality. This, then, is so sure that one cannot think of its not being so. For it is possible to think of something which one cannot conceive not to exist which is greater than that which cannot be conceived can be thought not to exist, it is not that a greater than which cannot be conceived. But this does not make sense. Therefore, it is true that something than which a greater cannot be conceived is not able to be conceived as not existing. This art Thou, O Lord, my God.

Source 7 from Lynn Thorndike, editor and translator, University Records and Life in the Middle Ages *(New York: Columbia University Press, 1944), pp. 66–67.*

7. Odofredus Announces His Law Lectures at Bologna, ca 1255

If you please, I will begin the *Old Digest*[10] on the eighth day or thereabouts after the feast of St. Michael[11] and I will finish it entire with all ordinary and extraordinary, Providence permitting, in the middle of August or thereabouts. The *Code*[12] I will always begin within about a fortnight of the feast of St. Michael and I will finish it with all ordinary and extraordinary, Providence permitting, on

10. **Old Digest:** the first part of the *Digest,* the emperor Justinian's collation of laws, commentaries, and interpretations of laws by Roman jurists.
11. **feast of St. Michael:** September 29.
12. **Code:** another part of Justinian's collation of laws reflecting the additions to Roman law that came about after Christianity became the official religion of the empire.

the first of August or thereabouts. The extraordinary lectures used not to be given by the doctors. And so all scholars including the unskilled and novices will be able to make good progress with me, for they will hear their text as a whole, nor will anything be left out, as was once done in this region, indeed was the usual practice. For I shall teach the unskilled and novices but also the advanced students. For the unskilled will be able to make satisfactory progress in the position of the case and exposition of the letter; the advanced students can become more erudite in the subtleties of questions and contrarieties. I shall also read all the glosses, which was not done before my time. . . .

For it is my purpose to teach you faithfully and in a kindly manner, in which instruction the following order has customarily been observed by the ancient and modern doctors and particularly by my master, which method I shall retain. First, I shall give you the summaries of each title before I come to the text. Second, I shall put forth well and distinctly and in the best terms I can the purport of each law. Third, I shall read the text in order to correct it. Fourth, I shall briefly restate the meaning. Fifth, I shall solve conflicts, adding general matters (which are commonly called *brocardica*) and subtle and useful distinctions and questions with the solutions, so far as divine Providence shall assist me. And if any law is deserving of a review by reason of its fame or difficulty, I shall reserve it for an afternoon review.

Source 8 from Anders Piltz, The World of Medieval Learning, *translated by David Jones (Totowa, N.J.: Barnes & Noble, 1981), p. 97.*

8. Introduction to *Digest* of Emperor Justinian, 6th century

Public law is the legislation which refers to the Roman state, *private law* on the other hand is of value to the individual. Common law contains statutes about sacrifices, the priesthood and civil servants. Private law can be divided into three parts: it comprises regulations based on natural law and regulations governing the intercourse of nations and of individuals. *Natural law* is what is taught to all living creatures by nature itself, laws which apply not only to mankind but to every living creature on the earth, in the heavens or in the seas. It is this that sanctions the union of man and woman, which is called marriage, and likewise the bearing and upbringing of children: we can see that other living creatures also possess understanding of this law. *International law* is the [commonly recognized set of] laws applied by every nation of the world. As can be seen it differs from natural law in that the latter is the same for all living creatures whereas the former only concerns human intercourse. . . . *Civil law* does not deviate completely from natural law but neither is it subordinate to it. . . . It is either written or unwritten. . . . Its sources are laws, popular decisions, decisions of the senate, the decrees of princes and the opinions of jurists. . . . *Justice* is the earnest and steadfast desire to give every man the rights he is entitled to. The injunctions of the law are these: live honestly, do no man injury, give to every man what he is entitled to.

Jurisprudence is knowledge of divine and human things, the study of right and wrong.

Source 9 from The Letters of St. Bernard of Clairvaux, *translated by Bruno Scott James (Chicago: Henry Regnery Company, 1953), pp. 321, 328.*

9. Extracts from the Letters of St. Bernard of Clairvaux, 1140

Master Peter Abelard is a monk without a rule, a prelate without responsibility. . . . He speaks iniquity openly. He corrupts the integrity of the faith and the chastity of the Church. He oversteps the landmarks placed by our Fathers in discussing and writing about faith, the sacraments, and the Holy Trinity; he changes each thing according to his pleasure, adding to it or taking from it. In his books and in his works he shows himself to be a fabricator of falsehood, a coiner of perverse dogmas, proving himself a heretic not so much by his error as by his obstinate defence of error. He is a man who does not know his limitations, making void the virtue of the cross by the cleverness of his words. Nothing in heaven or on earth is hidden from him, except himself. . . . He has defiled the Church; he has infected with his own blight the minds of simple people. He tries to explore with his reason what the devout mind grasps at once with a vigorous faith. Faith believes, it does not dispute. But this man, apparently holding God suspect, will not believe anything until he has first examined it with his reason. When the Prophet says, "Unless you believe, you shall not understand," this man decries willing faith as levity, misusing that testimony of Solomon: "He that is hasty to believe is light of head." Let him therefore blame the Blessed Virgin Mary for quickly believing the angel when he announced to her that she should conceive and bring forth a son. Let him also blame him who, while on the verge of death, believed those words of One who was also dying: "This day thou shalt be with me in Paradise."

Source 10 from Cecil Headlam, The Story of Oxford *(London: Dent, 1907), pp. 234–235.*

10. Anonymous Account of a Student Riot at Oxford, 13th century

They [the townsmen] seized and imprisoned all scholars on whom they could lay hands, invaded their inns, made havoc of their goods and trampled their books under foot. In the face of such provocation the Proctors[13] sent their bedels[14] about the town, forbidding the students to leave their inns. But all commands and exhortations were in vain. By nine o'clock next morning, bands of scholars were parading the streets in martial array. If the Proctors failed to restrain them, the mayor was equally powerless to restrain his townsmen. The great bell of S. Martin's rang out an alarm; oxhorns were sounded in the streets; messengers were sent into the country to collect rustic allies. The clerks,[15] who numbered three thousand in all, began their attack simultaneously in various quarters. They broke open warehouses in the Spicery, the Cutlery and elsewhere. Armed with bows and arrows, swords and bucklers, slings and stones, they fell upon their opponents. Three they slew, and wounded fifty or more. One band, led by Fulk de Neyrmit, Rector of Piglesthorne, and his brother, took up a position in High Street between the Churches of S. Mary and All Saints', and attacked the house of a certain Edward Hales. This Hales was a longstanding enemy of the clerks. There were no half measures with him. He seized his crossbow, and from an upper chamber sent an unerring shaft into the eye of the pugnacious rector. The death of their valiant leader caused the clerks to lose heart. They fled, closely pursued by the townsmen and country-folk. Some were struck down in the streets, and others who had taken refuge in the churches were dragged out and driven mercilessly to prison, lashed with thongs and goaded with iron spikes.

Complaints of murder, violence and robbery were lodged straight-way with the King by both parties. The townsmen claimed three thousand pounds' damage. The commissioners, however, appointed to decide the matter, condemned them to pay two hundred marks, removed the bailiffs, and banished twelve of the most turbulent citizens from Oxford. Then the terms of peace were formally ratified.

13. **proctor:** university official who maintained order and supervised examinations.
14. **bedel:** assistant to the proctor.
15. **clerks:** here, students and teachers.

Source 11 from Dana Carleton Munro, editor and translator, Translations and Reprints from the Original Sources of European History, *vol. 2, no. 3 (Philadelphia: University of Pennsylvania Press, no date), pp. 19–21.*

11. Jacques de Vitry's Description of Student Life at Paris, ca 1225

Almost all the students at Paris, foreigners and natives, did absolutely nothing except learn or hear something new. Some studied merely to acquire knowledge, which is curiosity; others to acquire fame, which is vanity; others still for the sake of gain, which is cupidity and the vice of simony. Very few studied for their own edification, or that of others. They wrangled and disputed not merely about the various sects or about some discussions; but the differences between the countries also caused dissensions, hatreds and virulent animosities among them, and they impudently uttered all kinds of affronts and insults against one another.

They affirmed that the English were drunkards and had tails; the sons of France proud, effeminate and carefully adorned like women. They said that the Germans were furious and obscene at their feasts; the Normans, vain and boastful; the Poitevins, traitors and always adventurers. The Burgundians they considered vulgar and stupid. The Bretons were reputed to be fickle and changeable and were often reproached for the death of Arthur. The Lombards were called avaricious, vicious and cowardly; the Romans, seditious, turbulent and slanderous; the Sicilians, tyrannical and cruel; the inhabitants of Brabant, men of blood, incendiaries, brigands and ravishers; those of Flanders, fickle, prodigal, gluttonous, yielding as butter, and slothful. After such insults, from words they often came to blows.

I will not speak of those logicians, before whose eyes flitted constantly "the lice of Egypt," that is to say, all the sophistical subtleties, so that no one could comprehend their eloquent discourses in which, as says Isaiah, "there is no wisdom." As to the doctors of theology, "seated in Moses' seat," they were swollen with learning, but their charity was not edifying. Teaching and not practicing, they have "become as sounding brass or a tinkling cymbal," or like a canal of stone, always dry, which ought to carry water to "the bed of spices." They not only hated one another, but by their flatteries they enticed away the students of others; each one seeking his own glory, but caring not a whit about the welfare of souls.

Having listened intently to these words of the Apostle, "If a man desire the office of a bishop, he desireth a good work," they kept multiplying the prebends,[16] and seeking after the offices; and yet they sought the work decid-

16. **prebends:** that part of church revenues paid as a clergyman's salary.

edly less than the preëminence, and they desired above all to have "the uppermost rooms at feasts and the chief seats in the synagogue, and greetings in the market." Although the Apostle James said, "My brethren, be not many masters," they on the contrary were in such haste to become masters, that most of them were not able to have any students, except by entreaties and payments. Now it is safer to listen than to teach, and a humble listener is better than an ignorant and presumptuous doctor. In short, the Lord had reserved for Himself among them all, only a few honorable and timorous men, who had not stood "in the way of sinners," nor sat down with the others in the envenomed seat.

Source 12 and 13 from Charles Homer Haskins, The Rise of Universities *(Ithaca, N.Y.: Cornell University Press, 1957), pp. 77–80; pp. 85–87.*

12. Two Letters, 13th century

B. to his venerable master A., greeting. This is to inform you that I am studying at Oxford with the greatest diligence, but the matter of money stands greatly in the way of my promotion,[17] as it is now two months since I spent the last of what you sent me. The city is expensive and makes many demands; I have to rent lodgings, buy necessaries, and provide for many other things which I cannot now specify. Wherefore I respectfully beg your paternity that by the promptings of divine pity you may assist me, so that I may be able to complete what I have well begun. For you must know that without Ceres and Bacchus Apollo[18] grows cold.

To his son G. residing at Orleans P. of Besançon sends greetings with paternal zeal. It is written, "He also that is slothful in his work is brother to him that is a great waster." I have recently discovered that you live dissolutely and slothfully, preferring license to restraint and play to work and strumming a guitar while the others are at their studies, whence it happens that you have read but one volume of law while your more industrious companions have read several. Wherefore I have decided to exhort you herewith to repent utterly of your dissolute and careless ways, that you may no longer be called a waster and your shame may be turned to good repute.

17. **promotion:** that is, attaining his degree.

18. **Ceres:** Roman god of grain. **Bacchus:** god of wine. **Apollo:** god of wisdom.

13. Three Anonymous Student Poems, 12th century

I, a wandering scholar lad,
  Born for toil and sadness,
Oftentimes am driven by
  Poverty to madness.

Literature and knowledge I
  Fain would still be earning,
Were it not that want of pelf[19]
  Makes me cease from learning.

These torn clothes that cover me
  Are too thin and rotten;
Oft I have to suffer cold,
  By the warmth forgotten.

Scarce I can attend at church,
  Sing God's praises duly;
Mass and vespers both I miss,
  Though I love them truly.

Oh, thou pride of N———,
  By thy worth I pray thee
Give the suppliant help in need,
  Heaven will sure repay thee.

Take a mind unto thee now
  Like unto St. Martin;
Clothe the pilgrim's nakedness,
  Wish him well at parting.

So may God translate your soul
  Into peace eternal,
And the bliss of saints be yours
  In His realm supernal.

We in our wandering,
Blithesome and squandering,
  Tara, tantara, teino!

Eat to satiety,
Drink with propriety;
  Tara, tantara, teino!

Laugh till our sides we split,
Rags on our hides we fit;
  Tara, tantara, teino!

Jesting eternally,
Quaffing infernally:
  Tara, tantara, teino!
    etc.

Some are gaming, some are drinking,
Some are living without thinking;
And of those who make the racket,
Some are stripped of coat and jacket;
Some get clothes of finer feather,
Some are cleaned out altogether;
No one there dreads death's invasion,
But all drink in emulation.

19. **pelf:** a contemptuous term for money.

QUESTIONS TO CONSIDER

You have now examined medieval universities and colleges from four points of view—those of the authorities who established them, the teachers who taught in them, the church officials who criticized them, and the students who attended them. In refining your description of university life, think first about points on which a number of sources agree. What role did religious and secular authorities play in the universities, both in their founding and in their day-to-day operations? What privileges were extended to teachers and students, and how did these benefits affect their relationship with townspeople? Given these privileges and student attitudes and actions, what opinion would you expect townspeople to have of students? Which of Sorbon's rules would you expect to have been frequently broken? What qualities did authorities and teachers alike see as vital to effective teaching? What qualities did both try to encourage in students? Would students have agreed about any of these? What problems did the authorities, teachers, and students all agree were most pressing for students?

Now turn to points on which you have contradictory information. How would you compare Abelard's beliefs about the role of logic in education with those of Bernard and de Vitry? How might Bernard and de Vitry have viewed Anselm's attempt to prove the existence of God through reason? Would Abelard have believed that the rules for students set out in Sources 1 through 4 helped or hindered the learning process? What suggestions for educational improvements might a philosopher like Abelard have made? A churchman like Bernard? Would Anselm and Odofredus have agreed about the proper methods and aims of education?

De Vitry's critique and the student poetry have pointed out that the rules for student life set out in Sources 1 through 4 were not always followed. The consequences of St. Bernard's criticism similarly demonstrate that Abelard's assertion of the need for free discussion of all topics was an ideal and not always the reality in medieval universities. In 1140, St. Bernard convinced the church leadership at the Council of Sens to condemn Abelard's teachings. Abelard appealed to the pope, who upheld the council's decision, and Abelard retired to a monastery, never to teach again. What does this incident indicate about where the ultimate authority in the university lay? Does this assertion of papal authority contradict any of the ideas expressed in other sources for this chapter besides Abelard's writings?

Some of the contradictions you have discovered are inherent in the highly different points of view of the four groups and are irreconcilable. You must, however, make some effort to resolve those contradictions that involve conflicting points of *fact* rather than simply conflicting *opinions.* Historians resolve contradictions in their sources by a variety of methods: by assessing the authors' intent and possible biases, giving weight to evidence that is likely to be most objective; by judging each source as partially valid, speculating on how each author's point of view might have affected his or her description; by trying to find additional information confirming one side or the other. At this point you can use the first two methods in your own thinking: Which observers do you judge to be most objective? Why did the students, teachers, and officials have different viewpoints in the first place? (You can also think about the third method historians use to resolve contradictions in their evidence: What other types of sources would you examine to confirm what you have discovered here?) Once you have made these judgments, you can complete your description of medieval university life.

Now move on to the second part of your task in this chapter, which is to compare medieval and modern university life. Some of the more striking contrasts have probably already occurred to you, but the best way to proceed is to think first about your evidence. What types of sources would give you the information for modern universities that you have unearthed for medieval ones? What are the modern equivalents of the medieval rules and ordinances? Of descriptions of student actions? Of student poetry? Of course announcements? Of philosophical treatises? Besides such parallel sources, where else can you find information about modern universities? What types of sources generated from modern universities, or from their students and teachers, have no medieval equivalent?

After considering these points of similarity and difference in sources, we are ready to make a specific comparison of university life in medieval and modern times. Because higher education in the United States is so diverse—some colleges and universities are public and some private, some religious and some nonsectarian, some residential and some commuter—it would be best if you compared your own institution with the more generalized description of medieval universities that you have developed. Do you see any modern equivalents to the privileges granted to students by popes and kings? To the frequent clashes between universities and their surrounding communities? To the pope's restriction of "academic freedom" in the case of Abelard? How would you compare the relationship between religious and political authorities in medieval universities and in your own institution? The concern of authorities for the methods and content of higher education? How would you compare student residential life? Student problems? The students themselves? Relations between students and their parents? How would you compare the subjects taught? The method of teaching? The status of the faculty? Relations between students and teachers? Teachers' and students' views of the ultimate aims of education?

Once you have drawn up your comparison, you will need to perform what is often the most difficult task of any historical inquiry: suggesting reasons for what you have discovered. In doing this, you need to speculate not only about why some things have changed, but also about why others have remained the same. In your view, what is the most important difference between medieval and modern universities, and why?

EPILOGUE

The pattern set by Paris and Bologna was a popular one; by 1500, more than eighty universities were in existence throughout Europe. Often a dispute at one university, particularly among the faculty of theology, would lead a group of teachers and students to move elsewhere to form their own university. Sometimes they left one city because they felt the townspeople were overcharging them for food and lodging. Students often traveled from university to university in search of the best teachers or the most amenable surroundings; because there were no admission forms or credits required for graduation, transferring from school to school was much easier in the Middle Ages than it is today.

As you have deduced from the sources, medieval students and teachers were criticized for all the seven deadly sins: greed, sloth, pride, lust, gluttony, envy, and anger. Toward the end of the Middle Ages, the university system itself came under increasing attack for being too remote from worldly concerns, providing students only with useless philosophical information that would never help them in the real world of politics and business. Especially in Italy, independent teachers of speech and writing began to offer young men who wanted an education an alternative to universities, setting up academies to teach practical rhetorical and literary skills for those who planned to engage in commerce, banking, or politics. This new program of study, called *humanism,* emphasized language and literature rather than theology and philosophy.

Though the universities initially opposed the humanist curriculum, by the sixteenth century a considerable number, especially the newer ones, began to change their offerings. They established endowed chairs for teachers of Latin, Greek, and Hebrew, particularly because students who had trained at humanist secondary schools demanded further language training. Some of the oldest universities, such as Paris, were the slowest to change, but eventually they modified their program to keep students from going elsewhere.

The gradual introduction of humanism set a pattern that universities were to follow when any new body of knowledge or subject matter emerged. Innovative subjects and courses were at first generally taught outside the universities in separate academies or institutes, then slowly integrated into the university curriculum. In the seventeenth and eighteenth centuries, natural science was added in this way; in the nineteenth century, the social sciences and modern languages; and in the twentieth, a whole range of subjects, such as agriculture, engineering, and the fine arts. (The University of Paris continued to be the slowest to change well into the twentieth century; for example, it did not add sociology as a discipline until the 1960s. Modernization of the curriculum was one of the demands of the 1968 student revolt in Paris.) Thus, even though the university has survived since the Middle Ages, Peter Abelard or Robert de Sorbon might have difficulty recognizing the institution in its present-day form.

CHAPTER FIVE

TWO FACES OF "HOLY WAR":[1]

CHRISTIANS AND MUSLIMS

THE PROBLEM

According to the Book of Matthew in the Christian New Testament, after his resurrection from the dead, Jesus appeared before his eleven remaining disciples in Galilee, where he commanded them, "Go ye, therefore, and teach all nations, baptizing them in the name of the Father, and of the Son, and of the Holy Ghost, [t]eaching them to observe all things whatsoever I have commanded you."[2] Similarly, in the Qur'an (Koran), the book containing the revelations to Islam's founder, Muhammad ibn Abdullah, the Prophet commanded his followers to "Invite [all] to the way of your Lord . . . For your Lord knows best who has strayed from His Path, and who receives guidance."[3] Thus Christianity and Islam, both of which saw themselves as the keepers of God's ultimate revelation of Himself to humanity, from their respective beginnings had built within their doctrines the commandment to proselytize and spread to include all peoples.

At their beginnings, neither Christianity nor Islam preached the expansion of the faith by use of the sword. Muhammad counseled his followers to make converts "with wisdom and beautiful preaching; and argue with them in ways that are best and most gracious,"[4] while earlier the apostle Paul, himself a convert to Christianity, wrote to his fellow Christians in Rome to "follow after the things that make for peace, and things therewith one may edify another," so that "through your mercy they also may obtain mercy."[5]

Yet ultimately both Christians and Muslims were willing to spread their respective faiths by force. As Christians swelled in numbers, they increasingly embraced violence both to punish unbelievers and heretics and to expand the faith. For justification, they often

1. The term *holy war* is of European origin, first coined by Friedrich Schwally in his book *Der Heilege Kreig im alten Israel [Holy War in Ancient Israel]* (Leipzig, 1901).

2. King James Version (KJV) 28:19–20. See also Acts 1:8.

3. Qur'an, Sūra 16:125.

4. Ibid.

5. Romans 14:19, 11:31, KJV.

reached back into the Old Testament, in which Israelites had been told to "utterly destroy them [unbelievers], as the Lord thy God hath commanded thee."[6] For their part, after the *hijra*[7] of Muhammad and his followers to Medina, the Prophet began to report revelations of *jihads al-sayf* (jihads of the sword). Originally the term *jihad* was shorthand for *jihad fi sabil Allah* (struggle in the path of God) and had no relation to warfare at all. Most often the term referred to an *internal* struggle of a Muslim against temptations, or a particular internal struggle against Muslim heretics or impious leaders. But, as noted above, within a few years of the *hijra,* Muhammad was saying such things as "Whoever fights in the path of God, whether he be killed or be victorious, on him We shall bestow a great reward," and "those who strive and fight has He distinguished above those who sit [at home] by a great reward."[8]

For centuries the proponents of these two religions maintained comparatively good relations with one another. In lands conquered by Muslims, Christians and Jews (known to Muslims as "People of the Book") were able to practice their respective faiths so long as they paid tribute and taxes to Muslim political authorities. Christians and Jews also were able to make pilgrimages to Jerusalem. And in Italy and Spain, Muslims lived in close proximity to Christians for hundreds of years without major altercations. Yet while their respective intellectual elites shared knowledge with one another, the two kept a careful—and enforced—distance. The papacy labeled Christians who dealt with Muslims as traitors and warned that such treason meant loss of all their property. For their part, most Muslims thought Western Christians were primitive and had little to teach them (Usamah ibn-Munqidh called Christians "animals").

Sometime after 1071 C.E., however, that brittle peace was broken. Seljuk Turks, new converts to Islam who interpreted the term *jihad* in its most warlike way, seized control of Jerusalem from the more tolerant Abbasid Muslims. The Muslim world was becoming fragmented and vulnerable to outside intrusions.

At the same time that the Muslim world was becoming increasingly divided, western Europe was showing signs of increased energy. After centuries of comparatively modest population increases, the population suddenly grew more rapidly, creating a surplus agricultural population and a resulting desire for more land. For example, it has been estimated that between about 950 and 1347 (the year the Black Death first appeared in Europe), the population of Europe increased threefold—in some areas, like Saxony, it increased tenfold. At the same time, trade with the eastern Mediterranean grew significantly, feeding the desire, especially in the commercial cities of Italy, for more trade connections with the Middle East. Finally, the social order produced a

6. Deuteronomy 20:17, KJV.

7. **hijra:** the flight or emigration of Muhammad from Mecca to Medina, in 622 C.E.

8. Qur'an, Sūra 4:74, 95. Muhammad's revelations in the Qur'an are in order of length, with the longest sūra first. For one interpretation of the *chronology* of the revelations, see Reuven Firestone, *Jihad: The Origins of Holy War in Islam* (New York: Oxford University Press, 1999), pp. 67–91, 115–125.

class of knightly warriors who were anxious to extend their power through combat.

Politically, however, Europe was even more fragmented than the Muslim world. Kings, for the most part weak, were unable to enforce peace within their domains. In an effort to keep the lords of Europe away from each other's throats as well as to enhance the power of the papacy, popes in the eleventh century attempted to promote the Peace of God movement among Christians. European nobles, the movement proclaimed, would not engage in warfare against one another.

The Peace of God movement shows that the power of the popes was increasing and that religious enthusiasm was on the rise in Europe. Itinerant preachers whipped up crowds into fevers of religious excitement in which visions and miracles of healing were reported. In about the year 1000, an old Christian myth was revived and spread throughout much of Europe. Before the second coming of Christ and the resulting end of the world, the story went, an emperor from the West would be crowned in Jerusalem and would battle the Antichrist in that holy city. The circulation of this myth was especially rampant during the widespread famine of 1033.

Hence a number of factors were pushing Christian Europe toward its own version of a "holy war." Population growth spurred a hunger for land, and, in turn, a drive for new lands to be brought under Europeans' control gained momentum. The knightly warriors could maintain the Peace of God among Christians while at the same time uniting to battle "pagans" elsewhere. Crusades could also increase the power of the papacy and would direct the religious enthusiasm toward a productive end.

On November 27, 1095, in a field of Clermont, France, Pope Urban II called on Western Christians to undertake a *peregrinatio* (pilgrimage) to capture Jerusalem from the Muslims.[9] Many Christians took up the cry "God wills it!" "You should be especially aroused," Urban challenged his listeners at Clermont, "by the knowledge that . . . the holy places are shamelessly misused and sacrilegiously defiled with their filth." The first armies set off in August 1097[10]; they captured Jerusalem on July 15, 1099.

Earlier Muslim incursions into North Africa, the eastern Mediterranean, Sicily, Italy, Spain, and southern France did not mean that Muslims had learned a great deal about Christian Europe, or that European Christians had learned a great deal about them. Instead, what is striking is the apparent utter lack of curiosity that each side displayed toward the other. Beginning about the time of the First Crusade, however, the number of written accounts by both Christians and Muslims increased dramatically. By the time the first Christian army arrived in Palestine in 1098, a number of written accounts by one side about the

9. Those Christians who went on these expeditions referred to themselves as "pilgrims." The term *crusade* (from the French word *croix*, "cross" in English) was not used for some time.

10. A ragtag army of peasants led by the itinerant holy man Peter the Hermit began its march earlier, slaughtered Jews on its way across Europe, and was wiped out before reaching Palestine. It has been estimated that one-fourth of all crusaders died on their way to the Holy Land.

other had been circulated and read (or listened to). Appearing as they did during the period Europeans refer to as the Crusades, there is little doubt that these accounts created perceptions and stereotypes in the minds of Christians who had never met Muslims, and vice versa. Moreover, it is clear that these accounts helped to formulate ideas in each camp of how the other should be treated.

Your tasks in this chapter are twofold. First, by examining the accounts written by Christians and by Muslims, determine the impressions that each side created of the other. Second, reach some conclusions about how those perceptions and stereotypes (whether accurate or inaccurate) might have influenced the ways in which Christians and Muslims chose to deal with one another. Thus, your tasks are to determine what the perceptions presented were *and* how they helped to shape opinion on how the other side was to be treated.

SOURCES AND METHOD

Before you begin, we must issue a note of caution. From the evidence provided by Christians, you will *not* be able to determine what Muslims were *really* like, but only what Christians perceived (or wanted their readers to perceive) Muslims were like. This is equally true of the Muslim accounts. Indeed, it is quite possible that some of the writers had never even met the people about whom they were writing. Even so, what you *do* learn will prove extremely important, for perceptions, impressions, and stereotypes are often just as powerful as facts in prompting individuals to action. To paraphrase historian Claude Van Tyne, what people *think* is true may be more important to them than what is *really* true.

The Evidence section of this chapter contains three Muslim accounts of European crusaders and two European Christian accounts of Muslims. Usamah ibn-Munqidh (1095–1188) was born in Syria and educated by private tutors; he was a merchant and government administrator, and knew Europeans quite well. Source 1 is his account of the "curious" crusaders. For his part, Ibn al-Athir (1160–1233) was one of three brothers, all of whom became noted Arabic scholars. He traveled extensively to collect material for his historical writing, and in Source 2, he glories in the 1187 retaking of Jerusalem. Imad ad-Din (1125–1201) was a scholar who was best known as a secretary to the sultan Saladin. Source 3 is an excerpt from his *History of the Fall of Jerusalem.*

As to the Christian sources, *History of the Jerusalem Journey* (Source 4) is by Peter Tudebode, a priest who accompanied the warriors on the First Crusade. One or possibly two of his brothers were killed in battle during the siege of Antioch. Some controversy continues to surround Peter Tudebode's account because many scholars believe that some of it was plagiarized from earlier writers. Since you are concerned with the perceptions that readers or listeners might have gleaned from the account, whether Tudebode actually saw some of what he chronicled or not is less important than those perceptions.

The final account, *A History of Deeds Done Beyond the Sea* by William of Tyre (Source 5), is almost certainly the most widely read account by a Christian of the Crusades. William was born around 1130 in or near Jerusalem to European parents. He was extremely well educated both in Palestine and in Europe and had command of six languages, including Arabic and Persian. He was ordained a Roman Catholic priest, returned to what Christians referred to as the Holy Land, and was made Archbishop of Tyre, a position he held from 1175 to approximately 1185. By the time Saladin conquered Jerusalem in 1187, William had disappeared from view and probably had died.

At first glance, all of these sources present some potential problems. To begin with, we cannot be certain that any of the authors were eyewitnesses to the events they describe. For example, some events that William of Tyre wrote about took place before he was born. To be sure, as secretary to Saladin, Imad ad-Din was in an excellent position to witness the events that he recounted. But that is not proof that he actually *did* see them, and we cannot be sure how much he embellished what he saw or heard.

And yet, in this chapter, these are not the obstacles that they might be elsewhere. This is because, as noted above, we are seeking the *perceptions* that each side had of the other and the images and stereotypes that were deliberately created for a myriad of purposes (one pilgrim on the First Crusade, the Fulcher of Charters, described people "so tall that they can mount elephants as easily as horses").[11] Each author is attempting to create an impression in the minds of readers. To that end, he may accurately report events, or he may liberally exaggerate, interpret, or simply invent. That these writers were helping to create or perpetuate what ultimately would become very unhealthy stereotypes that in some cases continue to exist today does not appear to have bothered them in the least. Indeed, for some of these men, such stereotypes were good things that people should believe when facing their enemies.

As you finish each selection, think of some adjectives that readers of the account might have used to describe "the enemy." Keep a running list of these adjectives as you proceed through the evidence. Be willing also to read between the lines. Sometimes a particular author, in genuinely trying to describe or explain a specific incident, may have nevertheless created a perception in the minds of his readers, intentionally or unintentionally. Be alert for such instances.

Keep the central questions of the chapter in mind: In the written accounts by Muslims and Christians, what impressions did each side create of the other? How might those perceptions or stereotypes have influenced

11. See Fulcher of Charters, *A History of the Expedition to Jerusalem, 1095–1127*, trans. Frances Rita Ryan (Knoxville: University of Tennessee Press, 1969), p. 287.

the way each side chose to deal with and treat the other, both during and after the period that Europeans refer to as the Crusades?

THE EVIDENCE

MUSLIMS ON CHRISTIANS

Source 1 from Usamah ibn-Munqidh, An Arab-Syrian Gentleman and Warrior in the Period of the Crusades, *translated by Philip K. Hitti (New York: Columbia University Press, 1929; reprint, Princeton: Princeton University Press, 1987), pp. 161–169.*

1. Usamah ibn-Munqidh Describes the Franks

Their lack of sense.—Mysterious are the works of the Creator, the author of all things! When one comes to recount cases regarding the Franks,[12] he cannot but glorify Allah (exalted is he!) and sanctify him, for he sees them as animals possessing the virtues of courage and fighting, but nothing else; just as animals have only the virtues of strength and carrying loads. I shall now give some instances of their doings and their curious mentality.

In the army of King Fulk, son of Fulk, was a Frankish reverend knight who had just arrived from their land in order to make the holy pilgrimage and then return home. He was of my intimate fellowship and kept such constant company with me that he began to call me "my brother." Between us were mutual bonds of amity and friendship. When he resolved to return by sea to his homeland, he said to me:

> My brother, I am leaving for my country and I want thee to send with me thy son (my son, who was then fourteen years old, was at that time in my company) to our country, where he can see the knights and learn wisdom and chivalry. When he returns, he will be like a wise man.

Thus there fell upon my ears words which would never come out of the head of a sensible man; for even if my son were to be taken captive, his captivity could not bring him a worse misfortune than carrying him into the lands of the Franks. However, I said to the man:

12. Most Muslims called all the crusaders "Franks" even though they knew full well that they were not all French.

> By thy life, this has exactly been my idea. But the only thing that prevented me from carrying it out was the fact that his grandmother, my mother, is so fond of him and did not this time let him come out with me until she exacted an oath from me to the effect that I would return him to her.

Thereupon he asked, "Is thy mother still alive?" "Yes," I replied. "Well," said he, "disobey her not." . . .

Their curious medication.—A case illustrating their curious medicine is the following:

The lord of al-Munayṭirah wrote to my uncle asking him to dispatch a physician to treat certain sick persons among his people. My uncle sent him a Christian physician named Thābit. Thābit was absent but ten days when he returned. So we said to him, "How quickly hast thou healed thy patients!" He said:

> They brought before me a knight in whose leg an abscess had grown; and a woman afflicted with imbecility. To the knight I applied a small poultice until the abscess opened and became well; and the woman I put on diet and made her humor wet. Then a Frankish physician came to them and said, "This man knows nothing about treating them." He then said to the knight, "Which wouldst thou prefer, living with one leg or dying with two?" The latter replied, "Living with one leg." The physician said, "Bring me a strong knight and a sharp ax." A knight came with the ax. And I was standing by. Then the physician laid the leg of the patient on a block of wood and bade the knight strike his leg with the ax and chop it off at one blow. Accordingly he struck it—while I was looking on—one blow, but the leg was not severed. He dealt another blow, upon which the marrow of the leg flowed out and the patient died on the spot. He then examined the woman and said, "This is a woman in whose head there is a devil which has possessed her. Shave off her hair." Accordingly they shaved it off and the woman began once more to eat their ordinary diet—garlic and mustard. Her imbecility took a turn for the worse. The physician then said, "The devil has penetrated through her head." He therefore took a razor, made a deep cruciform incision on it, peeled off the skin at the middle of the incision until the bone of the skull was exposed and rubbed it with salt. The woman also expired instantly. Thereupon I asked them whether my services were needed any longer, and when they replied in the negative I returned home, having learned of their medicine what I knew not before. . . .

Another wants to show to a Moslem God as a child.—I saw one of the Franks come to al-Amīr Mu'īn-al-Dīn (may Allah's mercy rest upon his soul!) when he was in the Dome of the Rock and say to him, "Dost thou want to see God as a child?" Mu'īn-al-Dīn said, "Yes." The Frank walked ahead of us until he showed us the picture of Mary with Christ (may peace be upon him!) as an infant in her lap. He then said, "This is God as a child." But Allah is exalted far above what the infidels say about him!

Franks lack jealousy in sex affairs.—The Franks are void of all zeal and jealousy. One of them may be walking along with his wife. He meets another man who takes the wife by the hand and steps aside to converse with her while the husband is standing on one side waiting for his wife to conclude the conversation. If she lingers too long for him, he leaves her alone with the conversant and goes away.

Here is an illustration which I myself witnessed:

When I used to visit Nāblus, I always took lodging with a man named Mu'izz, whose home was a lodging house for the Moslems. The house had windows which opened to the road, and there stood opposite to it on the other side of the road a house belonging to a Frank who sold wine for the merchants. He would take some wine in a bottle and go around announcing it by shouting, "So and so, the merchant, has just opened a cask full of this wine. He who wants to buy some of it will find it in such and such a place." The Frank's pay for the announcement made would be the wine in that bottle. One day this Frank went home and found a man with his wife in the same bed. He asked him, "What could have made thee enter into my wife's room?" The man replied, "I was tired, so I went in to rest." "But how," asked he, "didst thou get into my bed?" The other replied, "I found a bed that was spread, so I slept in it." "But," said he, "my wife was sleeping together with thee!" The other replied, "Well, the bed is hers. How could I therefore have prevented her from using her own bed?" "By the truth of my religion," said the husband, "if thou shouldst do it again, thou and I would have a quarrel." Such was for the Frank the entire expression of his disapproval and the limit of his jealousy. . . .

Ordeal by water.—I once went in the company of al-Amīr Mu'īn-al-Dīn (may Allah's mercy rest upon his soul!) to Jerusalem. We stopped at Nāblus. There a blind man, a Moslem, who was still young and was well dressed, presented himself before al-Amīr carrying fruits for him and asked permission to be admitted into his service in Damascus. The amīr consented. I inquired about this man and was informed that his mother had been married to a Frank whom she had killed. Her son used to practice ruses against the Frankish pilgrims and cooperate with his mother in assassinating them. They finally brought charges against him and tried his case according to the Frankish way of procedure.

They installed a huge cask and filled it with water. Across it they set a board of wood. They then bound the arms of the man charged with the act, tied a rope around his shoulders and dropped him into the cask, their idea being that in case he was innocent, he would sink in the water and they would then lift him up with the rope so that he might not die in the water; and in case he was guilty, he would not sink in the water. This man did his best to sink when they dropped him into the water, but he could not do it. So he had to submit to their sentence against him—may Allah's curse be upon them! They pierced his eyeballs with red-hot awls. . . .

2. Ibn al-Athir, The Capture of Jerusalem, 1187

When the Franks saw how violently the Muslims were attacking, how continuous and effective was the fire from the ballistas and how busily the sappers were breaching the walls, meeting no resistance, they grew desperate, and their leaders assembled to take counsel. They decided to ask for safe-conduct out of the city and to hand Jerusalem over to Saladin.[13] They sent a deputation of their lords and nobles to ask for terms, but when they spoke of it to Saladin he refused to grant their request. "We shall deal with you," he said, "just as you dealt with the population of Jerusalem when you took it in 492/1099, with murder and enslavement and other such savageries!" The messengers returned empty-handed. Then Baliān ibn Barzān asked for safe-conduct for himself so that he might appear before Saladin to discuss developments. Consent was given, and he presented himself and once again began asking for a general amnesty in return for surrender. The Sultan still refused his requests and entreaties to show mercy. Finally, despairing of this approach, Baliān said: "Know, O Sultan, that there are very many of us in this city, God alone knows how many. At the moment we are fighting half-heartedly in the hope of saving our lives, hoping to be spared by you as you have spared others; this is because of our horror of death and our love of life. But if we see that death is inevitable, then by God we shall kill our children and our wives, burn our possessions, so as not to leave you with a *dinar* or a *drachma* or a single man or woman to enslave. When this is done, we shall pull down the Sanctuary of the Rock and the Masjid al-Aqsa and the other sacred places, slaughtering the Muslim prisoners we hold—5,000 of them—and killing every horse and animal we possess. Then we shall come out to fight you like men fighting for their lives, when each man, before he falls dead, kills his equals; we shall die with honour, or win a noble victory!" Then Saladin took counsel with his advisers, all of whom were in favour of his granting the assurances requested by the Franks, without forcing them to take extreme measures whose outcome could not be foreseen. "Let us consider them as being already our prisoners," they said, "and allow them to ransom themselves on terms agreed between us." The Sultan agreed to give the Franks assurances

13. **Saladin:** Muslim sultan Salah ad-Din, whose real name was Yusuf ibn-Ayyub. *Salah-ad-Din* means "Rectifier of the Faith," a name Yusuf took up when he began his jihad against Christians.

of safety on the understanding that each man, rich and poor alike, should pay ten *dinar*, children of both sexes two *dinar* and women five *dinar*. All who paid this sum within forty days should go free, and those who had not paid at the end of the time should be enslaved. Baliān ibn Barzān offered 30,000 *dinar* as ransom for the poor, which was accepted, and the city surrendered on Friday 27 rajab/2 October 1187, a memorable day on which the Muslim flags were hoisted over the walls of Jerusalem. . . .

The Grand Patriarch of the Franks left the city with the treasures from the Dome of the Rock, the Masjid al-Aqsa, the Church of the Resurrection and others, God alone knows the amount of the treasure; he also took an equal quantity of money. Saladin made no difficulties, and when he was advised to sequestrate the whole lot for Islām, replied that he would not go back on his word. He took only the ten *dinar* from him, and let him go, heavily escorted, to Tyre.

At the top of the cupola of the Dome of the Rock there was a great gilded cross. When the Muslims entered the city on the Friday, some of them climbed to the top of the cupola to take down the cross. When they reached the top a great cry went up from the city and from outside the walls, the Muslims crying the *Allāh akbar* in their joy, the Franks groaning in consternation and grief. So loud and piercing was the cry that the earth shook. . . .

3. From Imad ad-Din, *History of the Fall of Jerusalem*

At the same time as the King was taken the "True Cross"[14] was also captured, and the idolaters who were trying to defend it were routed. It was this cross, brought into position and raised on high, to which all Christians prostrated themselves and bowed their heads. Indeed, they maintain that it is made of the wood of the cross on which, they say, he whom they adore was hung, and so they venerate it and prostrate themselves before it. They had housed it in a casing of gold, adorned with pearls and gems, and kept it ready for the festival of the Passion, for the observance of their yearly ceremony. When the priests exposed it to view and the heads (of the bearers) bore it along all would run and cast themselves down around it, and no one was allowed to lag behind or hang back without forfeiting his liberty. Its capture was for them more important than the loss of the King and was the gravest blow that they sustained in that battle. The cross was a prize without equal, for it was the supreme object of their faith. To venerate it was their prescribed duty, for it was their God, before whom they would

14. The religious excitement in Europe led to the "discovery" of numerous relics both before and during the Crusades. Some of these relics were portions of the "True Cross" of Christ's crucifixion (see above), the Holy Lance (that pierced Jesus' side), and the Crown of Thorns. Thus, the loss of what was believed to have been the cross to Saladin was a devastating blow to the crusaders.

bow their foreheads to the ground, and to which their mouths sang hymns. They fainted at its appearance, they raised their eyes to contemplate it, they were consumed with passion when it was exhibited and boasted of nothing else when they had seen it. They went into ecstasies at its reappearance, they offered up their lives for it and sought comfort from it, so much so that they had copies made of it which they worshipped, before which they prostrated themselves in their houses and on which they called when they gave evidence. So when the Great Cross was taken great was the calamity that befell them, and the strength drained from their loins. Great was the number of the defeated, exalted the feelings of the victorious army. It seemed as if, once they knew of the capture of the Cross, none of them would survive that day of ill-omen. They perished in death or imprisonment, and were overcome by force and violence.

Here[15] are pictures of the Apostles conversing, Popes with their histories, monks in their cells, priests in their councils, the Magi with their ropes,[16] priests and their imaginings; here the effigies of the Madonna and the Lord, of the Temple and the Birthplace, of the Table and the fishes, and what is described and sculpted of the Disciples and the Master, of the cradle and the Infant speaking. Here are the effigies of the ox and the ass, of Paradise and Hell, the clappers and the divine laws. Here, they say, the Messiah was crucified, the sacrificial victim slain, divinity made incarnate, humanity deified. Here the dual nature was united, the cross was raised, light was extinguished and darkness covered the land. Here the nature was united with the person, the existent mingled with the non-existent, the adored Being was baptized and the Virgin gave birth to her Son.

They continued to attach errors like this to the object of their cult, wandering with false beliefs far from the true forms of faith, and said: "We shall die in defence of our Lord's sepulchre, and we shall die in fear of its slipping from our hands; we shall fight and struggle for it: how could we not fight, not contend and join battle, how could we leave this for them to take, and permit them to take from us what we took from them?" They made far-reaching and elaborate preparations, stretching out endlessly to infinity. They mounted deadly weapons on the walls, and veiled the face of light with the sombre curtain of walls. They sent out their demons, their wolves ran hither and thither, their impetuous tyrants raged; their swords were unsheathed, the fabric of their downfall displayed, their blazing firebrands lit. . . .

When Jerusalem was purified of the filth of the hellish Franks and had stripped off her vile garments to put on the robe of honour, the Christians, after paying their tax, refused to leave, and asked to be allowed to stay on in safety, and gave prodigious service and worked for us with all their might, carrying

15. **Here:** refers to the Church of the Holy Sepulchre, a church that Christians believed enclosed the sites of Jesus' crucifixion and the tomb from which he was resurrected.

16. **Magi . . . ropes:** refers to the Qur'an XX, 69, which describes Egyptian Magi casting down ropes before Moses and making them appear to be serpents.

out every task with discipline and cheerfulness. They paid "the tax for protection permitted to them, humbly." They stood ready to accept whatever might be inflicted on them, and their affliction grew as they stood waiting for it. Thus they became in effect tribute-payers, reliant upon (Muslim) protection; they were used and employed in menial tasks and in their position they accepted these tasks as if they were gifts.

The Franks had cut pieces from the Rock,[17] some of which they had carried to Constantinople and Sicily and sold, they said, for their weight in gold, making it a source of income. When the Rock reappeared to sight the marks of these cuts were seen and men were incensed to see how it had been mutilated. Now it is on view with the wounds it suffered, preserving its honour for ever, safe for Islam, within its protection and its fence. This was all done after the Sultan left and after an ordered pattern of life had been established. . . .

There arrived by ship three hundred lovely Frankish women, full of youth and beauty, assembled from beyond the sea and offering themselves for sin. They were expatriates come to help expatriates, ready to cheer the fallen and sustained in turn to give support and assistance, and they glowed with ardour for carnal intercourse. They were all licentious harlots, proud and scornful, who took and gave, foul-fleshed and sinful, singers and coquettes, appearing proudly in public, ardent and inflamed, tinted and painted, desirable and appetizing, exquisite and graceful, who ripped open and patched up, lacerated and mended, erred and ogled, urged and seduced, consoled and solicited, seductive and languid, desired and desiring, amused and amusing, versatile and cunning, like tipsy adolescents, making love and selling themselves for gold, bold and ardent, loving and passionate, pink-faced and unblushing, black-eyed and bullying, callipygian[18] and graceful, with nasal voices and fleshy thighs, blue-eyed and grey-eyed, broken-down little fools. . . .

Among the Franks there were indeed women who rode into battle with cuirasses [armor breastplates] and helmets, dressed in men's clothes; who rode out into the thick of the fray and acted like brave men although they were but tender women, maintaining that all this was an act of piety, thinking to gain heavenly rewards by it, and making it their way of life. Praise be to him who led them into such error and out of the paths of wisdom! On the day of battle more than one woman rode out with them like a knight and showed (masculine) endurance in spite of the weakness (of her sex); clothed only in a coat of mail they were not recognized as women until they had been stripped of their arms. Some

17. Muslims believed that Muhammad ascended to heaven from the Dome of the Rock, located in Jerusalem on the very site of the Temple where Jesus taught, which was destroyed by Roman armies in the first century. In 691, Caliph Abd al-Malik built a pavilion on the rock. Both Christians and Muslims believed that the rock possessed curative powers, and pilgrims chipped off fragments to take them home.

18. **callipygian:** having shapely buttocks.

of them were discovered and sold as slaves; and everywhere was full of old women. These were sometimes a support and sometimes a source of weakness. They exhorted and incited men to summon their pride, saying that the Cross imposed on them the obligation to resist to the bitter end, and that the combatants would win eternal life only by sacrificing their lives, and that their God's sepulchre was in enemy hands. Observe how men and women led them into error; the latter in their religious zeal tired of feminine delicacy, and to save themselves from the terror of dismay (on the day of Judgment) became the close companions of perplexity, and having succumbed to the lust for vengeance, became hardened, and stupid and foolish because of the harm they had suffered. . . .

EUROPEANS ON MUSLIMS

Source 4 reprinted by permission of the American Philosophical Society from Peter Tudebode, Historia de Hierosolymitano Itinere (History of the Jerusalem Journey), *translated by John Hugh Hill and Laurita L. Hill (Philadelphia: American Philosophical Society, 1974), pp. 54–55, 58–59, 115.*

4. From Peter Tudebode, *History of the Jerusalem Journey*

The Turkish attack was so overwhelming that our men took to their heels over the nearest mountain or the most convenient path; and those who were swift of foot survived, but the laggards met death for the name of Christ. More than one thousand knights or footmen martyred on that day rose joyfully to heaven and, bearing the stole of customary white-robed martyrdom, glorified and praised our triune God in whom they happily triumphed; and they said in unison: "Our God! Why did you not protect our blood which was shed today for your name?"

Following a different road, Bohemond with a few knights gave his horse free rein and sped to the assembled group of beset crusaders. Burning with anger over the death of our men, we invoked the name of Jesus Christ and, being assured of the crusade to the Holy Sepulchre, moved as a united front against our foes and joined in battle with one heart and mind. The Turks, enemies of God and us, stood around stunned and paralyzed with fear because they thought that they could overwhelm and slaughter us as they had done the troops of Raymond and Bohemond.

But Omnipotent God permitted no such thing. Knights of the true God, protected on all sides by the sign of the Cross, rushed pell-mell and courageously struck the Turks. In the ensuing rout the besieged scurried to safety by way of the narrow bridge to Antioch. The survivors, who could not push their way through the jam of people and horses, were snuffed out in everlasting death, and their miserable souls returned to the devil and his legions. We knocked them in the head and drove them into the river with our deadly lances so that the waters of the swift Orontes seemed to flow crimson with Turkish blood. If by chance one of them crawled up the bridge posts or struggled to swim to land, he was wounded. All along the river banks we stood pushing and drowning the pagans in the pull of the rapid stream.

The din of battle coupled with the screams of Christians and Turks rang out to the elements, and the rain of missiles and arrows darkened the sky and obscured the daylight. Strident voices within and without Antioch added to the noise. Christian women of Antioch came to loopholes on the battlements, and in their accustomed way secretly applauded as they watched the miserable plight of the Turks. Armenians, Syrians, and Greeks, willingly or unwillingly, by daily orders of the tyrannical Turkish leaders, sped arrows against us. Twelve Turkish emirs in line of duty met death in soul and body as well as fifteen hundred of their most experienced and brave soldiers who were also the core of Antioch's defense.

The survivors in Antioch did not have the *esprit de corps* to shout and gibber by day and night as had been their custom. Only night broke off the skirmishing of crusaders and their opponents and so ended the fighting, the hurling of javelins, the thrusting of spears, and the shooting of arrows. So by the strength of God and the Holy Sepulchre the Turks no longer possessed their former spirit, either in words or deeds. As a result of this day, we refitted ourselves very well in horses and other necessities. . . .

On another day the Turks led to the top of an Antiochian wall a noble knight, Rainald Porchet, whom they had imprisoned in a foul dungeon. They then told him that he should inquire from the Christian pilgrims how much they would pay for his ransom before he lost his head. From the heights of the wall Rainald addressed the leaders: "My lords, it matters not if I die, and I pray you, my brothers, that you pay no ransom for me. But be certain in the faith of Christ and the Holy Sepulchre that God is with you and shall be forever. You have slain all the leaders and the bravest men of Antioch; namely, twelve emirs and fifteen thousand noblemen, and no one remains to give battle with you or to defend the city."

The Turks asked what Rainald had said. The interpreter replied: "Nothing good concerning you was said."

The emir, Yaghi Siyan, immediately ordered him to descend from the wall and spoke to him through an interpreter: "Rainald, do you wish to enjoy life honorably with us?"

Rainald replied: "How can I live honorably with you without sinning?"

The emir answered: "Deny your God, whom you worship and believe, and accept Mohammed and our other gods. If you do so we shall give to you all that you desire such as gold, horses, mules, and many other worldly goods which you wish, as well as wives and inheritances; and we shall enrich you with great lands."

Rainald replied to the emir: "Give me time for consideration"; and the emir gladly agreed. Rainald with clasped hands knelt in prayer to the east; humbly he asked God that He come to his aid and transport with dignity his soul to the bosom of Abraham.

When the emir saw Rainald in prayer, he called his interpreter and said to him: "What was Rainald's answer?"

The interpreter then said: "He completely denies your god. He also refuses your worldly goods and your gods."

After hearing this report, the emir was extremely irritated and ordered the immediate beheading of Rainald, and so the Turks with great pleasure chopped off his head. Swiftly the angels, joyfully singing the Psalms of David, bore his soul and lifted it before the sight of God for Whose love he had undergone martyrdom.

Then the emir, in a towering rage because he could not make Rainald turn apostate, at once ordered all the pilgrims in Antioch to be brought before him with their hands bound behind their backs. When they had come before him, he ordered them stripped stark naked, and as they stood in the nude he commanded that they be bound with ropes in a circle. He then had chaff, firewood, and hay piled around them, and finally as enemies of God he ordered them put to the torch.

The Christians, those knights of Christ, shrieked and screamed so that their voices resounded in heaven to God for whose love their flesh and bones were cremated; and so they all entered martyrdom on this day wearing in heaven their white stoles before the Lord, for Whom they had so loyally suffered in the reign of our Lord Jesus Christ, to Whom is the honor and glory now and throughout eternity. Amen. . . .

When our lords saw these atrocities, they were greatly angered and held a council in which the bishops and priests recommended that the crusaders hold a procession around the city. So the bishops and priests, barefooted, clad in sacred vestments, and bearing crosses in their hands, came from the church of the Blessed Mary, which is on Mount Zion, to the church of Saint Stephen, the Protomartyr, singing and praying that the Lord Jesus Christ deliver his holy city and the Holy Sepulchre from the pagan people and place it in Christian hands for His holy service. The clerks, so clad, along with the armed knights and their retainers, marched side by side.

The sight of this caused the Saracens to parade likewise on the walls of Jerusalem, bearing insignia of Mohammed on a standard and pennon. The Christians came to the church of Saint Stephen and there took their stations as is customary in our processions. In the meantime the Saracens stood on the walls, screamed, blared out with horns, and performed all kinds of acts of mockery. To add insult to injury they made from wood a cross similar to the one on which, pouring forth His blood, the most merciful Christ redeemed the world. Afterward they inflicted great sorrow upon the Christians when, in the sight of all, they beat upon the cross with sticks and shattered it against the walls, shouting loudly, *"Frango agip salip,"* which means "Franks, is this a good cross?"

Source 5 from William of Tyre, A History of Deeds Done Beyond the Sea, *2 vols., trans. Emily Atwater Babcock and A. C. Krey (New York: Columbia University Press, 1943), vol. 1, pp. 60, 68–69, 306–307; vol. 2, p. 323.*

5. From William of Tyre, *A History of Deeds Done Beyond the Sea*

In the time of the Roman Emperor Heraclius, according to ancient histories and Oriental tradition, the pernicious doctrines of Muhammad had gained a firm foothold in the Orient. This first-born son of Satan falsely declared that he was a prophet sent from God and thereby led astray the lands of the East, especially Arabia. The poisonous seed which he sowed so permeated the provinces that his successors employed sword and violence, instead of preaching and exhortation, to compel the people, however reluctant, to embrace the erroneous tenets of the prophet. . . .

There was a certain infidel living in the city, a treacherous and wicked man, who persecuted our people with insatiable hatred. This man was determined to devise some scheme that would bring about their destruction. One day, he stealthily threw the carcass of a dog into the temple court, a place which the custodians—and indeed the whole city as well—were most careful to keep scrupulously clean. Worshippers who came to the temple to pray the next morning found the mouldering body of the unclean animal. Almost frantic, they at once roused the whole city with their cries. The populace quickly ran to the temple, and all agreed that without question the Christians were responsible for the act. Need more be said? Death was decreed for all Christians, since it was judged that by death alone could they atone for such an act of sacrilege. The faithful, in full assurance of their innocence, prepared to suffer death for Christ's sake. As the executioners, with swords unsheathed, were about to carry out their orders, however, a young man, filled with the spirit, came forward and offered himself as the sacrifice. "It would be most disastrous, O brethren," he said, "that the entire church should die in this way. Far better were it that one man should give his life for the people, that the whole Christian race may not perish. Promise me that annually you will reverently honor my memory and that the respect and honor due to my family shall be maintained forever. On these terms, at the command of God, I will deliver you from this massacre." The Christians heard his words with great joy and readily granted what he asked. They promised that, on the day of palm branches, in perpetual memory of him, those of his lineage should bear into the city, in solemn procession, the olive which signifies our Lord Jesus Christ.

The young man then gave himself up to the chief men of Jerusalem and declared that he was the criminal. In this way he established the innocence of the other Christians, for, when the judges heard his story, they absolved the rest and put him to the sword. Thus he laid down his life for the brethren and, with pious resignation, met death, that most blessed sleep, confident that he had acquired grace in the sight of the Lord. . . .

There was a certain noble of the Turkish race named Balas living in that part of the country, who had formerly been the lord of Seruj. At that time, he had been allied by treaty with the count, and before the Latins arrived in such numbers the two had been on very friendly terms. This man perceived that Baldwin's affection toward him had become less. Led either by his own feelings of resentment, or possibly by the request of the citizens, he went to the count and begged as a favor that he would come personally to receive the one fortress which still remained in his [Balas's] possession. He declared that Baldwin's favor would be all-sufficient for him and would be esteemed as a valuable heritage. He said also that he intended to bring his wife and children, with all he possessed, to Edessa and pretended to stand in great fear of his fellow countrymen, because he had become so friendly with the Christians. To carry out this wish, the count was persuaded to set a day to visit the place. At the time appointed, he set out with two hundred knights and marched to the fortress, whither Balas had preceded him. The latter, however, had secretly strengthened the defenses of the castle by introducing a hundred valiant knights, splendidly armed. This force was concealed inside in such a way that not a man was visible.

When Baldwin arrived before the castle, Balas begged that he would take only a few of his staff with him into the fortress. He gave as an excuse for this request the risk of danger to his property if the entire force were introduced. His persuasive words almost induced the count to accede to his wishes in every respect. Fortunately, however, some of the wise noblemen in attendance on Baldwin had a certain foreboding of treachery. Almost by force they held the count back against his protest and prevented his entering the castle. They rightly distrusted the evil designs of the rascal and judged it safer that the trial be first made by others. The count acquiesced in this prudent counsel. He ordered twelve of his bravest men, well armed, to enter the place. Meanwhile, he himself with the rest of his band remained quietly outside near by until he should see with his own eyes the result of the experiment. No sooner had the gallant band entered than they fell victims to the perfidious treachery of the wicked Balas. For the hundred Turks mentioned above at once emerged from their hiding places, armed to the teeth. They seized the betrayed knights and, in spite of their efforts to resist, threw them into chains. This result distressed the count greatly. Anxious about the fate of his loyal men whom he had lost by so dastardly a trick, he drew nearer to the castle and earnestly admonished Balas to remember the oath of fidelity which he had taken. On the strength of this fealty, he urged him to return the prisoners so treacherously seized and to receive instead a large sum of money as ransom. Balas absolutely refused to consider this proposition, however, unless Seruj were returned to him. The count perceived that he could do nothing more, for the castle was situated on a steep precipice and was impregnable both because of its strength and because of the skill with which it was built. . . .

The reason for the title caliph is as follows: Muhammad, their prophet, or rather their destroyer, who was the first to draw the peoples of the East to this kind of superstition, had as his immediate successor one of his disciples named Abu-Bakr. The latter was succeeded in the kingdom by Omar, son of Khattab, who was likewise followed by Uthman, and he by Ali, son of Abu-Talib. All these prophets were called caliphs, as were also all who followed them later, because they succeeded their famous master and were his heirs. But the fifth in the succession from Muhammad, namely Ali, was more warlike than his predecessors and had far greater experience in military matters than his contemporaries. He was, moreover, a cousin of Muhammad himself. He considered it unfitting that he should be called the successor of his cousin and not rather a great prophet himself, much greater, in fact, than Muhammad. The fact that in his own estimation and that of many others he was greater did not satisfy him; he desired that this be generally acknowledged. Accordingly, he reviled Muhammad and spread among the people a story to the effect that the Angel Gabriel, the propounder of the law, had actually been sent to him from on high but by mistake had conferred the supreme honor on Muhammad. For this fault, he said, the angel had been severely blamed by the Lord. Although these claims seemed false to many from whose traditions they differed greatly, yet others believed them, and so a schism developed among that people which has lasted even to the present. Some maintain that Muhammad is the greater and, in fact, the greatest of all prophets, and these are called in their own tongue, Sunnites; others declare that Ali alone is the prophet of God, and they are called Shiites.

QUESTIONS TO CONSIDER

Begin with the three Muslim accounts of Christians. Usamah's account (Source 1) is extremely valuable, not only because he was well acquainted with Christians, but also because he offers his readers numerous examples to support his main view of his European Christian foes. Examine and analyze each of Usamah's illustrations. What point is he trying to make by relating the story of the Frank who wanted to take Usamah's son back to Europe to make him a "wise man"? How does this story shed light on Usamah's perception of the Franks? Similarly, Usamah describes in some detail two medical "case studies," comparing the

European remedies to the Muslim treatment. What does he intend his readers to think after reading about those two patients? Would readers get the same impressions from his account of the Christians' "ordeal by water"? What are those impressions likely to have been? In his "God as a child" story, Usamah is remarkably restrained (see later accounts by Muslims and Christians of each other's faith). What point is communicated?

Because it reappears in Imad ad-Din's account, the subject of male-female relations deserves to be examined a bit more closely. In the "lack of jealousy" story, Usamah offers a very curious tale of a Frank who returns home to find his wife in bed with another man. What impression of European Christians do you think Usamah intends to give? What would his readers' reactions have been?

Ibn al-Athir's account (Source 2) is primarily concerned with Saladin's conquest of Jerusalem in 1187, and his portraits of European crusaders seem extremely vague. From reading the two accounts (the first of Franks suing for surrender terms and the second of Franks leaving the city), what impressions would readers get of the European crusaders? What adjectives best describe their behavior?

It matters little that Imad ad-Din's view (Source 3) of Christianity contains a number of errors and misperceptions—each side was remarkably ignorant of the other's faith. What is important is the perception of Christian beliefs that he attempts to convey. What impressions would Imad's readers have gathered from his story of the devotion of the European crusaders to the "True Cross"? How is the Church of the Holy Sepulchre depicted by Imad? How does he describe the treatment of Muslim holy sites by Christians? What stereotypes of European crusaders would that have been likely to put into the minds of Imad's readers? Finally, Imad portrays two groups of Frankish women. What do the descriptions tell readers about European women—and men?

Finally, reexamine each of the Muslim accounts. Do you notice any threads that are common to all three sources?

Like their Muslim counterparts, Western writers also recounted the immediate transportation of fallen warriors' souls to heaven (see, for example, the immensely popular *Song of Roland*, written by an anonymous author around 1100 about the Battle of Roncesvalles in 778).[19] Roman Catholic priest Peter Tudebode also wrote of Christian souls transported immediately to heaven (the martyrdom of Rainald Porchet) and the "everlasting death" of the Turks. According to Peter Tudebode, how does the Turkish emir react to the faithfulness of Rainald? What perceptions was Peter Tudebode trying to communicate to his readers in that account? in his account of Muslims' mockery of crosses?

William of Tyre was the Christian chronicler most familiar with Palestine and its Muslim population. Yet the first paragraph makes it clear that,

19. *The Song of Roland* is based on a battle in which the rear guard of Charlemagne's army was overwhelmed and slaughtered by Basques. Writing during the First Crusade, however, the author substituted Muslims for Basques in the epic.

to William, Muhammad is the"first-born son of Satan," a false prophet whose successors were converted to Islam by force. Interestingly, the "dog carcass" story and the "Balas trap" story both sketch the same stereotype of Muslims. What is that stereotype?

Now repeat for the Christian writers the process that you followed for the Muslim writers; that is, look for any common themes or stereotypes that all the accounts share.

As you examined and analyzed the Muslim and the European accounts, you doubtless noticed that some of the perceptions held by Muslims and European Christians about each other were remarkably similar. What similarities did you identify? How do you account for them?

Finally, without being too explicit, all of the accounts advocate ways in which the other side should be treated. How do the perceptions (and misperceptions) lead directly to those conclusions? What attitudes and behaviors do you think might have been recommended? To answer these questions, you will have to exercise some historical imagination. Put yourself in the position of an intelligent but uninformed person who is reading these accounts soon after they were written. How do the implicit stereotypes affect your view of how the targeted group should be treated? Explain.

EPILOGUE

The perceptions that Muslims and European Christians had of each other made it almost inevitable that the wars later known in the West as the Crusades would be carried on with extreme ferocity. As some of the evidence in this chapter suggests, civilians and combatants often were slaughtered indiscriminately, as Christians were exhorted to "slay for God's love," and both Muslim and Christian warriors were promised immediate admission to heaven if they died while fighting in a holy war (jihad).[20] Although no accurate estimates of losses are available (some historians insist that the Crusades cost the West between 4 and 5 *million* people out of a total population of around 50 million, although most historians believe this figure is too high), it can be said that fewer than one-half of the pilgrims who set out on a crusade ever returned. Muslim losses, although not that high, were also frightful.

Gradually the crusading spirit declined in the West, partly because of the meager results the crusaders achieved and partly because Europe had turned to other concerns. The Black Death struck Europe in 1347, killing over five times the number felled in the Crusades. England lost between a quarter and a half of its total population to the plague, and the

20. St. Bernard wrote that "a Christian glories in the death of a pagan because Christ is glorified; the liberality of the King [God] is revealed in the death of the Christian, because he is led out to his reward." Quoted in Norman Daniel, *Islam and the West: The Making of an Image*, rev. ed. (Oxford: Oneworld Publishing, 1993), p. 136.

numbers of deaths were just as appalling in other parts of Europe and Asia (the plague had struck China in 1331, and a more serious outbreak occurred in 1353). In addition, the Hundred Years War (1337–1453) kept Europe in an almost perpetual state of upheaval, diverting its attention from any future crusades. In the Muslim world, political disunity and the Mongol threat turned Muslim attention away from Europeans. Too, the so-called crusader states (four European-ruled principalities on the eastern shores of the Mediterranean) all had succumbed again to Muslim control.

One would expect that the long period of contact between the Muslim and Christian worlds would have produced a great deal of cross-fertilization of culture, ideas, goods, and knowledge. Indeed, this was the case, although more of these kinds of exchanges took place in Spain and Italy than in the Middle East. From the Arabs, the West acquired a great deal of knowledge of medicine, astronomy, chemistry, physics, and mathematics. Paper, invented in China, was adopted by the Arabs and transmitted to Europe.[21] Arabs had preserved a great deal of Greek philosophy (much of which had been lost in the West), and it was by way of the Arabs that Europe "rediscovered" Aristotle. Arabic courtly literature (adab) was translated and became the basis of some European literature (including Shakespeare's *Taming of the Shrew*). Trade between the two worlds was intensified.

Not surprisingly, Muslims borrowed almost nothing from the West. The Islamic world simply didn't think it had much to learn from the West. Muslims did adopt some European clothing and liked some European food, but these were minor compared to what Muslims exported to Europeans.

Yet, although the spirit of holy warfare declined in both the Muslim and Christian worlds, the perceptions and misperceptions that each side created of the other remained strong for centuries, and one can find their unhealthy residues even today in the struggles between the West and Iran and (later) Iraq, in the Arab-Israeli conflicts, and in the reemergence of Islamic fundamentalism. Behind the struggles over oil and geopolitics lie images, perceptions, and stereotypes that are centuries old and durable even today.

Writing at the time of the Crusades, Friar Felix Fabari wrote of Muslims, "The easterners are men of a different kind to us, they have other passions, other ways of thinking, other ideas . . . they are influenced by other stars. . . ." Even as Westerners have come to learn a great deal more about Islamic religion, society, politics, and arts, the notions of Fabari and others remain.

21. In medicine, the Arab *al-Qanun* (The Canon) became *the* medical textbook in the West. In physics, the Arabs gave the West the pendulum; in astronomy, a more accurate method of predicting an eclipse; in mathematics, the field of algebra (practically an Arab creation), the zero, and the decimal point. Before Europeans borrowed paper from the Arabs, they wrote on papyrus or parchment.

CHAPTER SIX

THE "COMMERCIAL REVOLUTION"

THE PROBLEM

Western Europe during the Early Middle Ages was a largely rural society. The cities of the Roman Empire had shrunk into small villages, and the roads the Romans had built had been allowed to fall into disrepair. Manors and villages were relatively self-sufficient in basic commodities such as grain and cloth, and even in times of famine they could not import the food they needed because the cost of transportation was too high. When standardized Roman coinage was no longer available, villages, towns, monasteries, and individual nobles all minted their own coins, which were often accepted as legitimate tender only in very limited areas. Much local trade was carried out by barter; many people rarely used or even saw coins. Such long-distance trade as existed was handled by Jews, Greeks, and Syrians, who imported luxury goods like spices, silks, and perfumes from the Near East. These extremely expensive commodities were purchased only by nobles and high-ranking churchmen. The pervasive lack of trade is reflected in the almost complete absence of sources about trade before the tenth century. Commercial documents are extremely rare, and both public and private records testify to the agrarian nature of early medieval society.

This situation began to change in the tenth century, when Vikings in the north and Italians in the south revived European commerce. The Vikings initially raided and plundered along the coasts of northern Europe but soon turned to trading with the very people whose lands they had threatened. Their swift boats carried northern products like furs, timber, wax, and amber to all the towns of the North Sea and the North Atlantic. Swedish Vikings went eastward, trading down the Russian rivers as far as Constantinople and the Muslim world. Because these traders for the most part were illiterate, few written accounts of their far-flung enterprises survive. Those that we have often come from their eastern trading partners in the Byzantine and Muslim empires, who were much more likely to be able to read and write.

The Italians, on the other hand, have left voluminous records of their business activities. Most Italian merchants were literate, and Italian artisans learned from the Muslims how to make paper, which provided a writing surface that was much cheaper than parchment or vellum, products made from the skin of calves and goats. At the same time that the Vikings were trading in northern Europe, merchants from the cities of Genoa, Pisa, and Venice were taking over former Muslim trade routes in the western Mediterranean. After the Crusades in the twelfth century, merchants from these cities also became involved in the lucrative trade of the eastern Mediterranean, importing such oriental luxuries as spices and silks and exporting slaves, timber, and iron. When European cities began to produce manufactured products, including fancy wool cloth, armaments, and leather goods, Italian merchants traded these items both within Europe and to the East. They began to keep increasingly elaborate records of their transactions and devised new methods of bookkeeping to keep track of their ventures. They wrote manuals of advice for other merchants on these new business techniques, on practical arithmetic and geography, and on the customs and practices of the foreign lands they visited.

Though the profits of such trading ventures could be enormous, the risks were equally great. Travel was difficult and dangerous, for few inns were available for travelers and highway robbers and pirates posed a threat by land and sea. Shipwrecks were common, and in many places local residents claimed the right to anything that could be salvaged from a wreck. Italian merchants began to devise ways to share the risks, pooling their capital and talents and sharing the profits if the venture was a success. They formalized these agreements with various forms of contracts, ranging from temporary partnerships called *commenda* or *societas* that would be dissolved once the venture was over to more permanent partnerships called *compagnie* (literally, "bread together," i.e., sharing bread; the root of the word *company*). Many of these *compagnie* began as agreements between brothers or other relatives and in-laws but quickly grew to include non–family members. In addition, these partnerships began to include individuals who invested only their money, leaving the actual running of the business to the active partners. Along with long-distance trade, the *compagnie* became involved in purely banking activities, taking deposits, making loans, and investing in enterprises other than long-distance trade, primarily mining. Some partnerships also began to provide insurance for others, thus transferring the risk entirely.

This explosion of trade encountered two serious difficulties in medieval Europe. One was the problem of money. The amount of gold and silver available for coins was simply not adequate for the increased flow of commerce. How did merchants get around this obstacle? Records reveal a range of inventive ways that were employed to solve the need for money, the most important of which was the development of paper letters of exchange and deposit statements that could be used in place of metal coinage. This innovation freed up coinage for other business and also relieved merchants of the burden of always having to carry a cashbox with several guards to protect it.

The second problem was a moral and theological one. The Christian church in the West forbade *usury,* that is, the charging of interest on a loan. The Church had developed this doctrine in the Early Middle Ages, when loans were intended mainly for consumption—tiding someone over until the next harvest, for instance. Theologians reasoned that it was wrong for a Christian to take advantage of the bad luck or need of another Christian, so loans should be made *pro amore* (out of love), not with an eye to profit. This restriction on Christians is the reason that Jews were the primary moneylenders in early medieval society, for as a group outside the Christian community they were not subject to the same restrictions. Moneylending was also one of the few occupations at which Jews could make a living, for in many areas they were forbidden to own land or to engage in most trades. At the same time that Christians imposed these restrictions on Jews, they also harbored a deep grudge against the Jews for their moneylending activities. This economic resentment is one of the roots of Christian anti-Semitism, which was very strong in the Middle Ages and flared up in intermittent campaigns of persecution or mass murder.

The Church's prohibition on usury meant that merchants often felt compelled to hide their interest, which they did by adding the interest to the principal in a loan agreement without stating this practice explicitly or by repaying the loan in a different currency without noting that the amount repaid was more than the original sum. Gradually the Church relaxed its sanction against charging interest, declaring that some interest was legitimate as a payment for the risk the investor was taking and that only interest above a certain level would be considered usury. The Church itself then became a moneylender, opening pawnshops whose stated purpose was to help the poor by charging a lower rate of interest than secular moneylenders did.

The stigma attached to moneylending carried over in many ways to all the activities of a medieval merchant. Trade was not like agriculture or manufacturing, for a merchant merely handled goods produced by someone else. To the medieval sensibility, making a profit from manipulating money was a dubious undertaking; the investment of labor, skill, and time warranted a profit, but did the investment of mere money? Merchants themselves shared these attitudes to some degree; they gave generous donations to the Church and to charities and agreed, at least in principle, that profit should be limited to what was judged to be fair and just. They also took pains not to flaunt their wealth but to dress and furnish their homes in a way that would convey financial stability rather than flashy extravagance. By the end of the Middle Ages, society had somewhat come to accept the role of the merchant: Preachers in Italian cities compared merchants to Christ, who had "redeemed" the human race from the devil just as merchants redeemed loans and merchandise.

Historians often call this expansion and transformation of the European economy the *Commercial Revolution* and mark it as the beginning of our modern capitalist economy. Though you may be most familiar with the word *revolution* as a way to describe a violent political rebellion like the American Revolution or the French Revolution, the term is also used more broadly to describe economic and intellectual changes such as the Industrial Revolution or the Scientific Revolution. These social transformations do not necessarily involve violence and may occur over a much longer period of time than political revolutions. What makes them true revolutions is the extent of their effects on society. In calling this broad-based economic change the Commercial Revolution, historians point not only to the growth of new forms of business but also to the development of a "capitalist spirit"—of the idea that making a profit is good in itself, regardless of the uses to which that profit is put. Your task in this chapter is to use records left by medieval merchants to answer the question: Was the Commercial Revolution really a revolution in terms of business procedures and attitudes toward business?

SOURCES AND METHOD

In analyzing the development of medieval commerce and trade, historians have a wide variety of documents at their disposal. The most basic evidence, and the basis of business both then and now, consists of the contracts drawn up between individuals and firms. These were generally written by a notary and were witnessed by men who had a reputation for honesty. Copies of these notarial contracts were often preserved by towns that recognized the importance of business, such as Genoa or Florence, where they can be found today in city and private archives. Then as now, the language is matter of fact and often somewhat formalized and legalistic, quite similar to that found in contemporary legal documents. Because these contracts were written for other people in business and lawyers, they often assume a knowledge of the relevant laws and coinage systems, but they are still fairly straightforward because both parties to the contract wanted to make sure that the terms were clear and easily understood.

The first six documents are notarial contracts made by Italian merchants, arranged in chronological order. The first point to determine is the central purpose of each contract. Is it a loan? A business partnership? An insurance agreement? A deposit statement? Are the responsibilities of each party clearly laid out—that is, if you had been one of the parties, would you have known from this contract what was expected of you and what you could expect from the other parties? Did the contract end at a specific time, or was it ongoing? What were the penalties for failure to fulfill the contract? If merchandise was involved, what was it and where was it going?

Along with notarial contracts, historians also use personal letters and account books to document the expansion of commerce. Source 7 is a letter from an Italian merchant conducting business in southern France. Notice the dates of the letter and the payment ordered. What kind of transaction is being discussed here? What rate of interest is the investor to receive? Why does the merchant choose to call this an "exchange" rather than a "loan"? Sources 8 and 9 are extracts from two merchants' account books, the first from the early part and the second from the very end of the fourteenth century. Do you find any difference in the way the two merchants kept their accounts? Why did the second merchant divide his book into two columns? Which account do you find easier to use?

Though Source 7 and several of the notarial contracts openly mention interest, other records left by merchants provide evidence that this was not a unanimously accepted practice. Document 10 is a letter in the form of a contract written by a notary on behalf of a merchant and sent to a Church official. What does it reveal about the merchant? What does he promise to do? Why might he act in such a way at this point in his life? (The phrase "from this illness" provides a clue here.)

Think about the material you have read so far, which is only a small sample of the thousands of such contracts, letters, and personal accounts preserved in the archives of Italian cities. (And those surviving are themselves only a small portion of all the commercial documents drawn up during this period, for many were thrown away once the contract was no longer valid and many more were destroyed over time by flood, fire, mice, and rot.) How are these contracts and accounts similar to their modern counterparts? How are they different? Can we see in them the beginnings of our modern capitalist system?

Historians can tell a great deal about commercial practices from contracts, letters, and accounts, but such sources do not reveal much about what medieval merchants thought about themselves and their activities. For this we need to look at more reflective and introspective sources, the best of which are the manuals of advice written by merchants for their sons or other merchants. These manuals are all *prescriptive*—that is, they tell people how they should behave. Before using prescriptive sources, historians must first ask several questions: Who is writing? For whom is he or she writing? Why is he or she writing? Only after these questions have been answered is it possible to evaluate the actual content.

Because it is primarily based on theories about human nature, much prescriptive literature has a limited foundation in reality or personal experience. Such literature often gives us very little information about how people of this era actually conducted themselves, but the merchants' manuals we are examining here are somewhat different. All were written by older merchants, document 11 by an unknown thirteenth-century Norwegian merchant and the last three by fourteenth-century Florentines. Thus these documents not only tell us how these men thought merchants should behave but also reflect the writers' own experiences in trade. The problems and situations they describe were thus quite familiar to them and were not simply drawn from abstract theories.

As you read this evidence, keep in mind that even though the manuals are intended to instruct and guide, they also reflect real experience. What suggestions does each of the authors make for merchants? How do they feel merchants should behave? What should merchants avoid doing? What assumptions do the authors make about human nature? What judgment might these authors make about the contracts and accounts you have just read?

THE EVIDENCE

Sources 1 through 10 from Robert S. Lopez and Irving W. Raymond, editors and translators, Medieval Trade in the Mediterranean World *(New York: Columbia University Press, 1955), p. 145, no. 61; pp. 169–170, no. 78; p. 179, no. 84; p. 164, no. 73; p. 214, no. 103; pp. 260–261, no. 136; p. 231, no. 115; pp. 362–363, no. 179; p. 373, no. 182; pp. 159–160, no. 68. Reprinted with the permission of the publisher.*

1. Notarial Contract

[Genoa], January 14, 1156

I, Rinaldo Gauxone, promise you, Lamberto Grillo, or your accredited messenger, £6½ in pepper or in coin [to be delivered any time] up to next Easter; otherwise [I will pay] the penalty of the double, under pledge of my orchard in Sozziglia. And you may enter into [possession] of it for the principal and the penalty on your own authority and without order by the consuls. Done in the chapter house, 1156, on the fourteenth day from the beginning of January, third indiction. Witnesses: Sismondo Muscula, B. Papa Canticula Macobrio, notary, Baldo Rubeo, watchman.

2. Notarial Contract

Constantinople, December, 1158

In the name of the Lord God and our Savior, Jesus Christ. In the year of the Lord 1158, in the month of December, seventh indiction, in Constantinople. I, Pietro Cornaro of the section of Sant' Apollinare, together with my heirs, openly declare to you, Sebastiano Ziani of the section of Santa Giustina, and to your heirs that I have received from Stefano Ziani, your brother, 100 gold hyperpers of the old weight[1] belonging to you. And with these I am to go and to do business wherever it seems good to me. And I am to carry with me the aforesaid goods (*habere*) by the convoy of ships which will come to Venice from Constantinople or from Alexandria in this first coming September, or [I am] to send the same goods from the aforesaid territories to Venice by a reliable man in the wit-

1. **hyperpers of the old weight:** a type of Byzantine gold coin.

ness of good men. And then, within thirty days after that convoy of ships from the aforesaid territories enters [the waters of] Venice, I am to give and to deliver, personally or through my messenger, to you or your messenger in Venice, 125 gold hyperpers of the old weight. The aforesaid goods, however, are to remain at your risk from sea[2] and [hostile] people, provided [the risk] is proved. If I do not observe all these [conditions] for you as written above, then I, together with my heirs, am to restore to you and to your heirs all the aforesaid hyperpers in the double out of my lands and houses and of all that I am known to own in this world. And let the same capital and [the penalty of] the double bear interest of six per five every year from that time forward.

I, Pietro Cornaro, signed by my own hand.
I, Pietro Lambardo, witness, signed.
I, Marco Signorello, witness, signed.
I, Marco Bembo, witness, signed.
I, Giovanni da Noale, subdeacon and notary, completed and certified [this instrument].

3. Notarial Contract

[Genoa,] September 29, 1163

Witnesses: Simone Bucuccio, Ogerio Peloso, Ribaldo di Sauro, and Genoardo Tasca. Stabile and Ansaldo Garraton have formed a *societas* in which, as they mutually declared, Stabile contributed £88 [Genoese][3] and Ansaldo, £44. Ansaldo carries this *societas,* in order to put it to work, to Tunis or to wherever goes the ship in which he shall go—namely, [the ship] of Baldizzone Grasso and Girardo. On his return [he will place the proceeds] in the power of Stabile or of his messenger for [the purpose of] division. After deducting the capital, they shall divide the profits in half. Done in the chapter house, September 29, 1163, eleventh indiction.

In addition, Stabile gave his permission to send that money to Genoa by whatever ship seems most convenient to him [to Ansaldo].

4. Notarial Contract

Genoa [February 12, 1190]

Witnesses: Giovanni Patrio, Quilego, and Ugo Caniverga. We, Guglielmo Riccuomo and Egidio de Uxel, have received from you, Rufo, banker, and Bernardo,

2. Here Cornaro indicates that he is not assuming the risk for the merchandise.

3. Each city in Italy issued its own silver coinage, often called a pound (£) though it did not weigh a pound. Each city's pound contained a different amount of silver, so contracts generally specify which city's pound is involved.

banker, an amount of exchange for which we promise to pay to you or to your accredited messenger £69 Pavese[3] by mid-Lent. Otherwise we promise you the penalty of the double, [both of us liable] for the whole amount, etc. Done in Genoa, in the bank of Rufo, in the shop of Ogerio Vento, on the same day.

5. Notarial Contract

[Genoa,] November 7, 1200

I, Oberto, banker, of Pollanexi, acknowledge that I have received from you, Maria, wife of Rolando Generificio, £50 Genoese[3] in *accomendacio*,[4] which belong to your husband, the aforesaid Rolando. I am to keep them in the bank and to employ [them] in trade in Genoa as long as it shall be your pleasure; and I promise to give you the profit according to what seems to me ought to come to you. Moreover, I promise to return and to restore the aforesaid £50 or just as much instead of them, myself or through my messenger, to you or to your husband or to your accredited messenger, within eight days after you tell me and make the request, and similarly [to give you] the profit; otherwise the penalty of the double and the seizure of my goods as security. Done in the house of the late Baldovino de Arato. Witnesses: Rufo de Arato and Aimerico, cooper. In the year of the Nativity of the Lord 1200, third indiction, the seventh day of November.

6. Notarial Contract

[Palermo, March 24, 1350]

On the twenty-fourth of the same month. Luchino de Mari and Leonardo Cattaneo, of Genoa, of their own free will, each of them for one half, insured (*assecuraverunt*) Filippo Cavegra of Voltri, captain of that *panfilo*[5] called "Saint Ampelius," which today departed from the port of Palermo, for 200 gold florins[6] on said *panfilo* and its equipment and the right to the freight charges of the present voyage of the said *panfilo* against every risk, peril, and fortune of God, the sea, and [hostile] people which may happen to come to the aforesaid *panfilo* and its tackle and equipment from the port of Palermo and from that moment at which said *panfilo* departs from there [to the time of its arrival] at the shore of Sciacca, and from that shore as far as the port of Tunis, and from the port of Tunis as far as the port of Mazara or of Trapani—viz., as far as the one of the aforesaid ports to which said *panfilo* shall go in order to make port, going, loading, unloading, returning, [each insurer] pro rata, provided the voyage is not altered without a legitimate impediment of God, the sea, and [hostile] people. [The aforesaid is to be

4. **accomendacio:** a *commenda* contract.
5. **panfilo:** a type of ship.
6. **florin:** a large gold coin issued by the city of Florence.

done] in such a way that if perchance total disaster happens to overtake the aforesaid *panfilo* and its equipment and the right to the aforesaid freight charges, said Luchino and Leonardo are to be bound to give and to pay said 200 gold florins to the same Filippo in Palermo within one month after receiving positive news; and if a partial [disaster] occurs, [they are bound to give and to pay] by that proportion and part according to which [loss] has occurred. In consideration of this insurance thus made as above the said Luchino and Leonardo, in the presence and on request of the said Filippo, solemnly acknowledged that they have had and have received from the same Filippo 28 gold florins, waiving, etc.

Witnesses: Pellegrino Coccorello, Martino Leccavela, and Giovanni Salvago.

7. Letter from an Italian Merchant

Avignon, October 5, 1339

In the name of God, amen. To Bartolo and partners [*compagni*], Barna of Lucca and partners [send] greetings from Avignon.

You shall pay by this letter on November 20, [1]339, to Landuccio Busdraghi and partners, of Lucca, gold florins three hundred twelve and three fourths for the exchange [*per cambio*] of gold florins three hundred, because I have received such money today from Tancredi Bonagiunta and partners at the rate [*raxione*] of 4¼ per 100 to their advantage. And charge [it] to our account. •Done on October 5, [1]339.

Francesco Falconetti has ordered us to pay in your behalf 230 gold *scudi*[7] to the Acciajuoli [*compagnia*].

[*Address on the outside;*]

To Bartolo Casini and partners, in Pisa.

[*Mark of Barna of Lucca*]

8. Merchant's Account Book

Carcassonne, 1340

Senher Ber. of St. Esteve, nobleman, lord of Lastours, owes s.4[8] which we lent him. To be paid . . . on October 3.

Mosenher the major judge of Carcassonne owes s.18 for 3 palms of medley French [cloth], which was for the lining of the cape which Maestro Crestiá Rocafort took. Paid s.18. . . .

7. **scudi:** a gold coin issued by various Italian cities.

8. Most money systems in medieval Europe were based on the following equivalents: 1 pound (£) = 20 shillings (s) = 240 pence (d). A medal was worth ½ pence.

Riquart, wife of the late En Adam of Rovenay, of the city of Carcassonne, owes s.10 for 2 palms of vermilion and for 1½ palms of white [cloth], which was for hose with edging for her, which she took on Wednesday, October 4. Also, she owes d.1. Also, she owes d.1. Also, she owes d.1. Also, she owes d.1. Remains [to be paid] s.10 d.4. Also, she owes d.1. Paid s.3 d.11 medal. Paid s.6 d.5 medal.

Senher Uc Garie, £11 for 4 *canas* of *cameli.*[9] Paid £11.

Senher Peyre Fabre of Pomas owes s.4 which we lent to Jacme Rog of Villefranche de Conflent. Also, he owes 15 gold *dobles*[10] because of what we lent him on Sunday, October 8. Paid in full.

9. Merchant's Account Book

[Milan], 1396

Andreolo of Concorezzo must give—Credited to the account of Giovannino of Dugnano on folio 8 on March 17 £16 s.-d.-

Item—[credited] to Marco Serrainerio on folio 6 on March 31—[for money] which he [Marco] paid to him £4 s.16 d.-

Item—[credited] to said Marco on folio 6 on April 28—[for money] deposited in [the bank of] Manno, [son] of Ser Jacopo £10 s.-d.-

Item—[credited] to said Marco, on folio 6 on May 6—[for money] deposited in [the bank of] Paolino of Osnago £6 s.8 d.-

Item—[credited] to said Marco on folio 6 on May 16—[for money] deposited in [the bank of] Paolino of Osnago for the remainder £12 s.-d.-

Item—for the balance posted to the common credit, profit, and loss [of the partnership] on folio 20 on aforesaid day £ -s.7 d.6

Total £49 s.11 d.6

He [Andreolo] must have—Debited to the account of Merceries on folio 18 on March 6—for 12 thousand needles for sacks, marked Antonio £10 s.16 d.-

Item, posted as above on aforesaid day, for 12 thousand long needles, marked Masso, at s.13 [per thousand] £7 s.16 d.-

Item, posted as above; for 24 thousand long needles, marked Stefano, at s.12 d.9 [per thousand] £15 s.6 d.-

Item, posted as above, for 12 thousand old woman's needles . . . marked with a ship, at s.8 [per thousand] £4 s.16 d.-

Item, posted as above, for 12 thousand old woman's needles, large, marked with a ship, at s.12 d.9 [per thousand] £7 s.14 d.-

Item, posted as above, for 3 thousand needles for fine shoes, at s.21 d.6 [per thousand] £3 s.4 d.6

Total £49 s.11 d.6

9. **cameli:** a type of cloth.

10. **doble:** a gold coin issued in Spain.

10. Letter from a Merchant to a Church Official

[Siena, September 27, 1221]

On the same day, I, Aringhiero d'Altavilla, promise you, Magister Pietro, rector of the church of S. Pietro delle Scale, and I swear on the holy Gospels of God that if I escape from this illness I shall be and remain [obedient] to the order of the lord bishop of Siena in regard to the usuries which I have collected up to this day, satisfying whoever proves to me his legal [claims] in regard to them and making restitution of these [usuries] as he [the bishop] shall charge me. And in regard to the excommunication laid upon me in the case of the money of Boncompagno, late of the monastery, I shall likewise be [obedient] to his order, so far as it concerns my part.

And I, Mezzolombardo d'Altavilla, in his behalf promise you and swear that if said Aringhiero dies from this illness, I shall remain [obedient] to and shall observe, in regard to the aforesaid, the order of the lord bishop, according to the form and content mentioned above. In the presence of Tornampuglia, [son] of Salsidone, Rustichino, [son] of Sinibaldo, Bartolo of Leonessa, and many others invited.

Source 11 from L. M. Larson, editor and translator, The King's Mirror *(New York: American Scandinavian Foundation, 1917), pp. 79–81, 84–85. Reprinted by permission of the American Scandinavian Foundation from The King's Mirror. Copyright © 1917.*

11. Letter from a Norwegian Merchant, 13th century

The man who is to be a trader will have to brave many perils, sometimes at sea and sometimes in heathen lands, but nearly always among alien peoples; and it must be his constant purpose to act discreetly wherever he happens to be. On the sea he must be alert and fearless.

When you are in a market town, or wherever you are, be polite and agreeable; then you will secure the friendship of all good men. Make it a habit to rise early in the morning, and go first and immediately to church. . . .

When the services are over, go out to look after your business affairs. If you are unacquainted with the traffic of the town, observe carefully how those who are reputed the best and most prominent merchants conduct their business. You must also be careful to examine the wares that you buy before the purchase is finally made to make sure that they are sound and flawless. And whenever you make a purchase, call in a few trusty men to serve as witnesses as to how the bargain was made.

You should keep occupied with your business till breakfast or, if necessity demands it, till midday; after that you should eat your meal. Keep your table well provided and set with a white cloth, clean victuals, and good drinks. Serve enjoyable meals, if you can afford it.

Finally, remember this, that whenever you have an hour to spare you should give thought to your studies, especially to the law books; for it is clear that those who gain knowledge from books have keener wits than others, since those who are the most learned have the best proofs for their knowledge. Make a study of all the laws. . . . If you are acquainted with the law, you will not be annoyed by quibbles when you have suits to bring against men of your own class, but will be able to plead according to law in every case.

But although I have most to say about laws, I regard no man perfect in knowledge unless he has thoroughly learned and mastered the customs of the place where he is sojourning. And if you wish to become perfect in knowledge, you must learn all the languages, first of all Latin and French, for these idioms are most widely used; and yet, do not neglect your native tongue or speech.

And further, there are certain things which you must beware of and shun like the devil himself: these are drinking, chess, harlots, quarreling, and throwing dice for stakes. For upon such foundations the greatest calamities are built; and unless they strive to avoid these things, few only are able to live long without blame or sin.

Observe carefully how the sky is lighted, the course of the heavenly bodies, the grouping of the hours, and the points of the horizon. Learn also how to mark the movements of the ocean and to discern how its turmoil ebbs and swells; for that is knowledge which all must possess who wish to trade abroad. Learn arithmetic thoroughly, for merchants have great need of that.

If you come to a place where the king or some other chief who is in authority has his officials, seek to win their friendship; and if they demand any necessary fees on the ruler's behalf, be prompt to render all such payments, lest by holding too tightly to little things you lose the greater. . . . If you can dispose of your wares at suitable prices, do not hold them long; for it is the wont of merchants to buy constantly and to sell rapidly. . . .

If you attend carefully to all these things, with God's mercy you may hope for success. This, too, you must keep constantly in mind, if you wish to be counted a wise man, that you ought never to let a day pass without learning something that will profit you. Be not like those who think it beneath their dignity to hear or learn from others such things even as might avail them much if they knew them. For a man must regard it as great an honor to learn as to teach, if he wishes to be considered thoroughly informed. . . .

Keep your temper calm though not to the point of suffering abuse or bringing upon yourself the reproach of cowardice. Though necessity may force you into strife, be not in a hurry to take revenge; first make sure that your effort will succeed and strike where it ought. Never display a heated temper when you see that you are likely to fail, but be sure to maintain your honor at some later time, unless your opponent should offer a satisfactory atonement.

If your wealth takes on rapid growth, divide it and invest it in a partnership trade in fields where you do not yourself travel; but be cautious in selecting partners. Always let Almighty God, the holy Virgin Mary, and the saint whom you have most frequently called upon to intercede for you be counted among your partners. Watch with care over the property which the saints are to share with you and always bring it faithfully to the place to which it was originally promised.

Sources 12 through 14 from Robert S. Lopez and Irving W. Raymond, editors and translators, Medieval Trade in the Mediterranean World *(New York: Columbia University Press, 1955), p. 422, no. 204; pp. 423–424, no. 205; pp. 425–426, no. 208. Reprinted with permission of the publisher.*

12. An Italian Merchant's Advice

[Florence, 1393]

If you engage in the wool or French-cloth business, do [it] on your own and do not try to grow rich in two days. Manage on your own money and never borrow for profit's sake. Transact your business with trustworthy persons who enjoy good reputation and credit and who have something to show for their name. And if you ever get cheated by them, do not again fall into their clutches. Do not sell your merchandise to persons who may be willing to overpay for it; never be ensnared by greed for [high] prices; always demand flawless records; better go slowly, [but] do go safely.

If you exercise the wool craft (*Arte di Lana*), manage on your own money. Be not eager to send your merchandise abroad unless you have someone to whom it matters as much as to you. If you can do without a partner (*compagno*) do so. If you cannot, get a partner wisely—a good and rich man, and not one higher than you, especially in [social] status or in [connection with] families with overbearing manners.

Do not exercise any trade or business in which you have no experience. Do what you are able to do and beware of everything else, for [otherwise] you would be cheated. And if you want to become experienced in anything, practise it as a child, be in shops (*fondachi*) and in banks with others, go abroad, frequent merchants and merchandise, see with [your own] eyes the places and countries where you have in mind to do business. Try a friend—or rather the man whom you believe to be a friend—a hundred times before you rely upon him a single time, and never rely upon anyone so deeply that he may ruin you. Go cautiously in [placing] your confidence, and do not be gullible, and the more one shows himself loyal to you and wise in words, the less trust him. And do not trust at all one who makes overtures to you in anything. Enjoy listening to tall talkers, braggers, and men lavish of compliments, and give words [in return] for words; but do not give any credit that may bring harm to you, and do not rely upon them at all. As for Pharisees and hypocrites smiting themselves and covering themselves with the cloak of religion, rely not upon them but sooner [rely] upon a soldier. Have nothing to do with one who has often changed his business, partners, and masters. And with one who gambles, lives in luxury, overdresses, feasts himself, or is a scatterbrain—do not get involved by entrusting your goods or committing your business to him.

If you do business abroad, go often yourself—at least once a year—to see and to settle the accounts. Watch what [kind of] life the man who is abroad in your behalf leads—whether he spends too much. [Make sure] that he extends sound credits, that he does not rush to [start] things or lies down too low[?], that he acts cautiously and never oversteps instructions. Should he cheat you in anything, fire him.

And always behave with wisdom and do not get involved. And never show off your wealth but keep it hidden, and always by words and acts make people believe that you possess one half as much as you have. By following this course you cannot be too badly cheated, neither you nor those who will be left after you.

13. Giovanni Frescobaldi, *A Bit of Advice for Those Who Cross to England*

[Florence, early fourteenth century]

Wear modest colors, be humble, be dull in appearance but in fact be subtle: if the Englishman [tries to] floor you, woe to him!

Flee cares as well as any one who fights you; spend bravely, and do not show yourself mean.[11]

Pay on the day [when payment is due and be] courteous in collecting, showing that need is driving you to the grave. Make no more demands than you are entitled to.

Buy in [good] time if you have good prospects—and do not get involved with people at court. Obey the orders of those who are in authority.

It behooves you to club together with your nation, and see to it that your doors are well bolted early.

14. Dino Compagni, *Song on Worthy Conduct*

[Florence, beginning of the fourteenth century]

A merchant wishing that his worth be great
Must always act according as is right;
And let him be a man of long foresight,

11. **mean:** cheap.

And never fail his promises to keep.
Let him be pleasant, if he can, of looks,
As fits the honor'd calling that he chose;
Open when selling, but when buying close;
Genial in greeting and without complaints.
He will be worthier if he goes to church,
Gives for the love of God, clinches his deals
Without a haggle, and wholly repeals
Usury taking. Further, he must write
Accounts well-kept and free from oversight.

QUESTIONS TO CONSIDER

This period of European history has been dubbed the Commercial Revolution for three reasons: an increase in the sheer volume of trade in Europe, the increasing sophistication and complexity of business procedures, and a new attitude toward business and making money. The evidence you have examined does not give you information about the first reason, but it can help you assess the latter two.

To evaluate the change in business procedures, we need to return to the first ten documents, paying particular attention to their dates and to the smaller details that indicate change. Economic revolutions do not occur within a few years the way political revolutions do, but we should be able to notice economic change over time. Look again at these documents, one by one. What problem of the medieval economy does the first document reveal? Do any of the later documents refer to this method of payment? What did the borrower pledge as security for his loan? What does that pledge reveal about the flow of capital? Do any of the other documents hint at the source of the investors' money? What risks are described in the second document? Do any of the later documents discuss these same risks? Do they suggest any ways of avoiding these risks?

What does the third document reveal about family relationships? Do any of the other contracts give you further information about families? Why did the partners in document 3 get an equal return on their investments when their original investments were not the same? You have probably noticed that the original amount in document 4 was not specified. Why might this be? Document 5 is a male banker's contract with a woman. Who determined how much profit she is to receive? How does this arrangement differ from the practices in other contracts you have read? What might account for the differences? In document 7, the 4¼ percent interest rate mentioned is per month, rather than per year, though this is not explicitly stated. Why might the merchant choose to hide the true yearly rate?

Document 9 is an account book with debits and credits listed separately, a procedure known as *double-entry bookkeeping*. Why has this been called the most important change in the history of accounting? Did you also notice any differences in the types of currencies described in the two accounts? Why might the use of these currencies be significant?

Though the Church disapproved of charging interest on a loan, most of the contracts openly discuss interest. Why do you think they do this? Does your explanation fit with what you have learned from document 10? Do you think this merchant would have agreed with the advice given in the final four documents?

The new "capitalist spirit" toward making money is much harder to document than changes in business procedure. Why so? As you read the selections from the advice manuals, what attitude toward profit and money did you detect? Do you find evidence of older attitudes as well? How would you compare the advice given by these merchants with that you might expect to receive from a professor at the Harvard or Stanford Business School? Are you surprised by the similarities or the differences? You are now ready to answer the central question for this chapter: Was the Commercial Revolution really a revolution?

EPILOGUE

Like every major economic change, the Commercial Revolution was a slow and gradual process. The new business procedures developed by the Italians spread only very slowly to the rest of Europe; not until the fifteenth or sixteenth century, for example, did northern European merchants take up double-entry bookkeeping. As more small investors combined their resources to fund trading ventures, the concept of *limited liability* developed so that, in case of a shipwreck or failed venture, investors lost only their original investments and not all their property, as stipulated in the contracts you have just read.

The European banking and monetary system remained chaotic for several more centuries. The banks that developed out of the *compagnie* partnerships often made enormous loans to rulers and then collapsed when the rulers defaulted on their loans; when a bank collapsed, the investments of all depositors were lost. (This state of affairs remained unchanged until the bank collapses of the Great Depression of the 1930s, when governments began to see the need for insuring bank deposits.) Merchants continued to handle many different currencies, although gradually certain currencies, such as the Venetian ducat and the English pound, became more favored and automatically acceptable throughout Europe. All paper tender was still issued by private banks; not until the seventeenth century did any nation begin issuing paper currency.

Attitudes toward merchants also changed gradually. Though the Church relaxed its absolute position on usury and conceded that merchants might be allowed entrance to heaven, widespread resentment was still directed against merchants and bankers, especially when some merchant families began to accumulate wealth that was almost unimaginable by that era's standards. Less discreet about their wealth than the advice manuals recommended, merchants irritated and offended the often less wealthy noble class. As Italian bankers began to replace the Jews as Europe's prime moneylenders, they were insulted and occasionally physically attacked, though not to the degree that Jews were abused. (Shakespeare's plays, for example, refer to "greedy Lombards," or Italians.)

Despite the slow speed of these economic and attitudinal changes, Italian business practices gradually spread to the rest of Europe. Northern European merchants, especially the Dutch and the English, took the lead in the seventeenth century and developed such economic institutions as the stock market. They also turned medieval attitudes toward business upside down by formulating the idea that success in business was a sign of God's favor and poverty was a sign of moral and spiritual degeneracy. When the Europeans established colonies, they took capitalism with them. By the nineteenth century, most of the world had experienced a Commercial Revolution, though the business procedures and institutions developed by Europeans were modified when they were adopted by non-Europeans to fit their own cultural norms.

CHAPTER SEVEN

MEDICINE AND REPRODUCTION

IN THE MIDDLE AGES

THE PROBLEM

Along with ideas about how the world began, every human culture has also developed theories regarding what we now term "reproduction," that is, the process by which humans and other animals give rise to offspring. These have varied widely throughout history, and human reproduction in particular has often been linked to religious beliefs. In some religions, gods reproduce themselves in ways that are similar to human reproduction, thus giving reproduction divine sanction; in others, this divine sanction comes from the words or actions of a god or gods regarding reproduction; in still others, reproduction is regarded as evil or negative, established by malevolent deities or demons as a way to distract humans from their true spiritual pursuits.

The three Western monotheistic religious traditions—Judaism, Christianity, and Islam—all regard reproduction as established by the creator God at the beginning of time. In the words of Hebrew Scripture, also part of the Christian Old Testament, God says to the first humans, "Be fruitful and multiply." Jewish and Muslim tradition take these words to be divine commandments for all and frown on celibacy for either men or women. Christianity developed a more ambivalent attitude, praising individuals who chose a life of chastity but also cherishing children as a positive good; individuals and groups within Christianity who see sexuality and reproduction as unmitigated evils have been generally viewed as heretics—that is, as deviating from correct belief.

Reproduction is not only a religious issue, however; from very early times, it has also been a matter of medical concern. Though all aspects of health and disease were historically viewed as being influenced by divine will and action, human intervention was generally acceptable. (There were invariably some who opposed this view, as there continue to be today in groups such as the Christian Scientists.) This intervention might take the form of prayers and intercessions, but it also included treatments that were not primarily religious. Some of the earliest records from ancient Egypt, for example, indicate that doctors identified and treated such diseases as diabetes, bronchitis, hemorrhoids, and skin cancer. The Chinese pharmacology, which is currently undergoing a resurgence, has roots in a tradition that is thousands of years old. In ancient Greece, philosophers such as Aristotle (384–322 B.C.E.) and physicians such as Hippocrates (ca. 460–370 B.C.E.) were interested not simply in clinical practice, but also in developing medical theories about the way in which the body—and the mind—operates.

For many of these ancient practitioners and theorists, reproduction was an essential part of medical knowledge and practice; Aristotle, for example, wrote an entire treatise on it: *The Generation of Animals.* His ideas, and those of other ancient authorities, became the basis for theories of reproduction and treatment of reproductive difficulties—as well as most other ailments—for nearly two thousand years in the Near East, North Africa, and Europe. Later scholars within Judaism, Christianity, and Islam built on the work of the ancient Greeks, creating a body of medical literature that was translated into many languages and spread over a vast area.

The Greek tradition came primarily from Hippocrates and Galen (ca. 130–200 C.E.). Galen is credited with over five hundred works, mostly on medical topics, based on earlier medical knowledge and supported by his own observation and experimentation. His interests were so wide-ranging and his findings so influential that his work was considered the medical canon for centuries—until the seventeenth century or later in Europe and until the nineteenth through much of the Arabic world. Like the writings of Aristotle on other scientific subjects, the word of Galen was considered nearly as authoritative as the Hebrew and Christian Scriptures and the Muslim Qur'an.

Galen's ideas and writings were copied and taught within the Roman Empire (he lived for much of his life in Rome, though he continued to write in Greek) and, after the collapse of the western Roman Empire, within the eastern Roman, or Byzantine Empire, particularly at Alexandria, Athens, and Edessa. During the fifth and sixth centuries, the Byzantine emperors ordered many medical schools to close, and the physicians and scientists moved farther eastward, first to Jundishapur in Persia. Here they came into contact with Indian and Persian medicine and combined these with Greek teachings to form a single system. Once the Muslims conquered this area, many physicians moved to Baghdad, the capital of this part of the Islamic world, where they were welcomed at the caliph's court. Most of these physicians retained their allegiance to Christianity and Judaism, but also learned the native tongue and began to translate medical texts into Arabic. Under the leadership of Rhazes (Arabic al-Razi, 860–932), the main hospital in Baghdad became a center of clinical observation and the treatment of disease.

While Rhazes was celebrated for his accurate observations, the most influential Islamic medical writer was Avicenna (Arabic Ibn Sina, 980–1037), who was also a philosopher and an interpreter of Aristotle. Avicenna was dubbed "Prince of Physicians" throughout both

Europe and the Islamic world, and his major work, the *Canon of Medicine,* integrated medical traditions from a number of different cultures. Written originally in Arabic, this work was later translated into Latin and other languages; it became the most important book for all students of medicine within Islam and, in its Latin version, for medical students in Europe until the seventeenth century. In the *Canon* Avicenna discusses the general principles of health and disease, the diseases of particular organs and those like fever that affect the whole body, and simple and compound drugs. Ideas about reproduction and the treatment of reproductive ailments are found throughout the work.

At the time that physicians in the Islamic world were translating Greek works and developing their own theories of health and disease, medical treatment in Europe was largely in the hands of local healers. With the collapse of the Roman Empire in the West, the ability to read Greek declined and schools that taught medicine disappeared, so learned medicine lagged far behind that in Islam. Before the eleventh century, only two or three of Galen's works were available in Latin, whereas over one hundred were available in Arabic. This gap began to close in the tenth and eleventh centuries, when a few cities in Europe gradually developed first informal and then formal centers of medical training. The most prominent of these was at Salerno in southern Italy, where male and female medical practitioners received training through apprenticeship followed by instruction in an organized medical school. Individuals associated with Salerno, such as the convert from Islam and later Benedictine monk Constantine the African (f. 1065–1085), began to translate medical works out of Arabic. These translations included writings by Galen and Hippocrates, which had originally been written in Greek, and those by Rhazes, Avicenna, and other Islamic physicians, which were originally written in Arabic. Constantine often did not translate whole works, choosing instead to combine the ideas of many authors—and his own—on particular subjects; reproduction is a key issue in his treatises *On Coitus* and *On Human Nature.* Gradually copies of all of Constantine's works spread throughout Europe and, blended with those of other translators and commentators, formed the program of study under the medical faculties that were beginning to be organized within the newly developing universities in such cities as Paris and Bologna.

This shared Galenic/Islamic tradition was one in which medical ideas were very closely linked to philosophy and to ideas about the natural world in general. Prime among these was the notion of the four bodily *humors,* four fluids—blood, phlegm, black bile, and yellow bile—contained in the body that influenced bodily health. Each individual was thought to have a characteristic temperament, or *complexion,* determined by his or her particular balance of the four humors, in the same way that we might describe a person today as having a "positive outlook" or a "Type-A" personality. These four humors corresponded to four qualities—hot, cold, wet, and dry—and to the four basic elements in the Aristotelian universe—earth, air, fire, and water. The organs were viewed primarily as channels for the humors, rather than as having only one specific function. Disease was understood to be an imbalance of bodily humors, which could be diagnosed by taking a patient's pulse or examining his or her urine. Treatment was thus an attempt to bring the humors back into balance, which might be accomplished through diet or drugs—usually mixtures of therapeutic herbal or mineral substances—or through a direct attempt to rebalance the humors by using emetics, purgatives, or bloodletting. These therapies were somewhat gender-distinctive because the bodily humors were also gender-related: Women were regarded as tending toward the cold and wet, men toward the hot and dry. The exact balance of humors was different for each individual, however, with the healthy body capable of maintaining this balance on its own. Thus treatment, whether diet, drugs, or bloodletting, was aimed at eradicating any obstacles to this natural balance, rather than at altering the balance itself.

Blood was viewed as in some ways the dominant humor. According to Avicenna, phlegm was "imperfectly matured blood" that could be transformed into blood if heat were applied correctly. In his opinion, blood also carried phlegm, black bile, and yellow bile throughout the body, and it was these substances that were partially responsible for the different textures of body parts—the hardness of bones and the softness of the brain, for example. Though some commentators thought the source of semen was the brain, as both were soft and whitish, most saw semen—and milk— as transformed blood, gradually "cooked" until it was whitish. The agent in all of these transformations was heat, which was also a critical factor in many issues concerning reproduction. The sex of an infant, for example, was determined largely by the amount of heat present during intercourse and gestation: Males resulted when there was the proper amount of heat, which caused their sexual organs to be pushed outside the body, and females when there was too little heat, which caused their sexual organs to remain internal. Men's greater heat continued throughout their lives, causing them to burn up their hair and go bald and to develop broader shoulders and bigger brains (because heat rises and causes matter to expand).

Though medical theorists agreed about a great deal, irreconcilable conflicts divided certain schools of thought. In the area of reproduction, the sharpest disagreement was between the ideas of Aristotle and those of Galen and his followers regarding the role of the mother and father in conception. Aristotle held that the mother provided the matter out of which an infant was formed, and the father, though he did not provide any material part of the embryo, supplied the "active principle," the force that brought this inert matter to life; women were "passive" in reproduction, and their menstrual fluid was a deficient form of semen. Galen and his followers held that both the male and female produced seed, so that both contributed both materially and actively to the generation of the child. (The word *generation* was generally used in the ancient and medieval world to describe the process that we label *reproduction.*) Each sex produced both strong and weak seed, with strong seed being the source of males and weak seed, of females; the sex of a child depended on the balance of these two and the amount of heat present during generation.

Despite disagreements, the ideas of this body of medical literature spread throughout Europe, North Africa, and the Near East, and familiarity with this literature became the mark of a professional physician. In the Islamic world medical teaching was carried out largely in hospitals, and in Europe at the new universities, where medicine, along with law and theology, became one of the standard disciplines of advanced study. The influence of this Galenic/Islamic tradition did not stop with those who could read learned languages, however, for beginning in the fourteenth century in Europe, translations and compilations appeared in the vernacular languages. (Translation is less of an issue in the Islamic world; because the Qur'an was revealed to Muhammad in Arabic, study of that language was even more central to all learning than study of Latin was in Europe.) Once the printing press was developed in the mid-fifteenth century, these vernacular medical works and the Latin translations were very frequently reprinted. It is difficult to gauge how often the treatments they recommend were actually applied, but the ideas they contain were shared by most of the population, from the highly learned to the illiterate.

Though in many respects their cultures differed widely, in terms of medical understanding and practice the Muslims, Jews, and Christians who lived in the Near East, North Africa, and Europe during the medieval period shared a common tradition.

Your task in this chapter is to use medical literature to answer these questions: What central ideas regarding reproduction were shared by Jewish, Christian, and Islamic medical writers in the Middle Ages? How were these translated into practical advice for patients and medical practitioners?

SOURCES AND METHOD

One of the greatest dangers in exploring the history of science or medicine is viewing people who lived in earlier centuries as foolish or ignorant. How, we ask, could they have held such idiotic ideas? Couldn't they see what was in front of them? Many of the earliest historians of science, and even more the earliest historians of medicine, who were often retired physicians, themselves gave in to this intellectual arrogance, for they viewed the story of science and medicine in a linear fashion, as constant advance from the unenlightened past to the brilliant present. Increasingly, however, historians of science point out that in every era, including our own, scientific knowledge is shaped by people's pre-existing ideas; these ideas allow even the most "objective" scientists to see things only in certain ways. (This can perhaps best be seen in contemporary subatomic physics, in which attempts are now being made to trace the paths of types of particles whose existence was not known about until very recently, or in the discussions among astrophysicists and astronomers about the presence of "dark matter." Now that dark matter, or the neutrino, is a concept, scientists begin to see it and try to trace its effects.)

Thus it is important, as you examine the sources for this chapter, that you do not view them solely from the vantage point of medicine in the twenty-first century. Rather, try first simply to understand the view of the body and of reproductive processes that they contain. The sources are arranged roughly in chronological order, and they contain information on a variety of topics, for reproduction was linked to a number of other medical issues, such as general health, gynecology, obstetrics, and embryology, and to nonmedical issues such as ethics, religion, and astrology. Many of the medical works from which these sources come are extremely long, and some are still available in their entirety only in Latin or Arabic. As you read them, it might be best to make a list of the key ideas and topics that emerge. These might include such topics as basic anatomy and physiology, sexual intercourse, conception, gender differences, fetal development, difficulties in conception and birth, and the relations between general health and reproduction. Not every author covers every topic, but through this list you can begin to discern key ideas. At the same time, you will find it useful to keep a list of proposed remedies for ailments. This tool will help you answer the second main question and also give you further clues to the general medieval understanding of the reproductive process.

Source 1 includes selections from the *Canon* of Avicenna, written in Arabic at the beginning of the eleventh century and translated into Latin by Gerard of Cremona, translator of many medical and scientific works, during the second half of the twelfth century. How does Avicenna compare the male and female reproductive organs? What does he say happens at the moment of conception? How is the embryo formed in the uterus?

Source 2 is a short treatise about impotence, written by Constantine the African in the late eleventh century as part of his longer work *Pantechne.* It was frequently copied in later medical works, usually without naming him as the author, a very common practice. What sort of spells does Constantine view as interfering with intercourse? What remedies does he propose?

Source 3 is an excerpt from the treatise *The Diseases of Women,* attributed to Trota or Trotula of Salerno, a woman medical practitioner active in that city in the eleventh century. Trotula is a very mysterious figure whose work and even existence have been the source of great debate for centuries. By the twelfth century, several treatises were circulating in Europe under her name—this being one of them—and for the next several centuries they were the most widely circulated medical works on gynecological issues and were translated out of Latin into French, Irish, German, English, Flemish, and Catalan. By the sixteenth century, however, some medical authorities denied that works showing such familiarity with learned medicine could have been written by a woman. (Because women were excluded from the medical schools attached to universities in Europe, they could not receive theoretical training; their healing activities, along with those of men who had not been university trained, were often prohibited beginning in the thirteenth century as university-bred physicians sought to gain a monopoly on medical practice.) This debate was only finally laid to rest about a decade ago, when it was demonstrated that most of the works attributed to her, including the one excerpted here, were not written by her, but that she had, in fact, authored a different medical work, the *Practica secundam Trotam,* and thus was a real person. Most of the medical writers and practitioners of the Middle Ages, however, regarded Trotula as an important authority and cited her along with male authors when they were attempting to demonstrate the validity of a particular idea. It may seem ironic that they did this at the same time they were prohibiting women from studying or practicing medicine, but Trotula was thought to have written in the period before Salerno became an official medical school, and was simply regarded as transcending the normal rules applying to women. How does Trotula characterize the differences between men and women? Does she adopt an Aristotelian or a Galenic view about the role of the two sexes in reproduction? Why do women menstruate? Is menstruation harmful or beneficial? What are some of the causes for failure to conceive? What remedies are recommended? What does the author suggest to encourage the birth of a boy? Why do you think there is no corresponding advice to encourage the birth of a girl? How does a fetus develop, and what can be done to discourage miscarriage?

Source 4 contains excerpts from two works of Moses Maimonides (1135–1204), a Jewish rabbi, philosopher, and physician. Maimonides was born in Cordoba, Spain, but emigrated to Egypt and became the chief physician at the court of the sultan Saladin in Cairo. He was reputed to have been invited to become the physician for Richard the Lionhearted in England, but he never left Egypt. He wrote numerous religious and philosophical works, including a massive commentary on the Torah, and at least ten medical works. His religious works were penned in Hebrew and his medical works in Arabic, with many of these later translated into Hebrew, Latin, and other European languages. The selections included here are from two works, *Ethical Conduct* and *Regimen of Health.* What does Maimonides see as important to general health? How does this relate to his views about sexual intercourse?

Source 5 is another work with a spurious attribution—*On the Secrets of Women,* written in Latin in the late thirteenth or early fourteenth century by the pseudo–Albertus Magnus. The *real* Albertus Magnus was a prominent thirteenth-century theologian, philosopher, and scientist, and this work was most likely written by one of his followers, though we cannot be sure exactly which one. The fact that it was quickly attributed to the real Albertus Magnus—even though the text refers to him as a person different from the author—gave it weighty authority, and it became the most popular book of this type in the later Middle Ages. There are over eighty manuscript copies known today, and it was printed over fifty times in the period 1450–1500 and over seventy times in the sixteenth century. Read this evidence carefully. How does the author present the differences of opinion regarding the male and female role in conception? How does he describe the process of conception itself? What is the role and cause of menstruation? According to the author, how does the fetus receive nourishment and air? What general attitudes about sexual difference emerge from this text?

The works we have looked at so far, though they combine academic and popular medicine and were often eventually translated, were directed specifically to a learned—and therefore male—audience. Source 6 is somewhat different; it is an excerpt from one of the earliest printed midwives' manuals in Europe, the *Rosegarden for Midwives and Pregnant Women* written in German by Eucharius Rösslin, a pharmacist and physician in Frankfurt, and printed for the first time in Strasbourg in 1513. The *Rosegarden* was translated—often under a different title—into Latin, French, Czech, Polish, Spanish, Dutch, and English, with over one hundred known printed versions, and by the later sixteenth century was mentioned in city midwifery ordinances as recommended reading. Rösslin draws on a huge range of Greek and Arabic authorities, most prominently the Muscio translations of Soranus of Ephesus; these, rather than any hands-on experience, form the basis of his advice, though he also includes remedies grounded in popular traditions. The *Rosegarden* includes sections on diet and conduct for pregnant women, specific instructions for midwives during normal and difficult births, and instructions for the care of newborns. It also deals with rather grim topics, such as how to deliver a child that has died in the uterus. The portion included here covers the period just before and during a birth. As you read this, note Rösslin's advice to the mother and to the midwife. How does this fit with the more general ideas about health and bodily processes you have read so far? What is the midwife's role in a normal birth procedure?

Medical ideas were transmitted largely through words in the Middle Ages, but elaborate copies of treatises were occasionally illustrated, and after the development of the printing press, woodcuts and engravings became an important feature of medical works, particularly those designed at least in part for a popular audience. Sources 7 through 10 are four medical illustrations: Source 7, a manuscript illumination of Constantine the African doing a uroscopy for women and men; Source 8, a thirteenth-century manuscript illumination of a birth; Source 9, a caesarean section in a fourteenth-century manuscript of the Arabic writer al-Biruni's *Chronology of Ancient Nations*; and Source 10, a sixteenth-century engraving of a birth scene that was frequently used to illustrate pseudo–Albertus Magnus's *On the Secrets of Women*. How do these illustrations reinforce or refute the ideas presented in the written texts? How do they depict medical personnel? How do the attendants at the two births differ from those at the caesarean section? Do these figures attempt to portray actual medical procedures or to illustrate medical principles?

THE EVIDENCE

Source 1 from Avicenna, The Canon of Medicine, *tr. Gerard of Cremona, translated and reprinted in Danielle Jacquart and Claude Thomasset,* Sexuality and Medicine in the Middle Ages, *tr. Matthew Adamson (Cambridge, Polity Press, 1988), pp. 36, 55, 63, 77. Reprinted by permission of Blackwell Publishing Ltd.*

1. From Avicenna, *The Canon of Medicine*, 11th century

I say that the instrument of reproduction in the woman is the womb (*matrix*) and that it was created similar to the instrument of reproduction in the man, that is to say the penis and what goes with it. However, one of these instruments is complete and stretches outwards, whereas the other is smaller and held on the inside, to some extent constituting the opposite of the male instrument. The covering of the womb is like the scrotum, the cervix [= vagina] like the penis. There are two testicles in women as in men, but in men they are larger, turned outwards and tend to be spherical in shape; in women they are small, of a rather flattened roundness, and they are located on the inside, in the vulva. . . .

The sublime God created the testicles to be, as you know, the principal members which engender sperm from the moisture that is brought to them in the veins; this moisture is like the residue of the food that has reached the fourth stage in the whole body.[1] It is a better-digested and subtler blood. . . .

As soon as the two seeds have been mixed, the ebullition[2] of which we have spoken takes place and the swollen part and the first membrane are created; then all the sperm is suspended from the horn-shaped protuberances,[3] and it there finds its nourishment as long as it is still sperm, until it starts to draw its nourishment from the menstrual blood and from the cavities [the openings of the veins] to which the membrane which has been formed is attached. Accord-

1. Food was thought to be digested in stages within the body.

2. **ebullition:** the process of bubbling up.

3. The uterus was thought to have "horns," or growths sticking out on each side, which were shown in anatomical illustrations into the seventeenth century; these horns were thought to contain blood vessels.

ing to Galen, this membrane is like a protective coating left behind by the sperm of the female when it flows towards the place where the male's sperm also flows, and if it does not join with the sperm of the male at the very moment it is shed, it nonetheless mixes with it during intercourse. . . .

After that, the blood which is voided by the woman at the time of menses is used for nourishment. Part is transformed in accordance with its similarity to the spermatic substance: it forms the parts of the body that have come from the sperm, and it increases the sperm by nourishing it. Another part does not act as nourishment but, through coagulation, is used to fill the empty spaces of the principal parts of the body, and makes flesh and fat. A last part consists of superfluous matter and is no good for either of the above-mentioned purposes: it stays put until childbirth, when nature expels it as being superfluous.

Source 2 from Henry E. Sigerist, Essays in Biology *(Berkeley: University of California Press, pp. 541–546. Reprinted in Edward Grant,* A Source Book in Medieval Science *(Cambridge: Harvard University Press, 1974), pp. 768–769.*

2. Constantine the African's Treatise on Impotence, 11th century

A short treatise about the people who, impeded by spells, are unable to have intercourse with their wives.

There are people who, impeded by diabolical spells, are unable to have intercourse with their wives. We do not want to deprive our book of their applause, for the remedy, if I am not wrong, is most sacred.

Now, if this should happen to somebody, he must set his hope in the Lord and He will be merciful. Since, however, there are many kinds of spells, it is necessary that we discuss them. Some spells are made of animated substances such as the testicles of a cock. If they are put under the bed with blood of the cock, they bring it about that the people lying on the bed cannot have intercourse. Some are made of letters written with the blood of a bat. Some are made of inanimate substances, for instance if a nut or an acorn is divided in two, and one half is put on one side, the other on the other side, of the road along which the bride and bridegroom must proceed.

There are others also which are made from beans which are not softened with hot water nor cooked on the fire. This spell is very bad if four such beans are placed on the roof or on the road or over or under the door.

There are others also which are of metal, such as those that are of iron or lead, for instance, the iron ones made of the needle with which the dead men or women have been sewn. And because these spells are devilish and are particularly in women, they are sometimes cured by divine, sometimes by human measures.

If therefore bridegroom and bride are disturbed by the above-mentioned spells, it is better to talk about them than to keep silent, for if the victims are not succored they are separated and thus disgraced, and doing this evil they seem to sin not only against their relatives but also against the Holy Ghost.

If we wish to extirpate the spell properly, we must look out: if the above-mentioned spell is under the bed, it must be removed. But if the author of this spell removes it in daytime and puts it back at night, or vice versa, then bridegroom and bride must acquire another house and lie down there.

If the spell is made of letters, which is recognized by the fact that bridegroom and bride do not love each other, one must search above and under the threshold of the door, and if something is found it must be taken to the bishop or priest. If not, one must do what is indicated below.

If a nut or an acorn are the cause of this spell, the woman shall take a nut or an acorn and divide it in two. And with one half the man shall proceed on one side of the road and deposit it there; the woman, however, shall put the other half on the other side of the road. Thereupon bridegroom and bride shall take both parts of the nut without having removed the shell. And then the nut shall thus be made whole again and shall be kept for seven days. Having done this they shall have intercourse.

If, however, it happens on account of beans, it can be cured with divine rather than human means. If it is on account of the needles for the dead, the spells must be sought either in the pillow or in the mattress. If they are not found, the victims shall lie together in another house.

Bile of a male dog purifies the house and brings it about that no evil remedy be brought to the house.

Sprinkle the walls of the house with dog's blood, and it will be liberated from every spell. . . .

If, however, on account of impending sins, the above-mentioned measures did not help at all, they shall go to a priest or the bishop. And if the bishop has permitted it and no remedy is found, after having confessed to the bishop or an ordained priest they shall take Holy Communion on the day of the Holy Resurrection or Ascension in Whitsuntide. Having received the Body and Blood of the Lord, bridegroom and bride shall give each other the kiss of peace.

And after they have received the benediction of the bishop or priest, the bishop or priest shall give this verse of the prophet written on paper: The voice of the Lord is upon the waters: the great Lord is upon many waters [Psalms 28:3]. Thereafter they shall go home and shall abstain from intercourse for three days and three nights. Then they shall perform it, and thus all diabolical power is destroyed.

The little treatise on spells has come to an end. Thanks be to God. Amen.

Source 3 from Trotula of Salerno, The Diseases of Women, *translated by Elizabeth Mason-Hohl, M.D. (Los Angeles: Ward Ritchie Press, 1940), pp. 1–3, 16–25. Reprinted in Edward Grant,* A Source Book in Medieval Science *(Cambridge: Harvard University Press, 1974), pp. 761–763, 764–766.*

3. From Pseudo–Trotula of Salerno, *The Diseases of Women,* 12th century

PROLOGUE

Since God, the author of the universe, in the first establishment of the world, distinguished the individual natures of things each according to its own kind, He differentiated the human race above the other creatures by means of extraordinary dignity. To it, beyond the condition of other animals, He gave freedom of reason and of intellect. Moreover, desiring its generation to subsist perpetually, He created it male and female in different sexes that by means of their fertile propagation future offspring may never cease to come forth. Blending their embraces with a pleasing mixture, He made the nature of the male hot and dry and that of the female cold and wet so that the excess of each other's embrace might be restrained by the mutual opposition of contrary qualities. The man's constitution being hot and dry might assuage the woman's coldness and wetness and on the contrary her nature being cold and wet might soothe his hot and dry embrace. Likewise that the male having the stronger quality might pour seed into the woman as into a field and the woman endowed with a weaker quality, subject as it were to the function of the man, might naturally take unto her bosom the poured out seed. Since then women are by nature weaker than men it is reasonable that sicknesses more often abound in them especially around the organs involved in the work of nature. Since these organs happen to be in a retired location, women on account of modesty and the fragility and delicacy of the state of these parts dare not reveal the difficulties of their sicknesses to a male doctor. Wherefore I, pitying their misfortunes and at the instigation of a certain matron, began to study carefully the sicknesses which most frequently trouble the female sex. Since in women not so much heat abounds that it suffices to use up the moistures which daily collect in them, their weaknesses cannot endure so much exertion as to be able to put forth that moisture to the outside air as in the case of men. Nature herself, on account of this deficiency of heat, has assigned for them a certain specific purgation namely the menses, commonly called flowers. For just as trees do not produce fruit without flowers so women without menses are deprived of the function of conception. This purgation occurs in women just as 'pollutio'[4] occurs in men. . . . If such purgations have been of normal time and regularity, Nature

4. **pollutio:** nocturnal emissions, or "wet dreams."

sufficiently unloads women of superfluous moisture. If the menstruation has taken place too copiously various sicknesses arise from it. . . . Diarrhoea occurs too on account of excessive coldness in the womb, either because the veins are very slender as in thin women since in this case thick and excessive fluids do not have free channels through which they can break forth, or because the liquids are thick and viscous and because of clotting their egress is hindered. . . . Sometimes the periods fail because of excessive grief or anger or excitement or fear. If they have ceased for a long time there is a suspicion of serious future illness. Often the urine is changed into a red color or into a color like the washings from fresh meat; sometimes the woman's appearance is changed into a gray or leaden color, or into the color of grass. . . .

CHAPTER 11
ON THE HINDRANCES TO CONCEPTION AND OF THE THINGS WHICH MAKE FOR IMPREGNATION

Certain women are useless for conceiving either because they are too thin and lean or because they are too fat. In these latter the flesh folded around the opening of the womb binds it and does not permit the seed of the man to enter it. Some have a womb so soft and slippery that the seed having been received cannot be retained in it. Sometimes this happens through a defect of the male who has seed so thin that when it is poured into the vagina it slips out because of its own liquidness. Some men also have testicles cold and dry; these men rarely or never beget, because their seed is useless for procreation. It is evident therefore that conception is hindered as often by a defect of the man as of the woman. If it is by a defect of the woman it happens either from excessive warmth or from excessive moistures of the womb. Sometimes on account of its natural softness the womb cannot retain the seed injected into it, and often because of its excessive moisture it suffocates the seed. Often because of its excessive heat the womb burns the seed up and she cannot conceive. . . .

If conception be hindered because of a defect of the male it would be from a lack of force impelling the sperm, a defect of the organ, or a defect of heat. If it be from a defect of heat, the sign is that he is not eager for copulation. Hence he ought to anoint his loins with arrogon or take seed of colewort and euphorbia and reduce them to a fine powder. Then mix them with the oils of fleabane[5] and of weasel and with this anoint his loins. If it happens through a defect of the spirit the sign will be that he has desire but the penis is not erected. We aid him with an ointment that generates spirit. If it happens through a defect of the sperm the sign is that when he copulates he emits either none or too little seed. We aid him with things that increase sperm such as orris, domestic parsnips, and the like.

5. **arrogon, colewort, euphorbia** and **fleabane:** all plants.

If the woman or the man be sterile you will ascertain it by this method: take two jars and into each put bran. Into one of them put the urine of the man and into the other put the urine of the woman and let the jars be left for nine or ten days. If the barrenness be from a defect of the woman you will find many worms and the bran foul in her jar. On the other hand you will have similar evidence from the other urine if the barrenness be through a defect of the man. But if you have observed such signs in neither urine neither will be the cause of the barrenness and it is possible to help them to conceive by the use of medicines. If they wish to have a male child let the man take the womb and vulva of a hare and have it dried and pulverized; blend it with wine and let him drink it. Let the woman do the same with the testicles of the hare and let her be with her husband at the end of her menstrual period and she will conceive a male. . . .

CHAPTER 12
ON THE FORMATION OF THE SEED WHEN CONCEIVED

In the first month occurs a small clot of blood. In the second occurs the formation of the blood and of the body; in the third the nails and hair are produced. In the fourth motion and therefore women are nauseated. In the fifth the foetus receives the likeness of father or mother. In the sixth, the binding together of the sinews. In the seventh, the bones and sinews are strengthened; in the eighth nature helps and the child puts on flesh. In the ninth, it proceeds from darkness into light.

CHAPTER 13
ON THE POSITION OF THE FOETUS IN THE MOTHER'S WOMB

Galen gives the report that the foetus is fastened in the womb just as the fruit is on the tree, which when it comes forth from the blossom is very tender and falls from any occasion whatsoever. When it has become full grown, riper, and established, it clings to the tree and will not fall on slight occasion. When it has become completely ripe it will fall of itself and not of any other occasion. Thus when a child is first produced from a conceived seed the ligaments by which it is fastened to the womb are tender and unfirm and therefore it is easily let fall by abortion. On account of a cough, diarrhoea, dysentery, excessive activity or anger, or loss of blood, a woman can lose her foetus. But when a soul or life has been infused into the child[6] it clings a little more firmly and does not slip quickly. When the child has ripened it is quickly let out by the office of nature. Hippocrates says that if a woman requires bleeding or purgation, you should not do these things before the fourth month. In the fifth or sixth months she can

6. Many ancient and medieval authors thought that a child received its soul about the time the mother first felt movement. That point in a pregnancy is still termed *quickening*, which originally meant "coming to life."

be bled or purged cautiously, if there be necessity, with a mild . . . decoction according as the strength of the patient shall be able to tolerate. Beyond and before this time an evacuation will be dangerous. When the time for parturition has arrived the child moves more violently and struggles toward the exit. Nature in its own time causes the vulva to be opened, the foetus finds its own exit and thus it is expelled by the force of nature from its own resting place, the afterbirth.

CHAPTER 14
ON SIGNS OF PREGNANCY

For knowing whether a woman is carrying a male or female child take water from a spring and let the woman draw out two or three drops of blood or of milk from the right breast. Let them be poured into the water and if they seek the bottom she is bearing a male; if they float on top she is bearing a female. Hippocrates said that the woman who is bearing a male is well colored and has the right breast larger; if she is pale she is bearing a female and has the left breast larger.

Source 4 from Jacob Minkin, The Teachings of Maimonides *(Northvale, N.J.: Jason Aronson, 1987), pp. 384, 386–387; and "Moses Maimonides' Two Treatises on the Regimen of Health," trans. Ariel Bar-sela, Hebbel E. Hoff, and Elias Faris,* Transactions of the American Philosophical Society, *n.s. 52,4 (1964): 29.*

4. From Moses Maimonides, *Ethical Conduct* and *The Regimen of Health,* ca 1190s

ETHICAL CONDUCT

At every period of life, it should be one's care to secure free action of the bowels, approximating to a relaxed condition. It is a leading principle in medicine that if there is constipation or if the bowels move with difficulty, grave disorders result. How is a slight costive[7] condition to be remedied? If the patient is a youth, he should eat, every morning, salty foods well cooked and seasoned with olive oil, fish brine and salt, without bread. Or he should drink the liquid of boiled spinach or St. John's bread, mixed with olive oil, fish brine and salt. An old man should drink, in the morning, honey diluted with warm water, and wait about four hours before taking his breakfast. This regimen should be observed for one day, or, if necessary, for three or four successive days till the bowels move freely.

7. **costive:** constipated.

Honey and wine are bad for young children, but good for the aged, particularly in the winter. The quantity taken in the summer should be two-thirds of that consumed in the winter.

Another great principle of hygiene, physicians say, is as follows: As long as a person takes active exercise, works hard, does not overeat and keeps his bowels open, he will be free from disease and will increase in vigor, even though the food he eats is coarse. . . .

Whosoever indulges in sexual dissipation becomes prematurely aged; his strength fails; his eyes become dim; a foul odor proceeds from his mouth and armpits; the hair of his head, eye-brows and eye-lashes drop out; the hair of his beard, armpits and legs grow abnormally; his teeth fall out; and besides these, he becomes subject to numerous other diseases. Medical authorities have stated that for each one who dies of other maladies, a thousand are the victims of sexual excess. A man should, therefore, be careful in this regard if he wishes to lead a happy life. He should only cohabit when he finds himself in good health and vigor, experiences involuntary erections which persist after he has diverted his mind to other things, is conscious of a heaviness from the loins downwards as if the spermatic cords were being drawn and his flesh is hot. Such a condition calls for cohabitation which then is conducive to health. One should not cohabit when sated with food, nor when one is hungry, but only after a meal has been digested. Before and after coition, attention should be paid to the excretory functions.

THE REGIMEN OF HEALTH

The behavior of all men regarding coitus is known. And that is, that there is not one who uses it for the sake of the regimen of health, or for the sake of procreation, but merely for pleasure; thus they lust until fatigued, at all times, and at every opportunity. It is already manifest among those who know, that coitus is detrimental to all men except some few whose temperament is such that a little of it does no harm. But men differ only in the degree of harm; among them are those whom it harms greatly, and among them are those whom it harms but little. Its harm to the young that are of moist temperament is little. Its harm to the old, the convalescent, and those of dry temperament is very great. Among the convalescents we have already seen some who copulated and died that very day, or suffered syncope[8] and recurrence of fever, and died after a few days. On the whole, it is a pernicious matter for the sick and the convalescent, and very detrimental to the old and to all of dry temperament. It is improper for anyone to copulate before the food in the stomach is digested, or when hungry, or when thirsty, or in a state of inebriety, or after leaving the bath, or following exercise or before it, or for a day before bloodletting and for a day thereafter. Whoever desires the continuance of health, should drive his thoughts from coitus all he can.

8. **syncope:** fainting.

Source 5 from Helen Rodnite Lemay, Women's Secrets: A Translation of Pseudo–Albertus Magnus' *De Secretis Mulierum* with Commentaries *(Albany: State University of New York Press, 1992), pp. 63–64, 65, 69, 84, 85–86, 107, 109, 117.*

5. Pseudo–Albertus Magnus, *On the Secrets of Women,* late 13th or early 14th century

Now that we have finished our introductory remarks, designed to prepare the reader's mind toward this subject matter, let us turn to the matter of the book, and first let us examine the generation of the embryo. Note therefore that every human being who is naturally conceived is generated from the seed of the father and the menses of the mother, according to all philosophers and medical authorities. And I say "medical authorities" because Aristotle did not believe that the father's seed was part of the substance of the fetus, but rather that the fetus proceeded from the menses alone, and afterwards he states that the seed exudes like vapor from the menses. The doctors,[9] on the other hand, believe that the fetus is made up of male and female seed together.

Having set forth both opinions, we must now see how that seed is received in woman. When a woman is having sexual intercourse with a man she releases her menses at the same time that the man releases sperm, and both seeds enter the *vulva* (vagina) simultaneously and are mixed together, and then the woman conceives. Conception is said to take place, therefore, when the two seeds are received in the womb in a place that nature has chosen. And after these seeds are received, the womb closes up like a purse on every side, so that nothing can fall out of it. After this happens, the woman no longer menstruates. . . .

The menses in woman, just like the sperm in man, is nothing other than superfluous food which has not been transformed into the substance of the body. In woman it is called "menses" because it flows at least once every month when the woman reaches the proper age, that is, 12, 13, or, most frequently, 14. This flow takes place every month in order to purge the body. In some women it begins at the new moon, in some afterwards, and thus all women do not have their pain at the same time. Some have more suffering, some less; some have a shorter flow than others, and this is all determined by the requirement and the complexion of the individual woman.

The third question is why menses, which are superfluous food, flow in women, and sperm does not flow in men, for this is also superfluous food. To this I reply that woman is cold and humid by nature, whereas man is hot and dry. Now humid things naturally flow, as we see in the fourth book of the *Meteorology,*[10] and this is especially true of that humid substance which is in women,

9. **doctors:** that is, Galen and his followers.

10. *Meteorology* and *On Heaven and Earth* are two treatises attributed to Aristotle.

for it is watery. In men, on the other hand, the humid substance resembles air, and, further, man has natural heat, and this heat acts upon the humid. Since nature never does anything in vain, as is noted in the first book *On Heaven and Earth,*[10] and because the heat in women is weaker than that in men, and all their food cannot be converted into flesh, nature takes the best course. She provides for what is necessary, and leaves the excess in the place where the menses are kept. Enough has been said on this subject, for to go into more detail would be to give more than the subject demands. . . .

Now that we have examined the preceding questions, let us turn to the formation of the fetus in the womb. The first matter received in the womb has the nature of milk for the first six days, for the natural heat in the male sperm and in the womb causes it to become white as milk. Then that matter is changed to the nature or color of blood that is thickened, as if it were well cooked, and this lasts nine days. During the next twelve days the members of the fetus begin to be formed.

We note here that according to the philosopher[11] each living thing is composed from the four elements, such that terrestrial matter is used for the composition of bones and watery matter for the watery parts of the body, and thus with the others. During the following eighteen days the face is formed by nature, and the body is disposed according to three dimensions, namely length, width, and depth. After this, nature begins to strengthen the fetus until its exit. . . .

Certain women have more pain in childbirth than others, because sometimes the fetus presents its hand and sometimes its feet, and these are dangerous situations. . . . Therefore it is necessary that the women who assist in childbed be skillful, and expert in their work. I have heard from many women that when the fetus presents the head during birth, then the operation goes well, and the other members follow easily. . . .

If a woman dies from an illness before giving birth, the infant in the uterus can live for some time if he can get air. Thus doctors say that the mouth of the woman should be held open with a certain instrument so that air can enter, and if the body is then opened the child will live. In this manner, the first person to be called "Caesar" was born. *Caesar* means "cut" (*caesus*) from his mother's womb.[12]

When a child is born he immediately begins to cry. According to philosophers, this is because the baby finds birth painful because of the narrow openings, and also because of the cold air that he feels when he leaves the womb. If

11. **the philosopher:** that is, Aristotle.

12. Throughout the Middle Ages, both European and Arabic writers repeated the legend that Julius Caesar had been cut from his mother's womb. Though this story originated in a linguistic search for the roots of Caesar's name (hence the comment about "cut"), it came to be regarded as fact and this procedure became known as "caesarean section." During the Middle Ages, it was generally performed only on women who were dead, in order to extract the infant and—in Christian areas—baptize it.

a child is male he naturally has a coarser voice than a female. Women say that a male cries "Ah! Ah! Ah!" because "A" makes a coarser sound than "E," and the opposite seems to be true of girls, for they have a thinner voice and cry "Ay! Ay!"[13] . . .

In connection with this subject the most curious question of all arises: how does the baby lying in the womb receive food, since the womb is closed up everywhere? The child is enclosed in the womb by a natural power which is hidden in the complexion of the fetus. The first thing that develops is a certain vein or nerve which perforates the womb and proceeds from the womb up to the breasts. When the fetus is in the uterus of the mother her breasts are hardened, because the womb closes and the menstrual substance flows to the breast. Then this substance is cooked to a white heat, and it is called the flower of woman; because it is white like milk it is also called the milk of woman. After being cooked in this way, it is sent through the vein to the womb, and there the fetus is nourished with its proper and natural food. This vein is the umbilical cord which is cut off by the midwives at birth, and thus we see newborn babies with their cord tied with a piece of iron. This is to prevent anything from leaving the baby's body from this vein, which is called the umbilicus, and which is suspended in the mother's womb with the amniotic sac. . . .

Note that according to Avicenna if the semen falls in the left side of the womb a female is generated, and if it falls in the right side the child will be a male. If it should land in the middle, however, a hermaphrodite, participating in both the nature of male as well as female, is conceived. The hermaphrodite is given the masculine species, for the male is the worthier, although he really has both natures.

Source 6 from Caroline Gisela March-Long, "Early Modern German Obstetrical Manuals: Das Frawenbüchlein *(c. 1495) and* Der Rosengarten *(1513)," M.A. thesis, Duke University, 1993, pp. 125, 127–129. Reprinted by permission of Caroline Gisela March-Long.*

6. From Eucharius Rösslin, *Rosegarden for Midwives and Pregnant Women,* 1513

When the pregnant woman nears delivery, she should drink mature wine mixed with water. She should also have a regimen of food and drink, a regimen a month before birth which makes one moist but not too fat, and one should avoid what makes one dry, constipated, weighs down, presses or constricts. When the

13. The differences between the cries of male and female infants were explained by some medieval philosophers as resulting from their identification with Adam and Eve. Boys' initial cry was "Oh, A(dam)" and girls', "Oh, E(ve)"; both were wailing because of the burden of Original Sin, which Western Christianity after Augustine generally taught was passed down through sexual intercourse.

woman is even nearer to delivery, when she still has twelve or fourteen days and feels some pain and pressure, she should sit in a bath up to her navel every day, sometimes more often, but not too long (so that she doesn't get weak). She should move around with easy work and movements, walking and standing more than she did before. Such things help the fetus come into position.

Another regimen for the time of delivery which the woman should need if she feels pressure, pain and some moistness begins to show and flow out of the vagina. This regimen takes place in two ways. The first is that one brings on a quick descent and delivery. The other way to lessen complications, labour pains, and pain is for her to sit down for an hour and then stand up and climb up and down the stairs shouting loudly. The woman should force out and hold her breath (breathe heavily) so that she puts pressure on her intestines and bears down. ITEM: The woman should also drink those medicines that are written about afterwards for they force the child downward into delivery position. When she feels the uterus dilate and plenty of fluid flow to her genitals (i.e., water breaks), she should lie on her back, but not completely lying down or standing. It should be a middle position between lying and standing. She should tilt her head more towards the back than the front. In southern German and in Italian/French areas, the midwives have special chairs for delivery. They are not high, but hollowed out with an opening in the inside. The chair should be prepared so that the woman can lean on her back. One should fill and cover the back of the same chair with cloth and when it is time, the midwife should lift the cloth and turn them first to the right and then to the left side. The midwife should sit in front of her and pay careful attention to the child's movement in the womb. The midwife should guide and control her arms and legs with her hands which are coated with white-lily or almond oil or the like. And with her hands in the same way, the midwife should also gently grasp the mother, as she well knows. The midwife should also instruct, guide, and teach the mother, and strengthen her with food and drink. She should urge the woman on to work with soft, kind words so that she begins to breathe deeply. One should dry her stomach off gently above the navel and hips. The midwife should comfort the woman by predicting a successful birth of a baby boy. And if the woman is fat, she should not sit, rather lie on her body and lay her forehead on the ground and pull her knees up underneath so that the womb has pressure applied to it. Afterwards, she should anoint her internally with white-lily oil and, if necessary, the midwife should open the woman's cervix with her hands and afterwards, the woman will deliver quickly.

Source 7 from Loren MacKinney, Medical Illustrations in Medieval Manuscripts *(Berkeley: University of California Press, 1965), fig. 8. Original manuscript in Bodleian Library, University of Oxford, MS Rawl C. 328, folio 3.*

7. Constantine the African Performs Uroscopy, 15th-century Manuscript

Source 8 from the Osterreichische Nationalbibliothek. Bildarchiv d. ONB, Vienna.

8. Birth Scene, 13th-century Manuscript

Source 9 from University of Edinburgh Library, Oriental MS 161.

9. Caesarean Section, 14th-century Arabic Manuscript

Source 10 from Albertus Magnus, Daraus man alle Heimlichkeit des weiblichen Geschlechts erkennen kann *(reprint Frankfurt, 1977), p. 7.*

10. Birth Scene from Pseudo–Albertus Magnus, *On the Secrets of Women,* 16th-century Illustration

QUESTIONS TO CONSIDER

If you have been making lists of the ideas and treatments presented, you have probably assembled what appears to be a great amount of disparate material. Now it is time for you to pull this material together. Turn first to the issue of basic anatomy. What does the womb look like, according to Avicenna? How do pseudo-Trotula and pseudo–Albertus Magnus describe the connections between the womb and the brain? the womb and the breasts? How does pseudo–Albertus Magnus describe the ability of the fetus to breathe?

Now look at issues of physiology. Constantine the African and pseudo-Trotula both discuss impediments to sexual intercourse or conception. How do these fit with humoral theory? What else besides the humors can influence bodily functioning? Maimonides goes on at great length about the dangers of too much sexual intercourse for men; does this idea appear to come from humoral theory or from some other source? Several of the authors, including pseudo-Trotula, Maimonides, and Rösslin, discuss the dangers of diarrhea and constipation. Why do you think medieval authors saw these problems as so serious? Does this concern with digestive processes seem to come from humoral theory or from clinical and practical experience? Medical theory taught that inspecting the urine was a key way to diagnose illness. Based on the information in Source 3 about hindrances to conception, what might Constantine the African be looking for in the woman's urine he is examining in Source 7?

Avicenna, pseudo-Trotula, and pseudo–Albertus Magnus all describe anatomical and physiological differences between men and women. To what do they ascribe these differences? Do they see the reproductive organs in women and men as anatomically similar or completely distinct? How do the authors relate the process of menstruation to sexual difference? Why is there no similar process in men? How do they value anatomical and physiological differences (in other words, which is superior—male or female)? In the Middle Ages, the right/left dichotomy was a very strong intellectual concept, with right being seen as good and left as bad. (This is reflected in the word *sinister,* which comes from the Latin word for "left.") How does this dichotomy relate to that of male/female in matters of reproduction?

Now look at issues of fetal development, beginning with conception. Are Avicenna and pseudo–Albertus Magnus primarily Aristotelian or Galenist in their interpretations? What physiological changes do they describe happening in the uterus at the moment of conception? Several of the authors use words taken from food processing such as *coagulation* or *thickening* to describe the first part of fetal development. How does this fit with humoral theory and ideas about the role of heat? What are the significant milestones in fetal development?

Rösslin and the illustrations in Sources 8 through 10 all depict birth procedures. How would you compare Rösslin's advice to midwives with the births shown in Sources 8 and 10? What might the flasks on the table in the foreground of Source 10 contain? How would you compare these scenes with that of the caesarean section shown in Source 9? Given pseudo-Albertus's discussion of letting a fetus breathe in the womb before doing a caesarean, would you expect the delivery shown in Source 9 to save the life of the infant? In the background of Source 10, what might the men pointing to heavenly bodies indicate about astrological beliefs regarding birth? (A section of *On the Secrets of Women* not reprinted here also discusses the influence of the planets on fetal development.)

Now consider issues of medical treatment and advice. How would you compare the advice given by Constantine the African on neutralizing spells to the conception hints of pseudo-Trotula? How do these fit with Rösslin's suggestions for easing delivery? What might account for the differences between these authors? What range of treatment and action was available to medieval people who were concerned about their health? According to the authors represented here, what is the connection between general health and reproduction for either men or women? How would you summarize their primary advice for those who want to have a long life and many children?

You have probably recognized that the medical ideas and treatments in these documents do not all arise from strict humoral theory, but also come from other sources, such as local familiarity with the therapeutic properties of various plants and mixtures, learned ideas about the influence of the heavenly bodies, popular notions of black and white magic, general ideas about gender hierarchy, and—most important in the Middle Ages—religious belief in God as the ultimate source of healing and well-being. We may often view these ideas as contradictory and try to draw a sharp line between science and superstition. As you have noticed, that line was not sharp for medieval medical writers, nor was the line between magic and religion. As you answer the central questions for this chapter, ask yourself also how the variety of sources of medical "wisdom" might have benefited medieval people. Why might both physicians and patients have preferred a range of theories and treatments?

You are now ready to answer the questions for this chapter: What central ideas regarding reproduction were shared by Jewish, Christian, and Islamic medical writers in the Middle Ages? How were these translated into practical advice for patients and medical practitioners?

EPILOGUE

Ideas about reproduction changed very slowly in Europe and the Islamic world. During the seventeenth century, many university-trained physicians in Europe began to give up humoral theory for other systems of anatomy and physiology based largely on experiments and observation. In 1628, William Harvey discovered the circulation of the blood. (The circulation of blood through the lungs had been discovered in the thirteenth century by the Islamic physician Ibn-an-Nafis, although it was not widely recognized until the Spanish physician Michael Servetus's treatise on the subject in the sixteenth century.) The increasing use of human dissection slowly produced enough evidence to lead people to doubt Galen on a variety of anatomical and physiological issues.

However, observation alone was not enough to change ideas, and in fact it occasionally led to what appear to be even more bizarre notions than those held in the Middle Ages. During the seventeenth and eighteenth centuries, the debate between the Galenist and Aristotelian views of conception continued, but now both sides were armed with microscopes. Those who supported a basically Aristotelian position—that the active principle came from the man—claimed to have observed tiny men in human spermatozoa, complete with arms, heads, and legs. William Harvey thought that sperm was so powerful that it could act at a distance, like a magnet. He backed up this idea not by quoting ancient authorities as his medieval predecessors had, but by experimentation; he dissected large numbers of does just after sexual intercourse and, seeing no sperm in their uteruses, determined that sperm did not need to touch the egg to fertilize it. Those who supported a more active role for the ovum also claimed that humans were preformed in it, but they were somewhat hampered by the fact that the egg was not definitively identified until 1827, a remarkably late date considering its size relative to that of spermatozoa, which the Dutch scientist Anton von Leeuwenhoek identified correctly in the 1670s.

Misconceptions continued in the nineteenth and twentieth centuries. Until the 1840s most authorities believed that females—both human and other mammals—ovulated only with intercourse or orgasm, despite anatomical evidence to the contrary. That the female experience could be so different from the male was a notion that was very hard to give up, though by this point medical writers no longer believed, as Avicenna had, that the "womb is like the scrotum and the vagina like the penis." In the 1870s the removal of healthy ovaries became a popular treatment for women who were judged to be psychologically abnormal, though the physicians who performed the procedure were less clear about the exact link between the brain and reproductive organs than pseudo-Trotula had been seven centuries earlier. These high-minded misconceptions were accompanied by popular ones, many of which still exist. You probably know people who swear that they can tell the sex of a fetus by some aspect of the mother's body, and recently a state senator commented that he knew a woman's allegations of rape were false because she subsequently became pregnant, which was impossible if she had suffered "true" rape.

Except in cases such as those of the state senator, we don't yet know which of our contemporary ideas about reproduction will appear as far-fetched seven hundred years from now as those in this chapter do to us. What we do know is that today's ideas are just as connected to realms beyond medicine as were those of the Middle Ages. The kinds of issues that concerned medieval medical writers on reproduction—What can a couple do who cannot conceive? What is the source of differences between men and women? When does life begin? and more—are still with us, and not simply in medical textbooks.

CHAPTER EIGHT

FACING THE BLACK DEATH

THE PROBLEM

Ring around the rosies
A pocket full of posies
Ashes, ashes, all fall down.

For centuries, English and American children at play have chanted this seemingly nonsensical rhyme. For all their innocence, however, these children have been transmitters of historical memory. The "rosies" to which this song refers are "buboes," the ugly protuberances at the neck, armpits, or groin that are the horrible sign of bubonic plague. The "pocket full of posies" refers to the clump of flowers that medieval Europeans might clutch in their hands and hold before their noses in a futile attempt to keep the plague at bay. And when today's children collapse to the ground as they chant "all fall down," they unknowingly recreate piles of burning corpses.

This simple children's song records the terror of the Black Death, the epidemic of bubonic plague that struck Europe in the middle of the fourteenth century and killed somewhere between a quarter and a third of its people. Those who exhibited the telltale buboes usually had less than three days to live. Those who contracted the pneumatic form of the illness, spread by respiration from person to person, would be perfectly healthy one day and dead the next. "Ring around the rosies" shows how ancient memories of dramatic events can be retained in the popular imagination.

When the plague epidemic hit Europe in 1347–1348, people faced the crisis with little useful knowledge about how the plague was spread or how it could be treated. One thing they did know: The disease had come from the east. While most historical attention has been focused on the Black Death in Europe, historians have followed through on that single bit of knowledge and now understand that the fourteenth-century outbreak of the plague was a *pandemic*, that is, a widespread epidemic that struck most of Eurasia and North Africa almost simultaneously. The tragedy of the Black Death was not limited to a single corner of the world.

Where did the plague come from?

Why did it arise so suddenly and spread so rapidly? What could be done about it? Societies across Eurasia and North Africa were faced with these questions in the fourteenth century.

The answers to some of these questions are not absolutely clear even today, but we certainly know a great deal more about bubonic plague than did the Asian, European, and African victims of the fourteenth-century pestilence. Much of our scientific knowledge about bubonic plague comes from studies conducted in the late nineteenth and early twentieth centuries. In the 1890s a devastating new outbreak of plague afflicted Asia; millions died in India and China. Stirred to action, bacteriologists identified the bacterium that causes bubonic plague and the cycle of infection that produces epidemics of the disease. Fleas drink the blood of infected rats, after which the bacteria multiply in the flea's gut. When the flea bites another rat, the bacteria are regurgitated into the open wound. Usually this cycle of infection is limited to fleas and their rodent hosts. Under special circumstances, however, the fleas jump from their rodent hosts and bite people instead.

Thus the spread of the bubonic plague in the 1890s, like earlier epidemics, resulted from increasing human contact with infected fleas and rats. This knowledge, however, still does not explain why it is that in certain times and places bubonic plague spreads with such speed and ferocity. Plague-infested rodent populations have lived in close proximity to humans from time immemorial. In such areas plague is *endemic*, that is, always present. But its effects among humans are usually minimized and localized by the small size of the affected population, their lack of contact with the wider world, and popular knowledge of the local environment, which often permits the development of folk strategies that lessen human contact with infected rodents.

Plague becomes *epidemic*, spreading to previously unaffected areas, when these balances are upset. A sudden growth in the rat population, environmental changes that drive rats carrying infected fleas into closer contact with humans, economic or cultural changes that challenge the folk wisdom that had kept the plague at bay—all have been implicated in the spread of plague epidemics. Finally, in order for a pandemic to occur—for the plague bacillus to infect huge numbers of humans very suddenly across vast distances—even more substantial changes in the interactions between humans and the environment and among different societies must have taken place.

Such was indeed the case in the fourteenth century. One factor may have been environmental changes in Inner Asia. A period of drought may have forced infected rat populations in search of food and water into closer contact with human societies. But human actors were certainly involved as well, as we see in William McNeill's imaginative reconstruction.[1] In his view, it was the great Mongol warriors who unwittingly created the conditions for the Black Death. It was the Mongols' conquests and the vast expansion of trade that accompanied

1. William H. McNeill, *Plagues and Peoples* (New York: Anchor, 1977).

their empire building that facilitated the spread of plague from a localized outbreak in China in 1331, through the Central Asian steppes in the 1330s, to the ports of the Black Sea and the Mediterranean in the 1340s, and finally to the most densely populated areas of Europe, western Asia, and North Africa in 1347–1348.

The Mongol era saw an unprecedented unification of Eurasia, not only militarily and politically, but commercially and even environmentally as well. This was the thirteenth- and fourteenth-century world in which famous travelers such as the Italian Marco Polo (1254–1324) and the North African Ibn Battuta (1304–1368) crossed from one end of Eurasia to the other with unprecedented ease. Little did the merchants and other intercontinental travelers realize that in their saddlebags and on their carts and ships, plague-infested fleas had stowed away, ready to spread the disease to rodents and humans at the other end of their journey. By 1339 the plague was found in Samarkand, a famous Central Asian stopping point on the Silk Road. By 1345 it had reached the Volga River and the Caucasus Mountains. By 1347 it had reached the ports of the Black Sea, Constantinople, and Alexandria, and within a year it had spread to Mecca, Damascus, Tunis, Venice, and Paris. Far-away London was hit in 1349. In all of these areas the plague led to a devastating loss of population: By some estimates, the population of Egypt did not return to its pre-1347 level until the nineteenth century. The effects of the Black Death in Europe were so fundamental that the pandemic is often cited as one of the main causes of the decline of feudalism and the rise of the new ideas and institutions that would usher in the modern age.

Very little of this was known to the victims of the Black Death. Yet they could not have been expected to accept this scourge without attempts to find an explanation and a remedy. What caused the plague, and what could be done about it? There was, of course, no single answer to these questions. A great deal depended on religious beliefs: The responses of Latin Christians, Orthodox Christians, Muslims, Jews, Zoroastrians, Buddhists, and followers of other faiths were at least partially determined by the specific traditions of their religions.

In western Europe, the Black Death struck societies that had experienced several centuries of economic growth, population increase, and relative political stability. The "High Middle Ages" were a period of spiritual optimism, as demonstrated by the magnificent cathedrals erected in the twelfth through early fourteenth centuries. With the growth of cities came an expansion of long-distance trade; Europeans came into greater contact with the rest of the Eurasian world. They had no way of knowing that increased contact with the wider world would bring the danger of a plague epidemic.

The *Dar-al-Islam* ("Abode of Islam") was at the epicenter of political and military events in Eurasia, and was both more stimulated and more destabilized than western Europe by Asian-centered events such as the rise of the Mongols and the coming of the Turks. When the Mongols overran Baghdad in 1258, they not only brought the Abbasid caliphate to an end but also severed a link of authority between the Prophet and the caliphs ("successors") that has never to this day been reestablished. Muslims in western Asia had therefore experienced cataclysmic political change less than a century before the arrival of the Black Death. By the early fourteenth century, Muslims often felt a sense of faded glory, of the best times having already passed, whether one looked at the fairly recent fall of the Abbasid caliphate or at the glorious time when the Prophet Muhammad ruled the *umma* (community) with a perfect mixture of spiritual and political authority. Though the demographic effects of the Black Death were quite similar in Europe and the Middle East, these differences of experience and outlook conditioned the responses of various societies to this crisis.

Your task in this chapter will be to examine a number of contemporary accounts of the Black Death drawn from both Christian and Islamic sources. How did these authors answer the questions concerning the origin and spread of the plague and what could be done about it? What were some of the medical, religious, political, and economic reactions to the Black Death? Do you see any similarities between Christian and Muslim reactions? Or are there some fundamental differences in how people from the two religious traditions dealt with the plague?

SOURCES AND METHOD

As you consider the texts and images that follow, keep three side-by-side lists:

- On the first list, note every idea that you encounter that has to do with the ***cause*** of the pestilence. You may want to differentiate *ultimate* causes (e.g., divine intervention) from *immediate* causes (e.g., environmental factors and human activities).
- On the second list, write down every idea you find that has to do with the ***consequences*** of the plague for the societies and individuals concerned. You may want to differentiate the demographic, social and political, economic, religious, and psychological consequences of the Black Death as reported in the sources.
- On the third list, keep track of all the actions that are described or recommended for ***curing*** or in some other way ***coping*** with the Black Death. As you add items to this list, you may want to consider the question of how effective these measures might have been.

When you encounter the same idea in more than one document, make a note of how many times it occurs and whether it is found only in Christian documents, only in Muslim ones, or in both. When these lists are completed, you should have the material you need to make comparisons between the documents and to generalize about the main questions at issue: How did people interpret the causes of the plague, what were its effects, and how did people respond to this calamity?

Generalizations are just that; we should not let them obscure the very real differences that occur within given societies and between particular individuals. Even within a single tradition, people reacted to the trauma of the Black Death quite differently, and popular responses were frequently quite different from the policies adopted by secular and religious authorities. In western Europe, for example, groups known as *flagellants,* convinced that the plague was sent by God as a punishment for their sins, beat themselves bloody as a form of penance. Others sought solace and deliverance through quiet contemplation. In Islamic lands, some regarded the Black Death as a blessing, guaranteeing a place in heaven to those who suffered it in dignity as an unfathomable expression of God's will. But in these same societies there were also those who resorted to magic, trying to find some secret combination of words or numbers that would protect them. It is variations on these themes that you will explore in the readings.

The paragraphs below provide some historical context to help you make sense of each of the readings. You will want to refer back to this section as you consider the evidence.

The first document is taken from a book that many consider to be the greatest work of history written by a Muslim of this period, Ibn Khaldun's *Introduction to History* (Source 1). Ibn Khaldun, a well-known Arab philosopher, historian, and statesman, was centrally concerned with describing and analyzing various types of civilization; he anticipated the work of later world historians by placing a great emphasis on environmental conditions in explaining how different civilizations arise and develop.

The next three documents, by contrast, give us a much more immediate and intimate portrait of the plague as it affected three very different cities: Florence, Damascus, and Constantinople. Giovanni Boccaccio was a literary scholar as well as one of the great writers of his day. His *Decameron* (Source 2) is renowned for its glorious tales of late medieval Florentine life, for bringing us much closer to the real world of kitchens, bedrooms, shop fronts, and back alleys than any previous work in European literature. The *Decameron* is a work of fiction, but these opening pages, where Florentine reactions to the plague are described, have the ring of truth.

The passage from Ibn Battuta is similar to that from Boccaccio in its close description of civic reactions to the plague. The greatest of medieval Arab geographers, Ibn Battuta was one of the most widely traveled men of his age, and his *Travels in Asia and Africa* (Source 3) is an important source of information about the world of Islam in the fourteenth century. In this passage he describes a procession in the city of Damascus. Though he does not dwell on the fact, we know that Ibn Battuta was deeply affected by the Black Death: His own mother was carried away by the plague. Family tragedy also infuses the reading from Ioannes Cantacuzenos (Source 4), better known as the Byzantine Emperor John VI. Andronikos, the young man whose death is mentioned in this passage, was John VI's own son. In 1355, eight years after this tragic event, John VI abdicated his throne and retired to a monastery. This passage is taken from the history of the Byzantine Empire that he wrote while in retirement. While the other documents in this chapter come from either the Latin Christian or the Islamic tradition, this one represents an Orthodox Christian viewpoint.

Among the major elements of the account of Jean de Venette, a Carmelite friar (Source 5), are the great importance that Christians placed on dying a "good death" and the challenges that the huge mortality of 1348 posed to their doing so. Sudden death and the possibility of burial in unconsecrated ground were particularly horrible for people who believed that an eternity in hell awaited any soul that was not adequately prepared. Jean de Venette also comments, like Boccaccio, on the effects of the epidemic on standards of social conduct and morality. It is also important to note that this account indicates that some believed that the Black Death was caused by the evil actions of particular groups of people. The attacks on Germany's Jewish population that he describes are a chilling anticipation of the genocide that would take place six hundred years later; 1349 was neither the first nor the last time that one response to harsh times has been to find a scapegoat.

The next source is a visual one, a reproduction of a painting that is included because it gets at both human and cosmological dimensions of the Black Death as it was experienced in Europe (Source 6). In interpreting this painting, it might be helpful to think in terms of several sets of contrasts. First, compare the left and right sides of the lower part of the painting, with the corpse in the foreground as a bridge between the two. Second, compare the lower and upper portions of the painting. St. Sebastian, who is seen near the top of the painting in a position of prayer, was one of several saints who became identified as offering help to plague victims. Sebastian was a soldier in the Roman army who was put to death for his adherence to Christianity. St. Sebastian was always represented with arrows piercing his flesh, a torture equivalent to being pierced by the hidden arrows of the plague. (Muslims also made a connection between being shot with arrows and being infected by bubonic plague: There were those who thought that the disease entered the human body on invisible arrows shot by evil *jinn*, or spirits.) The prayer to St. Sebastian (Source 7) exemplifies the concept of the "intercession of the saints." If God himself seemed too distant to be appealed to directly, you could pray to a saint to intercede on your behalf.

The following four documents all relate to the Black Death in the Islamic world. The quotation from theologian and legal scholar Muhammad ibn Isma'il (Source 8), while very brief, is of the greatest importance. There is a strong tendency in Islam to judge current behavior and practice in relation not only to a sacred text but also to historical precedent. In addition to the Qur'an, the accounts of the life and times of Muhammad as given in the *hadith*, the stories of the Prophet's life collected and codified in later generations, give believers the guidance they need for correct behavior, individual as well as social and political, in almost every situation. While the Qur'an itself has little to say about the plague, the three statements from the hadith proposed by Ibn Isma'il helped establish an understanding of the plague that was shared by most Muslim theologians. They are therefore powerfully authoritative. Those in the Islamic world who thought differently had to justify their positions in relation to this orthodoxy. In contrast, Ibn al-Khatib's perspective (Source 9) is a medical one, and his conclusions do not necessarily conform to the orthodoxy. His perspective is that of a physician, interested in concrete causes and cures, rather than that of a lawyer or theologian interested in the interpretation of texts for their own sake.

In addition to the medical perspective, there were other Islamic responses to the Black Death. Mysticism and magic have long had a role in the Islamic world, and the catastrophe of the Black Death seems to have reinforced these trends. Muslims do not have saints to pray to, but in the Sufi brotherhoods they do have spiritual leaders whose blessings can continue even after death. Visiting the graves of departed holy men, while not sanctioned by some Islamic thinkers, became a much more common practice in this period. While Sufi mystics usually accept the basic theological premises of the Islamic legal traditions, they try to go beyond them by finding a direct connection with the Divine. Often this involves achieving a meditative state through constant repetition of one or more of the many names they attribute to God. It is possible that the surge of interest in Islamic mysticism in the late medieval period may be at least partly attributable to the spiritual quest of Muslims seeking solace from the harsh world of the plague.

The images reproduced in Source 10 point to another response to the plague: the use of cryptograms—combinations of numbers, letters, or words—to stave off the epidemic. Often these strategies relied on the use of specific Qur'anic verses or names for God. The use of devices such as amulets was not, of course, limited to the Islamic world. However, because Muslims are not allowed to find relief and help from the types of portraits and statues that were familiar to medieval Christians, they were more likely to use the type of figurative device shown in this source. The idea that salvation could come from writing a holy verse on a slip of paper, dissolving the ink in water, and then drinking it may have been opposed by orthodox thinkers like Ibn Isma'il, but it gave people a sense that there was something they could do other than simply accept their deaths as a martyrdom. The use of numbers to interpret the world, like the similar use of the stars by astrologers, could give people a sense of an underlying order of things when they were faced with the apparent randomness with which the plague chose its victims.[2] For Muslims, meditation on mathematical symbols or sacred words, like the Christian con-

2. Historian Michael Dols writes, "Obviously, the cryptograms show a great variety, being composed of words, letters, numbers, symbols,

templation of statues or other sacred images, could help believers focus on the divine.[3]

Ibn al-Wardi was an eyewitness to the spread of the plague in Aleppo (Syria) who died of the disease in 1349. The selection from his account of the plague (Source 11) seems less consistent than the accounts of some other authors, and in fact some of his arguments may even seem contradictory: If the plague for Muslims is really "a martyrdom and a reward," why would one seek to escape it? In spite of, or perhaps even because of, such inconsistencies, Ibn al-Wardi has a great deal to say about popular beliefs related to our core questions: Where did the plague come from, what were its consequences, and what could people do about it?

The following three selections give us varying European accounts of the causes of and remedies for the plague. The "Fifteenth-Century Treatise on the Pestilence," reproduced as Source 12, gives the conventional Christian interpretation of that time. Thus, just as Ibn al-Khatib had to struggle with Islamic religious orthodoxy in his assertion of medical causes and cures for the plague, so the Paris Medical Faculty (Source 13) had to justify their effort to go beyond this type of strictly religious explanation. The Paris doctors distinguished their mode of inquiry from that of religious authorities by grounding their analysis in the works of the classical tradition of medicine, with reference to such figures as Hippocrates and Galen. (Though they do not acknowledge it in this passage, these doctors were deeply indebted to the Iranian Muslim physician Ibn Sina, whose very influential medical text synthesizing classical and Islamic medical knowledge had been translated into Latin in the twelfth century.) While the references to astrology and the "four humors" may not seem very scientific to us, this document represents the most sophisticated medical thinking of its day. The selection entitled "A Wholesome Medicine Against All Infirmities" (Source 14) reminds us that while reaction to the plague in Europe could take such violent forms as self-flagellation and attacks on Jews,

or any combination of these. . . . Their symbolism is often not readily apparent. In some instances, there is a perfect square in which the sum is always the same whether the numbers are added horizontally, vertically or diagonally, or when any group of four contiguous numbers are added together. . . . The instructions state that when the quadrants were completed by the inclusion of the numbers outside the diagram the square would avert the plague. . . . These magic quadrants may have been used in numerous ways, but it is certain that they were often inscribed on metal amulets." (From Michael Dols, *The Black Death in the Middle East* [Princeton: Princeton University Press, 1977], pp. 138–139.)

3. Michael Dols elaborates, "Ibn Haydur relates that his teacher informed him that one night in the year 764/1362–63 he had gone to bed and thought about the epidemic of plague that was rampant in this year. He slept badly because of the distress caused by the epidemic. In his sleep, he saw a man take a small book from his own library and bring it to him. The man laid his hand on the last line on the right side of the page of the book and said: 'These names will intercede for you during the epidemic, and read them in this manner—"Oh Living One, Oh Patient One, Oh Loving One, Oh Wise One." . . . When it was morning he told his friends about the dream. Among them was [one] who, when he heard the recitation of the names of God in this manner, said that these names were engraved on rings. . . . The stone engraved in this way would guard a person against the burning fever that accompanied plague, if he drank water in which the ring had been submerged." (Dols, *The Black Death*, pp. 133–135.)

there were many other Christians who were more moderate and balanced in their response.

These readings on the Black Death have taken us across many intellectual and cultural frontiers. The final reading, in which the great Humanist philosopher Petrarch (Source 15) describes the death of his friends, brings us back down to the most basic, human level. As we read Petrarch's letter, can we really imagine what it would have been like to be living in such circumstances?

THE EVIDENCE

Source 1 from Michael Dols, The Black Death in the Middle East *(Princeton: Princeton University Press), 1977, p. 270; Ibn Khaldun,* The Muqaddimah; *trans. Franz Rosenthal (Princeton: Princeton University Press, 1967), pp. 136–137.*

1. From Ibn Khaldun, *The Muqaddimah: An Introduction to History*

Civilization in the East and West was visited by a destructive plague which devastated nations and caused populations to vanish. It swallowed up many of the good things of civilization and wiped them out. It overtook the dynasties at the time of their senility, when they had reached the limit of their duration. . . .

In the later (years) of dynasties, famines and pestilences become numerous. . . .

. . . There is much unrest and bloodshed, and plagues occur. The principal reason for the latter is the corruption of the air (climate) through (too) large a civilization (population). It results from the putrefaction and the many evil moistures with which (the air) has contact (in a dense civilization). Now, air nourishes the animal spirit and is constantly with it. When it is corrupted, corruption affects the temper of (the spirit). If the corruption is strong, the lung is afflicted with disease. This results in epidemics, which affect the lung in particular. (Even) if the corruption is not strong or great, putrefaction grows and multiplies under (its influence), resulting in many fevers that affect the tempers, and the bodies become sick and perish. The reason for the growth of putrefaction and evil moistures is invariably a dense and abundant civilization such as exists in the later (years) of a dynasty. . . . This is obvious. Therefore, it has been clarified by science in the proper place that it is necessary to have empty spaces and waste regions interspersed between civilized areas. This makes circulation of the air possible. . . .

God determines whatever He wishes.

Source 2 from Giovanni Boccaccio, The Decameron, *trans. Mark Musa and Peter Bondanella (New York: W. W. Norton, 1982), pp. 6–12. Used by permission of W.W. Norton & Company, Inc.*

2. From Giovanni Boccaccio, *The Decameron*

Let me say, then, that thirteen hundred and forty-eight years[4] had already passed after the fruitful Incarnation of the Son of God when into the distinguished city of Florence, more noble than any other Italian city, there came a deadly pestilence. Either because of the influence of heavenly bodies or because of God's just wrath as a punishment to mortals for our wicked deeds, the pestilence, originating some years earlier in the East, killed an infinite number of people as it spread relentlessly from one place to another until finally it had stretched its miserable length all over the West. And against this pestilence no human wisdom or foresight was of any avail; quantities of filth were removed from the city by officials charged with the task; the entry of any sick person into the city was prohibited; and many directives were issued concerning the maintenance of good health. Nor were the humble supplications rendered not once but many times by the pious to God, through public processions or by other means, in any way efficacious; for almost at the beginning of springtime of the year in question the plague began to show its sorrowful effects in an extraordinary manner. . . . Neither a doctor's advice nor the strength of medicine could do anything to cure this illness; on the contrary, either the nature of the illness was such that it afforded no cure, or else the doctors were so ignorant that they did not recognize its cause and, as a result, could not prescribe the proper remedy (in fact, the number of doctors, other than the well-trained, was increased by a large number of men and women who had never had any medical training); at any rate, few of the sick were ever cured, and almost all died after the third day of the appearance of the previously described symptoms (some sooner, others later), and most of them died without fever or any other side effects.

This pestilence was so powerful that it was transmitted to the healthy by contact with the sick, the way a fire close to dry or oily things will set them aflame. And the evil of the plague went even further: not only did talking to or being around the sick bring infection and a common death, but also touching the clothes of the sick or anything touched or used by them seemed to communicate this very disease to the person involved. . . . The plague described here was of such virulence in spreading from one person to another that not only did it pass from one man to the next, but, what's more, it was often transmitted from the garments of a sick or dead man to animals that not only became contaminated by the disease but also died within a brief period of time. My own eyes,

4. In Boccaccio's day, Florentines began each year not with the first of January, as is done today, but rather with the traditional date of the Annunciation (March 25).

as I said earlier, were witness to such a thing one day: when the rags of a poor man who died of this disease were thrown into the public street, two pigs came upon them, and, as they are wont to do, first with their snouts and then with their teeth they took the rags and shook them around; and within a short time, after a number of convulsions, both pigs fell dead upon the ill-fated rags, as if they had been poisoned. From these and many similar or worse occurrences there came about such fear and such fantastic notions among those who remained alive that almost all of them took a very cruel attitude in the matter; that is, they completely avoided the sick and their possessions, and in so doing, each one believed that he was protecting his own good health.

There were some people who thought that living moderately and avoiding any excess might help a great deal in resisting this disease, and so they gathered in small groups and lived entirely apart from everyone else. They shut themselves up in those houses where there were no sick people and where one could live well by eating the most delicate of foods and drinking the finest of wines (doing so always in moderation), allowing no one to speak about or listen to anything said about the sick and the dead outside; these people lived, entertaining themselves with music and other pleasures that they could arrange. Others thought the opposite: they believed that drinking excessively, enjoying life, going about singing and celebrating, satisfying in every way the appetites as best one could, laughing, and making light of everything that happened was the best medicine for such a disease; so they practiced to the fullest what they believed by going from one tavern to another all day and night, drinking to excess; and they would often make merry in private homes, doing everything that pleased or amused them the most. This they were able to do easily, for everyone felt he was doomed to die and, as a result, abandoned his property, so that most of the houses had become common property, and any stranger who came upon them used them as if he were their rightful owner. In addition to this bestial behavior, they always managed to avoid the sick as best they could. And in this great affliction and misery of our city the revered authority of the laws, both divine and human, had fallen and almost completely disappeared, for, like other men, the ministers and executors of the laws were either dead or sick or so short of help that it was impossible for them to fulfill their duties; as a result, everybody was free to do as he pleased.

Many others adopted a middle course between the two attitudes just described: neither did they restrict their food or drink so much as the first group nor did they fall into such dissoluteness and drunkenness as the second; rather, they satisfied their appetites to a moderate degree. They did not shut themselves up, but went around carrying in their hands flowers, or sweet-smelling herbs, or various kinds of spices; and they would often put these things to their noses, believing that such smells were a wonderful means of purifying the brain, for all the air seemed infected with the stench of dead bodies, sickness, and medicines.

Others were of a crueler opinion (though it was, perhaps, a safer one): they maintained that there was no better medicine against the plague than to flee from it; convinced of this reasoning and caring only about themselves, men and women in great numbers abandoned their city, their houses, their farms, their relatives, and their possessions and sought other places, going at least as far away as the Florentine countryside—as if the wrath of God could not pursue them with this pestilence wherever they went but would only strike those it found within the walls of the city! Or perhaps they thought that Florence's last hour had come and that no one in the city would remain alive.

And not all those who adopted these diverse opinions died, nor did they all escape with their lives; on the contrary, many of those who thought this way were falling sick everywhere, and since they had given, when they were healthy, the bad example of avoiding the sick, they in turn were abandoned and left to languish away without any care. The fact was that one citizen avoided another, that almost no one cared for his neighbor, and that relatives rarely or hardly ever visited each other—they stayed far apart. This disaster had struck such fear into the hearts of men and women that brother abandoned brother, uncle abandoned nephew, sister left brother, and very often wife abandoned husband, and—even worse, almost unbelievable—fathers and mothers neglected to tend and care for their children as if they were not their own.

Thus, for the countless multitude of men and women who fell sick, there remained no support except the charity of their friends (and these were few) or the greed of servants, who worked for inflated salaries without regard to the service they performed and who, in spite of this, were few and far between; and those few were men or women of little wit (most of them not trained for such service) who did little else but hand different things to the sick when requested to do so or watch over them while they died, and in this service, they very often lost their own lives and their profits. . . . Between the lack of competent attendants that the sick were unable to obtain and the violence of the pestilence itself, so many, many people died in the city both day and night that it was incredible just to hear this described, not to mention seeing it! Therefore, out of sheer necessity, there arose among those who remained alive customs which were contrary to the established practices of the time.

It was the custom, as it is again today, for the women relatives and neighbors to gather together in the house of a dead person and there to mourn with the women who had been dearest to him; on the other hand, in front of the deceased's home, his male relatives would gather together with his male neighbors and other citizens, and the clergy also came, many of them or sometimes just a few, depending upon the social class of the dead man. Then, upon the shoulders of his equals, he was carried to the church chosen by him before death with the funeral pomp of candles and chants. With the fury of the pestilence increasing, this custom, for the most part, died out and other practices took its place. And so not only did people die without having a number of women around them, but there were many who passed away without having even a single witness present, and very few were granted the piteous laments and bitter tears of their relatives; on the contrary, most relatives were somewhere else, laughing, joking, and amusing themselves; even the women learned this practice too well, having put aside, for the most part, their womanly compassion for their own safety. . . .

The plight of the lower class and, perhaps, a large part of the middle class was even more pathetic: most of them stayed in their homes or neighborhoods either because of their poverty or because of their hopes for remaining safe, and every day they fell sick by the thousands; and not having servants or attendants of any kind, they almost always died. Many ended their lives in the public streets, during the day or at night, while many others who died in their homes were discovered dead by their neighbors only by the smell of their decomposing bodies. The city was full of corpses. The dead were usually given the same treatment by their neighbors, who were moved more by the fear that the decomposing corpses would contaminate them than by any charity they might have felt toward the deceased: either by themselves or with the assistance of porters (when they were available), they would drag the corpse out of the home and place it in front of the doorstep, where, usually in the morning, quantities of dead bodies could be seen by any passerby; then they were laid out on biers, or for lack of biers, on a plank. . . . Moreover, the dead were honored with no tears or candles or funeral mourners; in fact, things had reached such a point that the people who died were cared for as we care for goats today. Thus it became quite obvious that the very thing which in normal times wise men had not been able to resign themselves to, even though then it struck seldom and less harshly, became as a result of this colossal misfortune a matter of indifference to even the most simpleminded people.

So many corpses would arrive in front of a church every day and at every hour that the amount of holy ground for burials was certainly insufficient for the ancient custom of giving each body its individual place; when all the graves were full, huge trenches were dug in all of the cemeteries of the churches and into them the new arrivals were dumped by the hundreds; and they were packed in there with dirt, one on top of another, like a ship's cargo, until the trench was filled. . . .

Oh, how many great palaces, beautiful homes, and noble dwellings, once filled with families, gentlemen, and ladies, were now emptied, down to the last servant! How many notable families, vast domains, and famous fortunes remained without legitimate heir! How many valiant men, beautiful women, and charming young boys, who might have been pronounced very healthy by Galen, Hippocrates, and Aesculapius (not to mention lesser physicians), ate breakfast in the morning with their relatives, companions, and friends and then in the evening dined with their ancestors in the other world!

Source 3 from Ibn Battuta: Travels in Asia and Africa, 1325–1354, *trans. and selected by H. A. R. Gibbs (New York: August M. Kelley, 1969), pp. 305, 68–69.*

3. From *Ibn Battuta: Travels in Asia and Africa, 1325–1354*

Early in June we heard at Aleppo that the plague had broken out at Gaza, and that the number of deaths there reached over a thousand a day. On travelling to Hims I found that the plague had broken out there: about three hundred persons died of it on the day that I arrived. So I went on to Damascus, and arrived there on a Thursday. . . .

One of the celebrated sanctuaries at Damascus is the Mosque of the Footprints (al-Aqdám), which lies two miles south of the city, alongside the main highway which leads to the Hijáz, Jerusalem, and Egypt. It is a large mosque, very blessed, richly endowed, and very highly venerated by the Damascenes. . . . I saw a remarkable instance of the veneration in which the Damascenes hold this mosque during the great pestilence, on my return journey through Damascus in the latter part of July 1348. The viceroy Arghún Sháh ordered a crier to proclaim through Damascus that all the people should fast for three days and that no one should cook anything eatable in the market during the daytime. For most of the people there eat no food but what has been prepared in the market. So the people fasted for three successive days, the last of which was a Thursday, then they assembled in the Great Mosque, amírs, sharífs, qádís, theologians, and all the other classes of the people, until the place was filled to overflowing, and there they spent the Thursday night in prayers and litanies. After the dawn prayer next morning they all went out together on foot, holding Korans in their hands, and the amírs barefooted. The procession was joined by the entire population of the town, men and women, small and large; the Jews came with their Book of the Law and the Christians with their Gospel, all of them with their women and children. The whole concourse, weeping and supplicating and seeking the favour of God through His Books and His Prophets, made their way to the Mosque of the Footprints, and there they remained in supplication and invocation until near midday. They then returned to the city and held the Friday service, and God lightened their affliction; for the number of deaths in a single day at Damascus did not attain two thousand, while in Cairo and Old Cairo it reached the figure of twenty-four thousand a day.

Source 4 from Christos S. Bartsocas, "Two Fourteenth Century Descriptions of the 'Black Death,'" Journal of the History of Medicine, *October 1966, pp. 395–397. Reproduced by permission of Oxford University Press.*

4. From Ioannes Cantacuzenos (John VI of Byzantium), *Historarum*

Upon arrival in Byzantium she [the empress] found Andronikos, the youngest born, dead from the invading plague, which starting first from the Hyperborean Scythians, attacked almost all the sea coasts of the world and killed most of their people. For it swept not only through Pontus, Thrace and Macedonia, but even Greece, Italy and all the islands, Egypt, Libya, Judaea and Syria, and spread throughout almost the entire world.

So incurable was the evil, that neither any regularity of life, nor any bodily strength could resist it. Strong and weak bodies were all similarly carried away, and those best cared for died in the same manner as the poor. No other [major] disease of any kind presented itself that year. If someone had a previous illness he always succumbed to this disease and no physician's art was sufficient; neither did the disease take the same course in all persons but the others, unable to resist, died the same day, a few even within the hour. Those who could resist for two or three days had a very violent fever at first, the disease in such cases attacking the head; they suffered from speechlessness and insensibility to all happenings and then appeared as if sunken into a deep sleep. . . .

Great abscesses were formed on the legs or the arms, from which, when cut, a large quantity of foul-smelling pus flowed and the disease was differentiated as that which discharged much annoying matter. Even many who were seized by all the symptoms unexpectedly recovered. There was no help from anywhere; if someone brought to another a remedy useful to himself, this became poison to the other patient. Some, by treating others, became infected with the disease. It caused great destruction and many homes were deserted by their inhabitants. Domestic animals died together with their masters. Most terrible was the discouragement. Whenever people felt sick there was no hope left for recovery, but by turning to despair, adding to their prostration and severely aggravating their sickness, they died at once. No words could express the nature of the disease. All that can be pointed out is that it had nothing in common with the everyday evils to which the nature of man is subject, but was something else sent by God to restore chastity. Many of the sick turned to better things in their minds, by being chastened, not only those who died, but also those who overcame the disease. They abstained from all vice during that time and they lived virtuously; many divided their property among the poor, even before they were attacked by the disease. If he ever felt himself seized, no one was so ruthless as not to show repentance of his faults and to appear before the judgment seat of

God with the best chance of salvation, not believing that the soul was incurable or unhealed. Many died in Byzantium then, and the king's son, Andronikos, was attacked and died the third day.

Source 5 from Rosemary Horrox, The Black Death *(Manchester: Manchester University Press, 1994), pp. 55–57. Reprinted with permission.*

5. From the Chronicle of Jean de Venette

In 1348 the people of France, and of virtually the whole world, were assailed by something more than war. For just as famine had befallen them, as described in the beginning of this account, and then war, as described in the course of the account, so now pestilences broke out in various parts of the world. In the August of that year a very large and bright star was seen in the west over Paris, after vespers, when the sun was still shining but beginning to set. It was not as high in the heavens as the rest of the stars; on the contrary, it seemed rather near. And as the sun set and night approached the star seemed to stay in one place, as I and many of my brethren observed. Once night had fallen, as we watched and greatly marvelled, the great star sent out many separate beams of light, and after shooting out rays eastwards over Paris it vanished totally: there one minute, gone the next. Whether it was a comet or something else—perhaps something condensed from some sort of exhalations which then returned to vapour—I leave to the judgment of astronomers. But it seems possible that it presaged the incredible pestilence which soon followed in Paris and throughout the whole of France, as I shall describe.

As a result of that pestilence a great many men and women died that year and the next in Paris and throughout the kingdom of France, as they also did in other parts of the world. . . .

. . . During the epidemic the Lord, of his goodness, deigned to confer such grace on those dying that, however suddenly they died, almost all of them faced death as joyfully as if they had been well prepared for it. Nor did anyone die without making confession and receiving the last sacrament. So that more of those dying would make a good end, Pope Clement mercifully gave the confessors in numerous cities and villages the power to absolve the sins of the dying, so that as a result they died the more happily, leaving much of their land and goods to churches or religious orders since their right heirs had predeceased them.

Men ascribed the pestilence to infected air or water, because there was no famine or lack of food at that time but, on the contrary, a great abundance. One result of this interpretation was that the infection, and the sudden death which it brought, were blamed on the Jews, who were said to have poisoned wells and rivers and corrupted the air. Accordingly the whole world brutally rose against them, and in Germany and in other countries which had Jewish communities many thousands were indiscriminately butchered, slaughtered and burnt alive by the Christians.[5] The insane constancy shown by them and their wives was amazing. When Jews were being burnt mothers would throw their own children into the flames rather than risk them being baptised, and would then hurl themselves into the fire after them, to burn with their husbands and children.

It was claimed that many wicked Christians were discovered poisoning wells in a similar fashion. But in truth, such poisonings, even if they really happened, could not have been solely responsible for so great a plague or killed so many people. There must have been some other cause such as, for instance, the will of God, or corrupt humours and the badness of air and earth; although perhaps such poisonings, where they did occur, were a contributory factor. The mortality continued in France for most of 1348 and 1349 and then stopped, leaving many villages and many town houses virtually empty, stripped of their inhabitants. Then many houses fell quickly into ruin, including numerous houses in Paris, although the damage there was less than in many places.

When the epidemic was over the men and women still alive married each other. Everywhere women conceived more readily than usual. None proved barren, on the contrary, there were pregnant women wherever you looked. Several gave birth to twins, and some to living triplets. But what is particularly surprising is that when the children born after the plague started cutting their teeth they commonly turned out to have only 20 or 22, instead of the 32 usual before the plague. I am unsure what this means, unless it is, as some men say, a sign that the death of infinite numbers of people, and their replacement by those who survived, has somehow renewed the world and initiated a new age. But if so, the world, alas, has not been made any better by its renewal. For after the plague men became more miserly and grasping, although many owned more than they had before. They were also more greedy and quarrelsome, involving themselves in brawls, disputes and lawsuits. Nor did the dreadful plague inflicted by God bring about peace between kings and lords. On the contrary, the enemies of the king of France and of the Church were stronger and more evil than before and stirred up wars by land and sea. Evil spread like wildfire.

What was also amazing was that, in spite of there being plenty of everything, it was all twice as expensive: household equipment and foodstuffs, as well as merchandise, hired labour, farm workers and servants. The only exception was property and houses, of which there is a glut to this day. Also from that time charity began to grow cold, and wrongdoing flourished, along with sinfulness and ignorance—for few men could be found in houses, towns or castles who were able or willing to instruct boys in the rudiments of Latin.

5. The Jews had been expelled from France by Philip the Fair in 1322.

Source 6: The Walters Art Gallery, Baltimore.

6. Lieferinxe, *St. Sebastian Interceding for the Plague-Stricken*

Source 7 from Rosemary Horrox, The Black Death *(Manchester: Manchester University Press, 1994), pp. 125–126. Reprinted with permission.*

7. A Prayer to St. Sebastian

O St Sebastian, guard and defend me, morning and evening, every minute of every hour, while I am still of sound mind; and, Martyr, diminish the strength of that vile illness called an epidemic which is threatening me. Protect and keep me and all my friends from this plague. We put our trust in God and St Mary, and in you, O holy Martyr. . . . Be with us always, and by your merits keep us safe and sound and protected from plague. Commend us to the Trinity and to the Virgin Mary, so that when we die we may have our reward: to behold God in the company of martyrs.

Source 8 from William H. McNeill, Plagues and Peoples *(New York: Anchor, 1977), p. 198.*

8. Citations from the Hadith

When you learn that epidemic disease exists in a county, do not go there; but if it breaks out in the county where you are, do not leave.

He who dies of epidemic disease is a martyr.

It is a punishment that God inflicts on whom he wills, but He has granted a modicum of clemency with respect to Believers.

Source 9 from Manfred Ullman, Islamic Medicine *(Edinburgh: Edinburgh University Press, 1978), pp. 94–95. Reprinted by permission of Edinburgh University Press.*

9. An Arab Doctor's Medical Perspective on the Black Death

If one asks, 'How can you admit the assertion, there is infection, when the revealed word (*ash-shar'*) denies this?' we answer: that infection exists, is confirmed by experience, research, insight and observation and through constantly recurring accounts. These are the elements of proof. For him who has treated or recognized this case, it cannot remain concealed that mostly the man who has had contact with a patient infected with this disease must die, and that, on the other hand, the man who has had no contact remains healthy. So it is with the appearance of the illness in a house or quarter because of a garment or a vessel;

even an earring can destroy him who puts it in his ear, and all the inhabitants of the house. The illness can first appear in a town in a single house; then, from there, it can break out among individual contacts, then among their neighbours, relatives, and especially their visitors, until the breach becomes even greater. The illness can appear in coastal towns that enjoyed good health until there lands in them a man with plague, come from across the sea, from another coast where the plague already exists, as reports tell. The date of the appearance of the illness in the town tallies with the date of debarcation of this man. Many remained healthy who kept themselves strictly cut off from the outside world, like the pious Ibn-Abī-Madyan in Salé. He belonged to those who believed in contagion. He had stored up provisions for a long period and bricked up his door behind him and his large family. The town succumbed but during that period, he was not deprived of a single soul. One had repeatedly heard that places which lie remote from highways and traffic remained untouched. But there is nothing more wonderful at this time than the prison camp of the Muslims—may God free them!—in the Arsenal of Seville: there were thousands but the plague did not touch them although it practically destroyed the town itself. The report is also correct that the itinerant nomads living in tents in North Africa and elsewhere remained healthy because there the air is not shut in and the corruption proceeding from it could only gain a slight hold. . . .

But it belongs to principles which one may not ignore that a proof taken from tradition (Hadīth), if observation and inspection are contrary, must be interpreted allegorically. In this matter it is essential that it should be interpreted in accordance with the views of those who hold the theory of contagion. There are numerous compassionate passages in revealed scripture, for example, the utterance of the Prophet: 'an owner of sick animals should not drive these to the owner of healthy animals.'

Source 10 from Michael Dols, The Black Death in the Middle East *(Princeton: Princeton University Press, 1977), pp. 139, 135. Copyright © 1977 by Princeton University Press. Reprinted by permission of Princeton University Press.*

10. Cryptograms

406	409	412	398
411	399	405	410
400		407	404
408	403	401	413

414

Source 11 from "Ibn al-Wardi's Risalah al naba' 'an al-Waba,' A Translation of a Major Source for the History of the Black Death in the Middle East," *in* Near Eastern Numismatics, Iconography, Epigraphy and History: Studies in Honor of George C. Miles, *ed. Dickran K. Kouymjian (Beirut: American University, 1974), pp. 447–450, 452–455.*

11. From Ibn al-Wardi, "An Essay on the Report of the Pestilence"

God is my security in every adversity. My sufficiency is in God alone. Is not God sufficient protection for His servant? Oh God, pray for our master, Muhammad, and give him peace. Save us for his sake from the attacks of the plague and give us shelter.

The plague frightened and killed. It began in the land of darkness. Oh, what a visitor! It has been current for fifteen years. China was not preserved from it nor could the strongest fortress hinder it. The plague afflicted the Indians in India. It weighed upon the Sind. It seized with its hand and ensnared even the lands of the Uzbeks. . . . The plague increased and spread further. It attacked the Persians, . . . and gnawed away at the Crimea. . . . The plague destroyed mankind in Cairo. . . . It stilled all movement in Alexandria. . . .

Oh Alexandria, this plague is like a lion which extends its arm to you.
Have patience with the fate of the plague, which leaves of seventy men only seven.

Then, the plague turned to Upper Egypt. It, also, sent forth its storm to Barqah. The plague attacked Gaza, and it shook 'Asqalān severely. The plague oppressed Acre. The scourge came to Jerusalem and paid the *zakāt* [with the souls of men]. It overtook those people who fled to the al-'Aqsā Mosque, which stands beside the Dome of the Rock. If the door of mercy had not been opened, the end of the world would have occurred in a moment. It, then, hastened its pace and attacked the entire maritime plain. The plague trapped Sidon and descended unexpectedly upon Beirut, cunningly. Next, it directed the shooting of its arrows to Damascus. There the plague sat like a king on a throne and swayed with power, killing daily one thousand or more and decimating the population. It destroyed mankind with its pustules. May God the Most High spare Damascus to pursue its own path and extinguish the plague's fires so that they do not come close to her fragrant orchards.

Oh God, restore Damascus and protect her from insult.
Its morale has been so lowered that people in the city sell themselves for grain. . . .

Oh God, it is acting by Your command. Lift this from us. It happens where You wish; keep the plague from us. Who will defend us against this horror other than You the Almighty? . . .

How many places has the plague entered. It swore not to leave the houses without its inhabitants. It searched them out with a lamp. The pestilence caused the people of Aleppo the same disturbance. . . .

Oh, if you could see the nobles of Aleppo studying their inscrutable books of medicine. They multiply its remedies by eating dried and sour foods. The buboes which disturb men's healthy lives are smeared with Armenian clay. Each man treated his humours and made life more comfortable. They perfumed their homes with ambergris and camphor, cyperus and sandal. They wore ruby rings and put onions, vinegar, and sardines together with the daily meal. They ate less broth and fruit but ate the citron and similar things.

If you see many biers and their carriers and hear in every quarter of Aleppo the announcements of death and cries, you run from them and refuse to stay with them. In Aleppo the profits of the undertakers have greatly increased. Oh God, do not profit them. Those who sweat from carrying the coffins enjoy this plague-time. Oh God, do not let them sweat and enjoy this. . . .

We ask God's forgiveness for our souls' bad inclination; the plague is surely part of His punishment. We take refuge from His wrath in His pleasure and from His chastisement in His restoring.

They said: the air's corruption kills. I said: the love of corruption kills.
How many sins and how many offenses does the crier call our attention to. . . .

This plague is for the Muslims a martyrdom and a reward, and for the disbelievers a punishment and a rebuke. When the Muslim endures misfortune, then patience is his worship. It has been established by our Prophet, God bless him and give him peace, that the plague-stricken are martyrs. This noble tradition is true and assures martyrdom. And this secret should be pleasing to the true believer. If someone says it causes infection and destruction, say: God creates and recreates. If the liar, disputes the matter of infection and tries to find an explanation, I say that the Prophet, on him be peace, said: who infected the first? If we acknowledge the plague's devastation of the people, it is the will of the Chosen Doer. So it happened again and again.

I take refuge in God from the yoke of the plague. Its high explosion has burst into all countries and was an examiner of astonishing things. Its sudden attacks perplex the people. The plague chases the screaming without pity and does not accept a treasure for ransom. Its engine is far-reaching. The plague enters into the house and swears it will not leave except with all of its inhabitants. "I have an order from the *qādī* to arrest all those in the house." Among the benefits of this order is the removal of one's hopes and the improvement of his earthly works. It awakens men from their indifference for the provisioning of their final journey.

One man begs another to take care of his children, and one says goodbye to his neighbors.
A third perfects his works, and another prepares his shroud.
A fifth is reconciled with his enemies, and another treats his friends with kindness.
One is very generous; another makes friends with those who have betrayed him.
Another man puts aside his property; one frees his servants.
One man changes his character while another mends his ways.
For this plague has captured all people and is about to send its ultimate destruction.
There is no protection today from it other than His mercy, praise to be God.

Nothing prevented us from running away from the plague except our devotion to the noble tradition. Come then, seek the aid of God Almighty for raising the plague, for He is the best helper. Oh God, we call You better than anyone did before. We call You to raise from us the pestilence and plague. We do not take refuge in its removal other than with You. We do not depend on our good health against the plague but on You. We seek Your protection, Oh Lord of creation, from the blows of this stick. We ask for Your mercy which is wider than our sins even as they are the number of the sands and pebbles. We plead with You, by the most honored of the advocates, Muhammad, the Prophet of mercy, that You take away from us this distress. Protect us from the evil and the torture and preserve us. For You are our sole support; what a perfect trustee!

Sources 12 through 15 from Rosemary Horrox, The Black Death *(Manchester: Manchester University Press, 1994), pp. 193–194; pp. 158–163; p. 149; pp. 248–249. Reprinted with permission.*

12. A 15th-Century Treatise on the Pestilence

It should be known to all Christians that pestilence, and every other manifestation of God's vengeance, arises because of sin. . . . Pestilence arises from a multitude of sins, but most especially from swearing worthless, deceitful and meaningless oaths.

If I am asked what is the cause of pestilence, what is its physical cause and by what means can someone save himself from it, I answer to the first question that sin is the cause, as set forth above. To the second question I say that it arises from the sea, as the evangelist says: 'There shall be signs in the sun and in the moon and in the stars; and upon the earth distress of nations, by reason of the confusion of the roaring of the sea and of the waves'.[6] For the devil, by the power committed to him, when the seas rise up high, is voiding his poison, sending it forth to be added to the poison in the air, and that air spreads gradually from place to place and enters men through the ears, eyes, nose, mouth, pores and the other orifices. Then if the man has a strong constitution, nature can expel the poison through ulcers, and if the ulcers putrify, are strangled and fully run their course the patient will be saved, as can be clearly seen. But if the poison should be stronger than his nature, so that his constitution cannot prevail against it, then the poison instantly lays siege to the heart, and the patient dies within a short time, without the relief which comes from the formation of ulcers.

To the third question I say that during the pestilence everyone over seven should be made to vomit daily from an empty stomach, and twice a week, or more often if necessary, he should lie well wrapped up in a warm bed and drink warm ale with ginger so that he sweats copiously, and he should never touch the sheets after that until they have been cleansed of the sweat, for if the person sweating had been in contact with the pestilence a healthy man could catch the plague from the sheets unless they have been well washed. And as soon as he feels an itch or prickling in his flesh he must use a goblet or cupping horn to let blood and draw down the blood from the heart, and this should be done two or three times at intervals of one or two days at most. And if he should feel himself

6. Luke 21.25. This occurs in a list of the signs that will precede Christ's second coming and the end of the world.

oppressed deep within the body, then he should let blood in the nearest veins, either in the arms or in the main veins of the feet. Likewise something which is extremely poisonous in itself may be of service in excluding the plague. And if a healthy adult does as I have described, they can save themselves whenever a great pestilence occurs.

13. From Report of the Paris Medical Faculty, October 1348

Seeing things which cannot be explained, even by the most gifted intellects, initially stirs the human mind to amazement; but after marvelling, the prudent soul next yields to its desire for understanding and, anxious for its own perfection, strives with all its might to discover the causes of the amazing events. For there is within the human mind an innate desire to seize on goodness and truth. As the Philosopher makes plain, all things seek for the good and want to understand.[7] To attain this end we have listened to the opinions of many modern experts on astrology and medicine about the causes of the epidemic which has prevailed since 1345. However, because their conclusions still leave room for considerable uncertainty, we, the masters of the faculty of medicine at Paris, inspired by the command of the most illustrious prince, our most serene lord, Philip, King of France, and by our desire to achieve something of public benefit, have decided to compile, with God's help, a brief compendium of the distant and immediate causes of the present universal epidemic (as far as these can be understood by the human intellect) and of wholesome remedies; drawing on the opinions of the most brilliant ancient philosophers and modern experts, astronomers as well as doctors of medicine. And if we cannot explain everything as we would wish, for a sure explanation and perfect understanding of these matters is not always to be had (as Pliny says in book II, chapter 39: 'some accidental causes of storms are still uncertain, or cannot be explained'), it is open to any diligent reader to make good the deficiency.

We shall divide the work into two parts, in the first of which we shall investigate the causes of this pestilence and whence they come, for without knowledge of the causes no one can prescribe cures. In the second part we shall include methods of prevention and cure. There will be three chapters in the first part, for this epidemic arises from a double cause. One cause is distant and from above, and pertains to the heavens; the other is near and from below and pertains to the earth, and is dependent, causally and effectively, on the first cause. Therefore the first chapter will deal with the first cause, the second with the second cause, and the third with the prognostications and signs associated with both of them. There will be two treatises in the second part. The first will deal with medical means of prevention and cure and will be divided into four chap-

7. "The Philosopher" is Aristotle.

ters: the first on the disposition of the air and its rectification; the second on exercise and baths; the third on food and drink; the fourth on sleeping and waking, emptiness and fullness of the stomach and on the emotions. The second treatise will have three chapters: the first on universal remedies; the second on specific remedies appropriate to different patients; the third on antidotes.

CHAPTER 1: OF THE FIRST PART: CONCERNING THE UNIVERSAL AND DISTANT CAUSE

We say that the distant and first cause of this pestilence was and is the configuration of the heavens. In 1345, at one hour after noon on 20 March, there was a major conjunction of three planets in Aquarius. This conjunction, along with other earlier conjunctions and eclipses, by causing a deadly corruption of the air around us, signifies mortality and famine—and also other things about which we will not speak here because they are not relevant. Aristotle testifies that this is the case in his book *Concerning the causes of the properties of the elements*, in which he says that mortality of races and the depopulation of kingdoms occur at the conjunction of Saturn and Jupiter, for great events then arise, their nature depending on the trigon in which the conjunction occurs. And this is found in ancient philosophers, and Albertus Magnus in his book, *Concerning the causes of the properties of the elements* (treatise 2, chapter 1) says that the conjunction of Mars and Jupiter causes a great pestilence in the air, especially when they come together in a hot, wet sign, as was the case in 1345. For Jupiter, being wet and hot, draws up evil vapours from the earth and Mars, because it is immoderately hot and dry, then ignites the vapours, and as a result there were lightnings, sparks, noxious vapours and fires throughout the air.

These effects were intensified because Mars—a malevolent planet, breeding anger and wars—was in the sign of Leo from 6 October 1347 until the end of May this year, along with the head of the dragon, and because all these things are hot they attracted many vapours; which is why the winter was not as cold as it should have been. And Mars was also retrograde and therefore attracted many vapours from the earth and the sea which, when mixed with the air, corrupted its substance. Mars was also looking upon Jupiter with a hostile aspect, that is to say quartile, and that caused an evil disposition or quality in the air, harmful and hateful to our nature. This state of affairs generated strong winds (for according to Albertus in the first book of his *Meteora*, Jupiter has the property of raising powerful winds, particularly from the south) which gave rise to excess heat and moisture on the earth; although in fact it was the dampness which was most marked in our part of the world. And this is enough about the distant or universal cause for the moment.

CHAPTER 2: OF THE FIRST PART: CONCERNING THE PARTICULAR AND NEAR CAUSE

Although major pestilential illnesses can be caused by the corruption of water or food, as happens at times of famine and infertility, yet we still regard illnesses proceeding from the corruption of the air as much more dangerous. This is because bad air is more noxious than food or drink in that it can penetrate quickly to the heart and lungs to do its damage. We believe that the present epidemic or plague has arisen from air corrupt in its substance, and not changed in its attributes. By which we wish it be understood that air, being pure and clear by nature, can only become putrid or corrupt by being mixed with something else, that is to say, with evil vapours. What happened was that the many vapours which had been corrupted at the time of the conjunction were drawn up from the earth and water, and were then mixed with the air and spread abroad by frequent gusts of wind in the wild southerly gales, and because of these alien vapours which they carried the winds corrupted the air in its substance, and are still doing so. And this corrupted air, when breathed in, necessarily penetrates to the heart and corrupts the substance of the spirit there and rots the surrounding moisture, and the heat thus caused destroys the life force, and this is the immediate cause of the present epidemic.

And moreover these winds, which have become so common here, have carried among us (and may perhaps continue to do so in future) bad, rotten and poisonous vapours from elsewhere: from swamps, lakes and chasms, for instance, and also (which is even more dangerous) from unburied or unburnt corpses—which might well have been a cause of the epidemic. Another possible cause of corruption, which needs to be borne in mind, is the escape of the rottenness trapped in the centre of the earth as a result of earthquakes—something which has indeed recently occurred. But the conjunctions could have been the universal and distant cause of all these harmful things, by which air and water have been corrupted.

CHAPTER 3: CONCERNING PROGNOSTICATION AND SIGNS

Unseasonable weather is a particular cause of illness. For the ancients, notably Hippocrates, are agreed that if the four seasons run awry, and do not keep their proper course, then plagues and mortal passions are engendered that year. Experience tells us that for some time the seasons have not succeeded each other in the proper way. Last winter was not as cold as it should have been, with a great deal of rain; the spring windy and latterly wet. Summer was late, not as hot as it should have been, and extremely wet—the weather very changeable from day to day, and hour to hour; the air often troubled, and then still again, looking as if it was going to rain but then not doing so. Autumn too was very rainy and misty. It is because the whole year here—or most of it—was warm and wet that the air is pestilential. For it is a sign of pestilence for the air to be warm and wet at unseasonable times.

Wherefore we may fear a future pestilence here, which is particularly from the root beneath, because it is subject to the evil impress of the heavens, especially since that conjunction was in a western sign. Therefore if next winter is very rainy and less cold than it ought to be, we should expect an epidemic round about late winter and spring—and if it occurs it will be long and dangerous, for usually unseasonable weather is of only brief duration, but when it lasts over many seasons, as has obviously been the case here, it stands to reason that its effects will be longer-lasting and more dangerous, unless ensuing seasons change their nature in the opposite way. Thus if the winter in the north turns out to be cold and dry, the plagues might be arrested.

We have not said that the future pestilence will be exceptionally dangerous, for we do not wish to give the impression that it will be as dangerous here as in southern or eastern regions. For the conjunctions and the other causes discussed above had a more immediate impact on those regions than on ours. However, in the judgement of astrologers (who follow Ptolemy on this) plagues are likely, although not inevitable, because so many exhalations and inflammations have been observed, such as a comet and shooting stars. Also the sky has looked yellow and the air reddish because of the burnt vapours. There has also been much lightning and flashes and frequent thunder, and winds of such violence and strength that they have carried dust storms from the south. These things, and in particular the powerful earthquakes, have done universal harm and left a trail of corruption. There have been masses of dead fish, animals and other things along the sea shore, and in many places trees covered in dust, and some people claim to have seen a multitude of frogs and reptiles generated from the corrupt matter; and all these things seem to have come from the great corruption of the air and earth. All these things have been noted before as signs of plague by numerous wise men who are still remembered with respect and who experienced them themselves.

No wonder, therefore, that we fear that we are in for an epidemic. But it should be noted that in saying this we do not intend to exclude the possibility of illnesses arising from the character of the present year—for as the aphorism of Hippocrates has it: a year of many fogs and damps is a year of many illnesses. On the other hand, the susceptibility of the body of the patient is the most immediate cause in the breeding of illnesses, and therefore no cause is likely to have an effect unless the patient is susceptible to its effects. We must therefore emphasise that although, because everyone has to breathe, everyone will be at risk from the corrupted air, not everyone will be made ill by it but only those, who will no doubt be numerous, who have a susceptibility to it; and very few indeed of those who do succumb will escape.

The bodies most likely to take the stamp of this pestilence are those which are hot and moist, for they are the most susceptible to putrefaction. The following are also more at risk: bodies bunged up with evil humours, because the unconsumed waste matter is not being expelled as it should; those following a bad life style, with too much exercise, sex and bathing; the thin and weak, and persistent worriers; babies, women and young people; and corpulent people with a ruddy complexion. However those with dry bodies, purged of waste matter, who adopt a sensible and suitable regimen, will succumb to the pestilence more slowly.

We must not overlook the fact that any pestilence proceeds from the divine will, and our advice can therefore only be to return humbly to God. But this does not mean forsaking doctors. For the Most High created earthly medicine, and although God alone cures the sick, he does so through the medicine which in his generosity he provided. Blessed be the glorious and high God, who does not refuse his help, but has clearly set out a way of being cured for those who fear him. And this is enough of the third chapter, and of the whole first part.

14. A Wholesome Medicine Against All Infirmities

The advice of the reverend father Dom Theophilus of Milan, of the order of St Benedict, against the plague; also a most wholesome medicine against all infirmities. Note it well.

Whenever anyone is struck down by the plague they should immediately provide themselves with a medicine like this. Let him first gather as much as he can of bitter loathing towards the sins committed by him, and the same quantity of true contrition of heart, and mix the two into an ointment with the water of tears. Then let him make a vomit of frank and honest confession, by which he shall be purged of the pestilential poison of sin, and the boil of his vices shall be totally liquified and melt away. Then the spirit, formerly weighed down by the plague of sin, will be left all light and full of blessed joy. Afterwards let him take the most delightful and precious medicine: the body of our lord and saviour Jesus Christ. And finally let him have himself anointed on the seat of his bodily senses with holy oil. And in a little while he will pass from transient life to the incorruptible country of eternal life, safe from plague and all other infirmities.

Compared with this all other remedies of doctors are futile and profit little against the plague, which God keeps for the chastisement of sin and which is without remedy save through him and his power.

15. From Petrarch, "Letters on Familiar Matters"

a. What are we to do now, brother? Now that we have lost almost everything and found no rest. When can we expect it? Where shall we look for it? Time, as they say, has slipped through our fingers. Our former hopes are buried with our friends. The year 1348 left us lonely and bereft, for it took from us wealth which could not be restored by the Indian, Caspian or Carpathian Sea. Last losses are beyond recovery, and death's wound beyond cure. There is just one comfort: that we shall follow those who went before. I do not know how long we shall have to wait, but I know that it cannot be very long—although however short the time it will feel too long. . . .

b. There remained to me at least something salvaged from the wreck of last year: a most brilliant man, and (you must take my word for it) one great in action and counsel, Paganino da Milano, who after numerous proofs of his virtue became very dear to me, and seemed worthy of your friendship as well as mine. He was on the way to becoming another Socrates, displaying almost the same loyalty and good fellowship, and that friendship which lies in sharing good and bad fortune and in baring the hidden places of the heart in a trusting exchange of secrets.

How much he loved you, how much he longed to see you—you whom he could see only with the eyes of imagination. How much he worried about your safety during this shipwreck of the world. I was amazed that a man unknown to him could be so much loved. He never saw me graver than usual without becoming anxious himself and asking, 'Is something wrong? How is our friend?' But when he heard that you were in good health he would cast aside his fears with wonderful alacrity.

And this man (I speak it with many tears, and would speak it with more but my eyes are drained by previous misfortunes and I should save some tears for whatever may befall in the future), this man, I say, was suddenly seized by the pestilence which is now ravaging the world. This was at dusk, after dinner with his friends, and the evening hours that remained he spent talking with us, reminiscing about our friendship and shared concerns. He passed the night in extreme pain, which he endured with an undaunted spirit, and then died suddenly the next morning. None of the now-familiar horrors were abated, and within three days all his children and household followed him.

Go, mortals, sweat, pant, toil, range the lands and seas to pile up riches you cannot keep; glory that will not last. The life we lead is a sleep; whatever we do, dreams. Only death breaks the sleep and wakes us from dreaming. I wish I could have woken before this.

QUESTIONS TO CONSIDER

Now that you have looked at the evidence and made a list of the causes and consequences of the Black Death and the reactions to it, we can draw out some more detail and make some more systematic comparisons.

What, ultimately, caused the Black Death? Astrological causation is mentioned by the doctors of Paris, and several other authors refer to the alignment of the heavens or the actions of heavenly bodies. But was this really the ultimate cause? For most Christians and Muslims, the ultimate cause almost certainly had to be God. The documents you have examined make this clear, but a question still remains: *Why* would God bring such a pestilence to humanity? Taking the documents from Christian writers first, what seems to have been the most common answer to that question? The "Fifteenth-Century Treatise on the Pestilence" is characteristic in this regard, and also gives us an idea of the larger historical framework within which medieval Christians might understand the cause of the Black Death.

If we then compare the Islamic documents, a contrast becomes apparent:

Meditations on God's intentions seem to be much less prominent in these sources. As Ibn Khaldun says, "God determines whatever He wishes." In general, Muslims are more reluctant than Christians to make authoritative pronouncements about God's intentions. The most rigid position articulated in these texts, Ibn Isma'il's relation of the *hadith,* implies that the plague is sent directly by God to the victim, as a punishment to the infidel and as a martyrdom (and therefore a blessing) to the Believer. No other explanation is necessary: God's will is unknowable. Nevertheless, you may be able to identify at least one passage from a Muslim writer who, like his Christian counterparts, ascribes a specific motivation for God's activities.

We find a greater range of possibilities when we turn from the ultimate causes in heaven to the immediate causes on earth. The first reading, from Ibn Khaldun, introduces us to the general area of environmental and demographic causation. While Ibn Khaldun locates the Black Death in a great scheme of the rise and fall of civilizations, other authors look more closely at particular environmental factors. As you look through the list of possible causes that you have identified in the documents, select those that have to do with environmental conditions or the size and distribution of population. From what you know of the "real" causes of the plague, how astute were these observations?

Many of our texts also refer to the means by which the plague is *transmitted* from one place to another and from one person to another. Again, issues of environment and demography are involved. How would you characterize the various theories of transmission, and which do you find to have been closest to the mark? Again, some variation between Christian and Islamic sources may be noted. The "orthodox" Islamic position, represented here by Muhammad ibn Isma' il, relies on an interpretation of the *hadith* that claims that since the disease is sent directly by God, there can be no belief in transmission through infection or contagion. How do the other Islamic authors react to this position?

Apart from theories of causation and transmission that refer to divine, heavenly, or environmental causes, there are also some texts that refer to the conscious activities of evil human beings who spread the disease on purpose. How were they said to have done so, and why? What groups were most likely to be singled out for such accusations, and what fate did they suffer as a consequence?

If we move from the question of causation to the question of the consequences of the Black Death, the most likely thing to notice first is the reports of mortality. How many people are said to have died? What percentage of the population is said to have been affected? How accurate do you think these reports might be?

Apart from the sheer number of people who died, many of the texts comment on the social, political, and economic effects of the Black Death. How did people's responses to the calamity affect social relationships within communities, between neighbors, between different social groups, and within families? According to the various authors, did the plague bring people closer together or push them apart? Were previously established forms of authority strengthened or weakened? How might some people benefit economically from the devastation of the plague? Does it seem that the changes in these societies brought about by the plague were temporary or permanent? Do the social, political, and economic effects of the plague seem to have been more concern to Christian or to Islamic commentators?

Many of these questions are posed in our sources in terms of public and private morality. As you compare entries in your list of consequences of the Black Death, also be aware of the contrast between those authors who saw standards of morality declining in the wake of the plague and those who reported that at least some people were becoming more virtuous. What were some of the most striking examples of the breakdown of social conventions and the decline in morality? Under what circumstances might some people actually improve their behavior, and how might that positive response be shown?

What about the psychological effects of the plague? Several of the documents give us a close and immediate sense of the despair felt by survivors of the plague who had seen their friends and family carried away: Ioannes Cantacuzenos and Petrarch come to mind. Apart from those human emotions, to which we can no doubt relate, however, there is another set of psychological concerns with which we may not immediately empathize. For medieval Christians in particular, it was of the greatest importance to die a "good death." This meant that one was properly prepared to leave this world for the next. One needed to be spiritually prepared, having made confession and received the last rites of the Church. It was best if one had an opportunity to take leave of friends and family. After death, an elaborate wake and funeral ceremony would help the soul of the departed into heaven, as would the continued prayers of those left behind. Burial in consecrated ground was absolutely essential. From your reading of the documents in which such questions are raised, what might have been the psychological and emotional effects of the Black Death on medieval Christians? How might the reactions of Muslims have differed if they interpreted the *hadith* to mean that for Believers the plague was a martyrdom that guaranteed them a place in Heaven?

The ultimate logic of despair is to do nothing. If the plague really was sent by God and the doctors could do nothing about it, then why do anything other than simply wait to die? Perhaps you can find evidence of such attitudes in some of the documents, but clearly most people were on the lookout for things they could do to protect themselves and their communities. The Christian painting and Islamic cryptograms demonstrate how people might use visual images both to externalize their fears and to invoke divine aid as a protection from the plague.

In fact, many of the responses intended to remedy the situation were religious in nature. What seem to have been the most common religious activities that groups and individuals could pursue to protect themselves from the plague, or at least alleviate their suffering? Which ones seem to have been most approved of by religious leaders, or organized by them on behalf of the community? Were there other remedies that, while religious in inspiration, might have been disapproved of by the Catholic Church or by the most orthodox Islamic thinkers?

Other remedies that people might take involved changes in their living situations: People might change either where they lived, with whom they lived, or both. What different types of examples of this pattern did you find in the documents? How much of a change did they represent from previous social practices? Did the commentators seem to approve or disapprove of these strategies? Were they effective?

There were also attempts at medical solutions to the problem, involving both diagnosis and remedy. The prescriptions could involve changes of diet, alteration of lifestyle, and the use of specific medications and cures, as well as "civic" solutions involving urban authorities. Which sources do you think are the most "medical" in their approach? Did you find any diagnoses or remedies that you thought were more sensible than others?

Now that you have drawn some comparisons and reached some conclusions, you may want to step back and consider more generally the people who lived through the Black Death as depicted in these documents. It is difficult for us, perhaps, to suspend our judgment when looking at the thoughts and beliefs of people who lived long ago in very different cultural, religious, and technological circumstances. But if we make the effort, we will be better able to engage the people of the past on their own terms. What, then, have you learned about the inner worlds of medieval Christians and Muslims through your work in this chapter?

EPILOGUE

The world afflicted by the Black Death more than seven centuries ago may seem quite remote from our own. Advances in medical science now shield us from such devastation. Or do they? Is the lesson to be drawn from an examination of epidemic disease in medieval history really all that comforting? Two of the essential preconditions for the plague pandemic of the fourteenth century, increasing population density and a growth in intercontinental trade, should sound familiar to us today. In fact, Ibn Khaldun saw it as a general rule of history that civilizations create the conditions for their own collapse. The growth of population in general, and of cities in particular, and the growth of trade and overall prosperity seem to Ibn Khaldun to lead almost inevitably to a catastrophic decline marked by famine and pestilence.

We do not need to be as fatalistic as Ibn Khaldun to recognize that the connection between plagues and peoples is not merely a matter of history. Yet the tremendous strides of medical science have tended to blind us to this fact. Over the past century, sustained efforts to bring cleaner food, water, and living conditions to growing populations made significant headway, at least in the world's more prosperous regions. At the same time, medical science grew ever more sophisticated at identifying and attacking epidemic diseases—witness the development of the polio vaccine, the eradication of smallpox, the creation of more and more powerful antibiotics, and a huge reduction in the rates of tuberculosis and syphilis. It seemed that the age-old problem of epidemic disease was well on its way to solution.

This complacency was shattered by the AIDS outbreak of the 1980s. Differences of opinion are still to be found concerning the origin of AIDS. Since it is often the case that viruses develop in wild or domesticated animals and then somehow make the leap to human beings, it is possible that one or more of the HIV-related viruses endemic amongst certain species of monkeys in Africa made such a transition, perhaps when a hunter was infected by the blood of his kill. In the past, such a virus would probably have had only a local impact. In today's world, however, that infected hunter is likely to travel to a city, spreading the virus outside its original confined environment. That city is likely to be connected to an international airport. A disease that might once have been confined to a small group or region now stands a much better chance of becoming a global epidemic. Whatever the origin of HIV-AIDS, there is no doubt that the conditions of modernity have contributed to the spread of the disease.

HIV-AIDS is only the most notorious of the new diseases that have appeared in the past two decades. We could add Ebola virus, Lyme disease, Legionnaire's disease, Lassa fever, and many others to the list. At the same time, there has been a resurgence of old scourges that we once thought were on their way out, and the rise of more deadly forms of diseases such as malaria and encephalitis. As Arno Karlen points out, we are constantly and unwittingly creating the conditions that make this possible:

> We provide new ecological niches for microbes by tilling fields and domesticating animals, and by bringing into existence gardens and second-growth forests, villages and cities, homes and factories. We give them new homes in discarded truck tires and water tanks, air conditioners and hospital equipment. We transport them by automobile, ship and airplane. We alter their opportunities and affect their evolution when we change our abodes, our sex behavior, our diets, our clothing. The faster we change ourselves and our surroundings, the faster new infections reach us. In the past century we have changed the biosphere as much as any glacial change or meteor impact ever has. So we and microbes are dancing faster than ever in order to survive each other. As we do so, the burdens on our environment and our immune defenses increase.[8]

8. Arno Karlen, "The New Epidemic," in *The Black Death,* ed. Dan Nardo (San Diego: Greenhaven, 1999), p. 126.

Far from having conquered epidemic disease, we seem to have speeded up the process in a way that threatens to get out of hand. As in the period reviewed in this chapter, population growth and expanded intercontinental trade bring both opportunity and danger.

Karlen advises us to be concerned, but not to despair. Our immune systems are very powerful and highly adaptable. Perhaps even more important, history shows that the human race has been through this before and has always survived. Then as now our responses are conditioned by our cultural presuppositions. As we think back on the tragic story of the Black Death, perhaps our attitude should be one of understanding and appreciation for the way our forebears dealt with problems that we still face today.

CHAPTER NINE

THE FAMILY IN MEDIEVAL ENGLISH VILLAGES

THE PROBLEM

In medieval England, the vast majority of people lived in small family groups within villages or small towns, and made a living predominantly by raising crops and animals. Most of the villages were *nucleated*; that is, the houses were clumped together, with the fields stretching out beyond the group of houses. Most houses sat in the middle of a *toft*, a yard that had pens for animals and storage sheds, and many houses also had a *croft* or garden next to them, which was cultivated by a spade and hoe rather than a plow.

In many parts of England, the fields of the village were farmed in what is termed *open-field agriculture*, a pattern that differs sharply from modern farming practices. In open-field agriculture, the village as a whole decided what would be planted in each field, rotating the crops according to tradition and need. Some fields would be planted in crops such as wheat or rye for human consumption, some would be planted in oats or other crops for both animals and humans, and some would be left unworked or *fallow* to allow the soil to rejuvenate. The exact pattern of this rotation varied from location to location, but in most areas with open-field agriculture the holdings farmed by any one family did not consist of a whole field, but included strips in many fields. These strips were traditionally measured in the width that a team of oxen (or oxen and horses, for these animals were often yoked together) could plow, and in lengths called *furlongs*. The plowed strips were divided by a *balk* (an unplowed ridge) or by a row of stones. At each end there was an unplowed *headlong* for turning the plow team around. The boundaries between fields were marked by hedges or ditches. In parts of England with heavy clay soil, the plow team might consist of eight animals, too many to be owned by any but the richest villagers, so that families worked their strips together, though they held them separately. Most families were also allowed to run some animals in the woods or meadows outside of the fields.

Though the open-field system and many other local issues were largely handled by the village itself, with regard to other economic and political matters, villages were under the jurisdiction of lords—members of the nobility or gentry who might live in a large house in the village but often lived elsewhere. The territory controlled by a lord is generally termed a *manor*, and it might consist of one village, a number of villages, or even only part of a village. Within each manor, the lord established the duties that each villager or village family owed; he also occasionally took surveys, termed *extents*, that listed what services or rents were due him from each head of household and how much land each household held. In addition, the lord controlled some of the land of the village—his land was called the *demesne*—which he could rent out, hire workers to farm, or demand that the villagers farm as part of their obligations to him.

Lords generally appointed officials termed *bailiffs* and *reeves* from outside the village to oversee the legal and business operations of their manors, but because the village itself took care of so many economic and legal issues, additional officials such as constables and ale-testers were chosen by some of the village residents themselves. We do not know how these officials were chosen or elected in many cases, but we do know that they were always adult men and generally heads of households. Women had no voice in the running of the village, though they could hold land independently and, especially as widows, head households; when they did hold land, they were required to pay all rents and taxes. Women could, with some limitations, buy and sell land and make other sorts of financial transactions, but in general they appeared in court much less often than men. Thus, they are also less visible in the types of legal records we will be using for this chapter. Female and male servants, who often worked for and lived with wealthier village families, also had no political voice.

In most English villages, several times a year the villagers gathered for court proceedings, during which the legal and financial affairs of both the lord and the village were handled. This court was sometimes termed a *hallmote*, and such courts began keeping formal records in the thirteenth century. These records were written on pieces of parchment that were stitched end to end and then rolled up; they were generally made while the court was in session, not written up afterwards. Such *court rolls* are the most important type of document surviving for exploring the lives of English medieval villagers and their families. Manorial courts collected fees due the lord, such as *chevage*, a payment to the lord from a serf for permission to live off the manor; *merchet*, a fee paid by a bride, her father, or the bridegroom in order to receive a marriage license; *heriot*, a fee due on the death of a tenant, usually the best animal owned by the family (though this later changed to a money payment); and *gersuma* or *entry fine*, a fee due when someone other than the widow took over land on the death of a villager.

The manorial courts also handled breaches of the peace such as fights, assaults, or robberies; litigation between villagers; and infractions of laws or customs regarding the fields, roads, or public places. The courts often went beyond what we would recognize as judicial activities and issued new ordinances, which historians now term *bylaws*, in order to regulate activities in the village or its fields and woods. Generally these bylaws were passed not after a period of reflection or long-range planning, but in order to stop activities that were already being carried out—activities the village leaders judged harmful. Thus the bylaws reflect both what people were doing on a small scale to improve their economic position, and the attitudes of the more powerful men in the village toward such activities.

In addition to their legislative function of issuing bylaws, many of the concerns and activities of medieval manorial courts were very different from those of modern courts. The medieval village did not have police as we know them, and so when villagers saw a crime or infraction, they were expected to chase the perpetrator themselves and yell to others to join in. This was termed *raising the hue and cry*; villagers could be fined for not doing this, and also *for* doing it when it was unwarranted.

This idea of community responsibility for law and order may be traced in a number of other court activities as well. Each male villager over the age of twelve was expected to enroll in a *frankpledge* or *tithing*, a unit of ten or so men who were responsible for each other's behavior. Each tithing was headed by a *capital pledge*, usually a villager from a more prominent family who also often acted as a juror in cases brought before the manorial court. The village jurors rendered judgments as a group and were also expected to bring cases to court. The manorial courts relied more on the collective memory of village traditions and customs than on written laws, so that jurors—or some group of responsible adult men—were often asked to decide issues, such as who had the rights to a certain piece of land, by simply talking among themselves or to others who might know. Because of this, jurors were chosen from among those who were most likely to know the facts of the case, which is the opposite of the principle of modern jury selection. Both plaintiff and defendant often brought in others who would swear to their view of the case or to their good character. In fiercely contested cases, the jury would ask the whole village to back its judgment. Punishment was typically a fine or, occasionally, banishment; imprisonment and corporal punishments were quite rare. (Serious criminal cases were handled not by the manorial courts but by the royal courts.) Villagers were expected to bring to court cases against other villagers, and they could be fined if they failed to report such violations as debt or trespass.

Villagers whose land carried heavy labor obligations were generally termed *serfs* or *villeins*, and in theory they were required to remain on a manor forever in order to fulfill their obligations to the lord. Such villagers were personally unfree. Villagers with few or no labor obligations were regarded as free, though they still had obligations to the lord, which they generally paid in cash or in goods such as wheat or animals.

Though today we might think that the distinction between serfdom and freedom would have been the most important distinction between villagers, at the time of the Black Death (1347–1348) wealth mattered more than personal status, and it is often difficult to tell from the records if a person was a serf or free. Serfs did have labor obligations, but by 1330 they were often paying these off in money rather than in labor, and using any extra money they acquired to buy more land rather than their freedom. In fact, their obligations might actually be *lower* than those of free peasants because their rents were set by custom. Based on studies of many villages, historians have found that a more useful division is that among what we might call the well-off, those of average wealth, and the poor villagers.

In general, well-off villagers were those families that farmed about twenty-five to thirty acres, or what is often termed a *virgate* or *oxgang.* (The size of the acre and the number of acres in a virgate varied throughout England, and so it is hard to figure exactly what medieval measurements mean in modern terms.) These families often had some disposable income left once their taxes and rents were paid, and we might expect this group to be the one most able to do things that furthered its own interests. Average village families farmed a *half-virgate,* about ten to fifteen acres. Historians estimate that this was the minimum needed to sustain a family, and a family farming this amount would have been susceptible to hunger and poverty in times of poor harvests. Poor villagers, often termed *cottars* or *cottagers,* were those who held less land than ten acres and who were dependent on activities other than farming to survive; they might hire themselves out to wealthier villagers during harvest time, or as servants during the entire year. In many villages and small towns, individuals and families belonging to all three groups also carried out craft or retail activities such as brewing, blacksmithing, baking, or selling food in addition to farming.

Through the various records left by manorial lords and the villages themselves, we can begin to discover not only the history of the relationships between lords and peasants, but also that of relationships among peasants themselves. This provides us with information about nonelite individuals, and also about the medieval family, for economic activities were carried out most often within the context of the family. Your task in this chapter will be to explore the actions of family members in relation to each other and to the world beyond the family. How did common people in medieval England seek to strengthen the economic and social position of their families? How did they define "family" and relate to those they saw as members of this group?

SOURCES AND METHOD

Until about thirty years ago, we knew very little about most families throughout history, other than very prominent families who left extensive records. This has changed dramatically, both because the interests of historians have changed and because new techniques are available for research into family life, particularly the use of computers to handle and sift large amounts of quantitative data. Questions that were once regarded as unanswerable for those who were not among the elite—When did people marry? How many children did they have? How did they feel about their children? How did they feel about their spouses? How did families respond to change or crisis? What did they do to improve their situation?—are now being researched for earlier and earlier time periods. An entire journal, *The Journal of Family History,* is devoted to such research. Though historians do not always agree on their answers, they see such questions as an important part of our understanding of the past.

Some of the most interesting questions being asked by historians of the family may best be answered cross-culturally and comparatively, but this work must be based on intensive local studies of the way in which families in one particular place behaved and operated. Thus our focus in this chapter will be narrower than in many of the other chapters in the book, for we will be using a variety of types of records to look at families in villages and small towns of late medieval England, with sources dating from the 1350s to the 1490s. This is, in fact, a broader focus than many studies of pre-modern families, which look at only one village, and we will rely on such studies to provide the context for our investigation.

One of the reasons that most studies of pre-modern common people focus on one village or small town is the difficulty of tracing large numbers of people over time in an era before there were birth, marriage, or death records. Historians must use the records they have creatively to try to determine the makeup of families and households, and to trace the ways in which family members related to one another. First, the historian often simply makes an entry in a computer file each time a name is mentioned in court records or elsewhere and then gradually groups all references to a single individual together. Next, the historian looks at records of how that individual was linked to others, either by having the same name or by being described as a relative. In this way, a number of family groupings become apparent. Finally, the historian studies how these family groupings were linked to other family groupings through marriage or legal transactions. The result is an extremely complex picture of at least some of the village residents, with conclusions or speculations about characteristics such as age, number of children, or number of marriages based on various references.

Deciding when references are to the same person is not always easy, however. Before the fourteenth century people in many places did not have surnames, so that they might be referred to simply as "John" or "Agnes." In England, surnames gradually became more common in the thirteenth century, usually based on a father's or mother's name, an occupation, a place of origin, or a physical characteristic. By the time our sources begin, most men, though not all, had surnames that stayed with them their entire lives, and identification problems come primarily from a number of people having the same first name and surname—John Miller, for example, or Richard Smith. This problem is exacerbated by the fact that first names varied little: In one fifteenth-century English village, for example, 90 percent of the men were named John, Thomas, Richard, or Robert. Married women in England at this time usually adopted their husband's surname. Tracing a woman's identity can be more complicated, though it is eased by references to male members of her birth family that show up in the sources. We will not be tracing individuals to the extent that village historians do, but we will use this method as we investigate people's activities through the court rolls.

Once historians have identified individuals, they can begin to count them and arrange them into groups to note trends and changes. To do this, they need to correct for various types of deficiencies in the records. When using any type of record to count people, whether medieval court rolls or the modern census, historians must determine whether certain groups were likely to be underrepresented. In the modern census, underrepresented groups include illegal aliens, who for obvious reasons do not want to be counted by a census taker. In medieval court records, underrepresented groups include those who were less likely than others to appear in court—children, those who never engaged in any financial transactions because they were too poor, and women, who did not serve as jurors and were much less likely than men to bring cases to court.

For this chapter you will be using four types of sources: court rolls, bylaws, wills, and quantitative tables recently created by historians from medieval court rolls. The original documents are all in Latin and all handwritten. Source 1 is an example of what a court roll actually looks like, from the village of Gnossal in 1492. Unless your Latin and paleographic skills are very good, you will find this impossible to read, although you can probably tell that it is arranged in groupings with headings to the left. The third grouping down lists the jurors by name.

Source 2 is the court roll from one sitting of a manorial court from the small town of Ramsey in 1460, edited somewhat for length. First read it and the accompanying notes carefully to make sure you understand what is being discussed. What types of problems are the focus of items 9 and 11? How does the bylaw passed by all male household heads ("the whole homage") in item 11 seek to solve this? Why is Thomas Tyler fined in item 14? If this had not been discovered, how would his actions have improved his family's situation? What types of problems are the focus of items 17 through 32? From the way the actions here are described, can you recreate what might have gone on? What information does item 22 give us about relations between spouses? About the way villagers expected these relations to be? What does item 31 tell us about relations between siblings? Why might the town have chosen to pass the new ordinance noted in item 35? Items 36 through 50 concern activities other than farming that residents of Ramsey engaged in. How might these have improved a family's economic position? Do you notice anything about the surnames of some of the artisans? If you were beginning a study of individuals and families in the town of Ramsey, you would now note each instance in which an individual is mentioned. Try it here for five individuals: William Wayte, John Newman, William Clerk, John Water, and Katherine Love. (All of the entries that mention these people are included in Source 2.) Note carefully each circumstance in which each person is mentioned. Do any of the combinations of circumstances surprise you?

Sources 3 and 4 are selections from court rolls that describe legal agreements between family members, Source 3 from the village of South Elmham in 1408 and Source 4 from the village of Wymondham in 1421. Read Source 3 carefully. What does the younger Henry Pekke gain from his grandmother? What does he agree to do in return? What provisions are made if he does not carry out this maintenance agreement? In Source 4, what do John and Joan Notte receive from John's father, William? What do they agree to do in return? What do these sources tell you about relations between parents and children, or between grandparents and grandchildren?

Source 5 is a translation of a brief court roll from the small village of Winterborne in Lancastershire from 1494. What concerns of the village and the lord are addressed in items 3 and 4? Read items 5 and 6 carefully, for they discuss related matters. What provisions are being made for the young daughters of William Barcoll? Why might William Webbe wish to do this? What assistance is he providing for his own sons?

Source 6 is a selection from the court rolls of Bromsgrove and King's Norton, a small town in Worcestershire, from 1496, concerning two conflicting claims to the same piece of land. In order to sort this out and understand what is being debated, it will be useful for you to do what medieval historians do as the second stage of tracing families—make a family tree linking the parties to the dispute. In item 1, what does Henry Banard ask the twelve tenants to decide? Who owned this piece of land originally? Who were his children, according to Henry's claim? How did Henry Banard inherit what he sees as his rights to the land? In item 2, do the jurors agree with what Henry Banard is asserting? Items 3 and 4 concern Peter Parre's claim to the same land. What does he say the original owner did with the land? How did he inherit what he sees as his rights to the land? Why might Henry Banard have neglected to mention that William had given the land to his brothers Richard or Robert, or even that Richard and Robert (who appear to have been his uncles) existed? Why might William have given the land to his two brothers when it was really for the work and use of one of them? (Here you will have to speculate about motivation, which is something historians of the premodern period often have to do.) Look at the lists of jurors in items 2 and 4. Why do you think none of the men are the same? Based simply on the evidence here (and there are no more records about this case, nor do we know who got the land in the end), can you judge which man has the stronger claim to the land? What does this case tell you about family land transactions?

Sources 7 and 8 are bylaws, Source 7 from the village of Wistow in Huntingdonshire from 1410 and Source 8 from the village of Hitchin in Hertshire from 1471. Like the bylaws contained in Source 2, they concern activities that some villagers were probably already engaged in. Why might people let their animals loose in the meadows or stubble? Why might this be a problem? Why would people dig pits in the road? Item 6 in Source 7 and all of Source 8 concern *gleaning*, or picking up loose heads of grain that fell off when the sheaves were gathered. Villages generally tried to reserve this for those who were very old, very young, or physically infirm, and so could not work a normal day helping with the harvest. Bylaws about gleaning are repeated frequently (here item 6 in Source 7 and item 1 in Source 8), and so apparently gleaning by able-bodied people was a common problem. Why might people choose to glean instead of work for wages in the harvest? According to item 2 in Source 8, what opportunities could gleaning provide? What does item 3 in Source 8 tell you about the legal responsibilities of a head of household? How might this have affected relationships within the family?

Sources 9, 10, and 11 are wills from the small town of Cranbrook in Kent from the late fifteenth century, the earliest time period from which many wills of common people survive. Just as they do today, people in medieval England used wills to set out how their property and possessions were to be divided and handled after their deaths. When a number of wills survive from any one area, historians can use them quantitatively to trace things such as religious and charitable donations, kinship and friendship networks, the role of professional lawyers, the relative wealth of a region or group of people, remarriage of widows and widowers, changing patterns of investment, or book ownership and literacy. We will not use enough wills to make a large-scale, quantitative study, but we can use the amounts mentioned within some of them to help us answer our questions for this chapter. Again it will be helpful if you make a family tree for each will, to see whom the person making the will—the testator—decides to include, and to make comparisons within a family; alongside this tree, keep a chart of all bequests that are *not* to family members, to help you assess the relative importance of other concerns, such as religion. When you make these charts, you will want to translate all amounts into the same type of money in order to make comparisons, for the English monetary system in the fifteenth century was not a decimal one. The basic unit was the penny (Latin *denarius*, abbreviated *d.*). Twelve pennies made a shilling (Latin *solidus*, abbreviated *s.*), and 20 shillings or 240 pennies a pound (Latin *libra*, abbreviated £). A mark was 13 s. 4 d., or two-thirds of a pound. Amounts were often written simply as numbers without the abbreviations: 2/13/6 equals £2, 13 s., 6 d. and 13/6 equals 13 s. 6 d.

Read Source 9 carefully, making your chart. Which family members does the testator, John Jalander, mention by name? Who are his executors? Why is this role important? Although at the beginning of the will it is not clear what relation Richard Crysp is to Jalander, who does he turn out to be? How would you compare the inheritance of the two brothers Robert and William? (This is not possible to do with complete assurance because we do not know the value of Jalander's land, but you can still get some impression of this from other aspects of the will, such as the distribution of animals or the instructions about what to do if Robert died without issue, that is, without children.) Based on this will, how would you assess the importance of godchildren to people in late medieval England? Of their own siblings or nieces and nephews? Along with Jalander's family, who else benefits from the will? How would you assess the relative importance of these bequests outside of the family?

Now go on to Source 10, and again make a chart. What special provisions does the testator, Robert Lurker, make for his wife? How do these compare with those of the previous testator? How would you compare the inheritance of his son William (who probably is the eldest) with that of his other sons and daughters? How would you compare the inheritance of the younger sons with that of the daughters? Do the same with Source 11. How do the inheritances of the two sons and daughter of the testator, Thomas Herenden, compare? How would you compare Herenden's donations to the church for his funeral expenses and the expenses of the later memorial ceremony with his gifts to his children?

You can tell from the three wills you have read that there were differences in wealth among families in English villages and small towns. So far, however, we have not paid great attention to economic differences and how these might have affected family strategies. This is difficult to do by reading only a few sources, for it is best done quantitatively. Sources 12 and 13 are charts for the period 1350–1400 made by the medieval historian Zvi Razi. They are based on his study of the village of Halesowen, in Worcestershire, with the bulk of his information coming from court rolls. Razi has carried out the laborious task of identifying individuals and determining family connections to arrive at the figures you see here. Look carefully at Source 12, which gives the adjusted mean number (average number) of offspring over the age of twelve for rich, middling, and poor village families. (The "adjusted" in this refers to the fact that Razi had to add daughters to arrive at an accurate count because girls and young women were so much less likely to appear in the court rolls than boys and young men. If he had not done this, it would have appeared that families were having twice as many sons as daughters, which is not biologically possible.) Why do you think the numbers are what they are? (Remember this is offspring who lived to age twelve.) In a largely agrarian economy such as medieval England, what are the advantages and disadvantages of having more children who survived? Source 13 traces the sale and leasing of land. What differences do you see in the ability of rich and poor families to improve their economic status through buying or leasing land? Looking at this chart, does it appear that economic differences among families were increasing or decreasing during this period? How might the differences in number of children who survived have affected this? Adding up the columns of lessor, lessee, vendor, and buyer in Source 13, how many families were involved in land transactions during this time? (There might be some overlap because members of one family might both buy and lease, or even buy and sell land, but this overlap is not likely to be too large, according to Razi.) From Source 12, you can see that Razi has traced 253 families in Halesowen during this period. Roughly what percentage were involved in land transactions of some type?

Just as any medieval historian would, at this point you have a lot of what may seem like quite disparate information about how families and family members acted and related. Before you answer the central questions for this chapter, it will be helpful to turn to the Questions to Consider section, which makes some suggestions on tying this all together.

THE EVIDENCE

Source 1 from Nathaniel J. Hone, The Manor and Manorial Records *(Port Washington, N.Y.: Kennikat Press, 1971; first published, 1906), p. 183.*

1. Court Roll, Village of Gnossal, England, 1492

Gnowshale [illegible] Curia magna ibidem tent' decimo die Aprilis [illegible] ibidem anno [illegible] Henrici septimi septimo

Esson — ad hunc diem Johes [illegible]

xii Jurat — Johes Banastre, Johes Podmore, Thomas Faldewall [illegible] Thomas a [illegible], Johes a More, Ricus [illegible] [illegible] Hugo [illegible], Ricus [illegible], Thomas Jones [illegible] Ricus Sutton [illegible] jurati [illegible]

[illegible] Willmus [illegible] Ricus [illegible] Humfridus [illegible] Robertus [illegible]

[illegible] Thomas [illegible] Thomas [illegible]

Willmus [illegible] Robertus [illegible] Willmus [illegible] Humfridus [illegible]

Johes [illegible] Johes [illegible] Willmus [illegible] Johes [illegible] Thomas [illegible] Humfridus [illegible]

Johes [illegible] Willmus [illegible] fecerunt defaltam ad hunc diem // Et ultimo

[illegible] presentant [illegible] Thomas [illegible] non [illegible] apud Littelfelde [illegible]

[illegible] presentant Thomam [illegible] consilit Thomas Faldewall [illegible]

Thomas [illegible] consilit in eodem campo // Et presentant [illegible] consilit in le [illegible]

[illegible] consilit [illegible] Thomas [illegible]

[illegible] consilit [illegible] in Wellesfeld // Et [illegible] Johem [illegible] Johes [illegible]

[illegible] Ricus Sutton [illegible] Thomas [illegible] Thomas

[illegible] Thomas [illegible] Johem [illegible] Thomas [illegible] Thomas Sutton

[illegible] ordinacionem [illegible] in [illegible]

[illegible] presentant [illegible] Thomas [illegible] Thomas [illegible] consilit

[illegible]

[illegible] ordinacionem [illegible] ad hunc diem [illegible]

[illegible]

[illegible] Weston [illegible]

[illegible]

[illegible] magna [illegible]

2. Court Roll of Ramsey, 1460

RAMSEY. VIEW OF FRANKPLEDGE[1] WITH COURT HELD THERE ON MONDAY AFTER THE FEAST OF ST. ANNE, IN THE THIRTY-EIGHTH YEAR OF THE REIGN OF KING HENRY VI AND THE TWENTY-FIFTH YEAR OF THE LORD ABBOT JOHN STOWE.[2]

1. (ESSOINS:[3]) None.

2. [JURORS:] Thomas Cok, John Baker, Thomas Plomer, Henry Brampton, Philip Aleyn, John Browse, Richard Baker, John Fen, William Abbot, Richard Toute, John Ridman, Thomas Vigerous, William Clerk, John Betcod, Robert Stone, William Wayte.

3. 3 d. from John Newman for not prosecuting a plea of debt against William Freman of Upwood. . . .

8. 2 d. from John Newman for having a dung heap too near the common lane, opposite his tenement[4] in the Wyght, to the nuisance of all passers-by.

9. 2 d. from John Thomas, 1 d. from Alice Shelford, [no amercement[5]] from John Bryan (beggar), 2 d. each from John Kent, Richard Glasyer and William Wayte for not cleaning their ditches at the end of their orchards towards Little Wyght. . . .

11. Ordinance by the whole homage that each tenant sufficiently clean his ditch opposite his tenement and make brinks[6] with piles and undergrowth before the next feast of All Saints[7] after this view, under an individual penalty of 40 d. . . .

14. 12 d. from Thomas Tyler, tenant of the Cellarer,[8] for making an encroachment by ploughing at the land he holds from the Cellarer, [appropriating] 24 feet from the common balks[9] leading towards the pond upon Pilcham. Order to correct before the feast of St. Michael[10] next, under penalty of 40 d.

15. 6 s. 8 d. each from Thomas Porter, John Bothby, John Whytwell and Peter Marche for putting dung near the Chapel of St. Thomas, contrary to the ancient ordinance. . . .

1. **view of frankpledge:** inspection of all those sworn in to the frankpledge.
2. July 28, 1460.
3. **essoins:** people's excuses for not appearing in court, brought in by others.
4. **tenement:** house.
5. **no amercement:** no fine levied, usually because the defendant was too poor.
6. **brinks:** banks.
7. **All Saints:** November 1.
8. **Cellarer:** steward of the lord or a local monastery.
9. **balks:** ridges of land left unploughed between fields.
10. **Feast of St. Michael:** September 29.

17. 6 d. from John Faukes for assaulting Matthew Kelew Wever and attempting to strike him, against the peace.

18. 6 d. from the same John Faukes for similarly assaulting Richard Merwyk and attempting to stab him with his dagger and for knocking him down and throwing him into the river, against the King's peace. . . .

20. 3 d. from John Kent for similarly assaulting Thomas Wode and striking him with a cudgel and drawing blood from him, against the King's peace.

21. 6 d. from William Stedeman for assaulting Thomas Wode and drawing blood from him by fracturing his skull.

22. 6 d. from Thomas Wode for unjustly raising the hue and cry on (his) wife, and [no amercement recorded] from his wife for unjustly raising the hue and cry on him, to the serious nuisance of their neighbors, which is something they do regularly, both day and night. . . .

25. 6 d. from John Water for assaulting Thomas Baker Junior and slightly wounding him in the chest with his dagger, against the King's peace.

26. 4 d. from John Water for assaulting Thomas Rolf and his wife, against the King's peace.

27. 1 d. from the same John for entering the lord's park and carrying off wood and undergrowth.

28. 6 d. from William Clerk for assaulting John Love, against the peace.

29. 6 d. from the same John Love for assaulting the said William, against the peace.

30. 6 d. from Thomas Love for assaulting William Clerk by shooting arrows at him and mistreating him, against the peace.

31. 12 d. from Robert Love, chaplain, for assaulting Thomas Love, his brother, with a drawn knife, against the King's peace.

32. 1 d. from Katherine Love for unjustly raising the hue and cry on William Clerk, to the nuisance and annoyance of their neighbors.

33. A half-mark from William Warde for regularly having diverse men within his dwelling playing tennis, contrary to the decree concerning this. . . .

35. A new ordinance: If anyone within the precincts of this leet[11] has pigs, piglets and sows wandering regularly in the street, the Bailiff, through his servant or deputy, is permitted to drive them and impound them in the lord's park, charging 1 d. for each pig or sow and 1/2 d. for each piglet, to the use and profit of the lord, and charging for his labour 1 d., as often as it happens that they have to be impounded.

36. 8 d. each from Joan Overton and Mariot Amy, 6 d. from Agnes Depyng, 8 d. each from Alice Couper and Agnes Faunt, 6 d. each from Marion Baveyn, Katherine Love and Joan Filhous, and 8 d. each from Agnes Symmes and Audrey Cooke, common brewers, for selling ale contrary to the assize.[12] . . .

11. **leet:** court.

12. **contrary to the assize:** against the ordinances regulating weights and measures.

38. 1 d. each from Joan Brampton, Isabelle Stedeman, Agnes Gelam, Margaret Baker, Juliana Baker, Joan Shirwode and Agnes Webster for not bringing their gallons and pottles[13] before the steward of this leet on this day. . . .

40. 16 d. from Thomas Plomer and 20 d. from John Asplond, bakers of bread, for selling bread contrary to the assize. . . .

42. 20 d. from William Faunt, 40 d. from Thomas Cokk, 20 d. from John Awbys and 8 d. from William Warde Sadeler, butchers, for charging too much in selling meat. . . .

44. 4 d. each from Thomas Cok, William Faunt and John Hunt, [no amercement] from John Berforth (because he is dead), 2 d. each from John Awbys and Marion Amy, 4 d. each from Walter Pamlion and John Asplond, 2 d. each from Alice Keteryng and John Whete, 1 d. each from John Treygo and Finetta Water, and 4 d. from Thomas Plomer, common victualers,[14] for charging too much in selling victuals.

45. 6 d. each from John Brouse and William Wayte, ale-tasters, for not performing their office.

46. 3 d. from William Wayte, 2 d. from Richard Wayte, 1 d. from Robert Grene, 2 d. from John Sowle, 12 d. from Richard Toute, 2 d. from Robert Tayllor, 3 d. from John Wryght Tayllor, 3 d. from John Hyll and 1 d. from Thomas Bonfaye, tailors, for charging too much in their art.

47. 6 d. from Richard Geyte, 2 d. from John Missangle, 6 d. from William Geyte (dead), 1 d. from John Boller (dead), and 3 d. from John Denby, cobblers, for charging too much.

48. 3 d. from John Webster, 6 d. from John Faukes, 2 d. from Richard Faukes, and 3 d. each from Robert Hyde and Matthew Kelew, weavers, for charging too much.

49. 3 d. from Roger Glover and 2 d. from John Pecok, glovers, for charging too much in their art.

50. 3 d. from Robert Skynner and 6 d. from Gilbert Skynner, skinners, for charging too much in their art. . . .

52. Election and swearing-in of William Wayte and Richard Baker as Constables.

53. Election and swearing-in of William Clerk and John Fen as ale-tasters.

13. **gallons and pottles:** measures for ale, which the steward must regularly inspect for accuracy.

14. **victualers:** food-sellers.

3. Court Roll of South Elmham, 1408

The jury presented that Henry Pekke died seised[15] of 1 messuage,[16] 10 acres, ½ rod of customary land. His grandson, Henry Pekke, is his heir and is of legal age. He requests admittance to the tenement. But Joan Recher, the late Henry's widow, requests half of the tenement as dower.[17] She is admitted. Henry is admitted to the other half with reversion of dower etc. to hold to himself and his heirs for services etc. Henry surrenders his half to the use of Joan for life. She resurrenders the entire tenement to him and to his heirs, but reserves 1 lower room (*camera*) and 1 upper room (*solar*), also a parcel of land, with free entry and exit for herself and her friends for life. Conditions: she is to receive yearly at 30 November 1 quarter of faggots[18] valued at 12d.; yearly for life, 8s. paid in quarterly installments at 30 November, Easter, 24 June, 29 September; Henry to keep her 2 rooms fully repaired; he is to provide her with the same food and drink that he himself has, and if she is not pleased with this fare, she is to have 12d. yearly on account of her displeasure; entry to the main house whenever she wishes.

4. Court Roll of Wymondham, 1421

From William Notte to John, his son, and Joan, his wife, and their heirs and assigns 1 messuage, 10 acres of the tenement "Banymouth," 4½ acres of the tenement "Rewald," 1 rod of the tenement "Hardened," ½ acre at Shirwod, ½ acre called "Qwythed," and 1 property with appurtenances[19] in Watt. Conditions: reservation of 1 room with solar at northern end of hall; food and clothing; William to warm himself at their fire and to have a horse, a saddle and a bridle in order to ride whenever he wishes; annually they will plow and seed 4 acres of his in a field called "Kalleye"; they will maintain 24 ewes. Entry fine £3.

15. **seised:** in possession of.
16. **messuage:** land surrounding a house, also called a croft.
17. **dower:** right of a widow to a portion of an estate.
18. **faggot:** bundle of sticks for firewood.
19. **appurtenances:** that which belongs to the property, such as buildings.

Source 5 from Nathaniel J. Hone, The Manor and Manorial Records *(Port Washington, N.Y.: Kennikat Press, 1971), pp. 164–166.*

5. Court Roll of Winterborne, 1494

Court held there the 18th day of April the ninth year of the reign of King Henry the Seventh.

1. Essoins—none.
2. The homage there come and are sworn. And they present that all things are well.
3. A penalty is imposed upon all the tenants there that they shall well and competently make all repairs of their tenements, under penalty for each one of them not doing so 20^{s}.
4. The suitors[20] there come and are sworn, and present that Thomas Hatt hath overburdened the common pasture there with his sheep, therefore he is in mercy.[21] And so it is commanded him for the future not to do so under penalty of 10^{s}.
5. Also they present that William Barcoll, freeholder, hath closed his last day, who held of the lord certain lands by knight service. And they say that Alice and Sibell are daughters and next heirs of the said William. And that Alice is five years of age and not more. And that the aforesaid Sibell is three years of age and over. And upon this comes William Webbe[22] and gives to the lord of fine for the minority of the aforesaid heirs 3^{s}4^{d}.
6. Also they present that the said William Barcoll held of the lord, according to the custom of the manor there, 3 messuages with their appurtenances, after whose death there falls to the lord by way of heriot, a horse of a roan colour value 10^{s}. And upon this comes the aforesaid William Webbe, and takes of the lord the aforesaid 3 messuages with all their appurtenances. To have and to hold to him, and Thomas, and John, sons of the said William for the term of their lives, or of the one of them longest living, according to the custom of the manor there, by rent and other services therefrom aforetime due and of right accustomed. And moreover it was granted to the aforesaid William, Thomas, and John, that each of them shall have a sufficient deputy dwelling in the said 3 messuages with their appurtenances, during the term aforesaid. And he gives to the lord of fine for entry, and for possession of his estate, 6^{s}8^{d}. And further, the tenants shall give to the lord by way of heriot 10^{s}.

20. **suitors:** those bringing cases to the court.
21. Thomas Hatt has placed more sheep there than he is entitled to do by his tenancy.
22. William Webbe seeks the wardship or custody of the children till they come of age.

Source 6 from A. F. C. Baber, The Court Rolls of the Manor Bromsgrove and King's Norton, 1494–1504 *(Kineton, Warwick, England: Worcestershire Historical Society, 1963), pp. 84–85.*

6. Court Roll of Bromsgrove and King's Norton, 1496

1. To this court came Henry Banard and paid 12d as a fine to the lady[23] to have an inquest of office[24] according to the custom of the manor of Bromsgrove and King's Norton to enquire on the oath of twelve of the tenants of the said manor as to what legal right Richard Sharpe had to grant any estate to Peter Parre and to enquire whether Giles Sharpe had issue[25] William and Elizabeth and whether the said William died without issue or not and to enquire whether the said Elizabeth married a certain William Banard or not and to enquire whether the said William Banard and Elizabeth his wife had issue Henry Banard and whether the said . . . Henry . . . is the true heir of the said Elizabeth or not. And he asked that the next steps might be taken according to the custom of the manor and Roger Bydell the bailiff of King's Norton was ordered to summon twelve of the tenants of King's Norton by good summoners to be at the next court at Lykehay that is on Monday (4 April) next ready to make an examination in the said inquest of office and the same day was given to the said Henry.

2. At this court the jurors empanelled, charged and sworn for the inquest of office of Henry Banard appeared that is William Benton, Thomas Reynold, Thomas Grene, Humphrey Rotton, Thomas Blyke, Richard Slough, Baldwin Sye, John Holyok junior, Thomas Holme, Thomas Byssehill senior, Baldwin Feld of Geyhill, Richard Lette and Thomas Lee and each of them say on oath that a certain William Sharpe gave an estate in the land to Richard Sharpe and they say that Giles Sharpe had issue William and Elizabeth and that the said William died without issue and they say that the said Elizabeth married a certain William Banard and that the said William Banard and Elizabeth had issue Henry Banard and that the said Henry Banard is the true heir of the said Elizabeth.

3. To this court came Peter Parre and paid 12d as a fine to have an inquest of office according to the custom of the manor to enquire on the oath of twelve of the tenants of King's Norton as to whether William Sharpe son and heir of Giles Sharpe at any time was seised of a tenement in Wrednale with appurtenances . . . and thus seised whether by charter he gave the said tenement to Roger Sharpe and Richard his brothers in fee and whether the said tenement was only for the work and use of Richard Sharpe and not of Roger Sharpe or not

23. The domina or lady of the manor was the widow of the previous lord.

24. **inquest of office:** official inquiry.

25. **issue:** children.

and whether the said Richard Sharpe after the death of the said William Sharpe his brother by virtue of the said charter entered alone into the whole of the said tenement and occupied the tenement throughout his life taking for himself all the profits without claim or blame from Roger Sharpe or not and if the said Richard Sharpe during his life time gave the said tenement with its appurtenances to Peter Parre and Alice his wife daughter of the said Richard Sharpe in fee[26] or not and if the said Peter and Alice by virtue of the said gift were alone peaceably seised of the said tenement . . . taking the profits thereof or not. And he asked that the next steps might be taken according to the custom of the manor of Bromsgrove and King's Norton. Therefore Thomas Reynold the under-bailiff of King's Norton was ordered to summon twelve of the tenants of King's Norton by good summoners according to the custom of the said manor to be at the next court at Lykehay on Monday (23 May) to make an examination in the said inquest of office and the said Peter has the same day.

4. At this court Roger Bedull the under-bailiff of King's Norton as ordered at the last meeting of the court appeared with the men empanelled to make the inquest of office of Peter Parre that is Roger Norton, John Feld in le hole, Baldwin Feld senior, John Freth, John Greve, Edward Kyteley, John Lyndon, William Hawkes, William Oldenhale, John Vitter, Richard Marten, John Feld of Gorshaw, William Halle, Robert Taillor, John Sergeaunt, John Chamber and John More junior and each of them sworn and charged of and in the said premises say upon oath that William Sharpe son and heir of Giles Sharpe was seised of the said tenement with its appurtenances in Wrednale . . . and thus seised by his charter gave the said tenement to Roger Sharpe and Richard Sharpe his brothers . . . and that the gift of the said tenement was for the work and use only of Richard Sharpe and not of Roger Sharpe and they say that Richard Sharpe after the death of the said William his brother by virtue of that charter himself entered into the whole of the said tenement with appurtenances and occupied it peaceably all his life taking the profits thereof to his own use alone without claim or blame from Roger Sharpe and they say that Richard Sharpe (gave) the said tenement . . . to Peter Parre and Alice his wife daughter of the said Richard and they say that the said Peter and Alice by virtue of the said gift are alone peaceably seised of the tenement in their demesne . . . taking the profits thereof etc.

26. **in fee:** with the right to pass it on to heirs.

Sources 7 and 8 from Warren O. Ault, Open-Field Farming in Medieval England: A Study of Village By-Laws *(London: George Allen and Unwin, 1972), p. 117; p. 133.*

7. Bylaws of Wistow, 1410

1. It is ordered by the lord and the whole homage that each tenant shall fill the pits which he made in the low way [*loway*] under pain[27] for each one of 12d.

2. Item that no one shall let his colts go loose so they are taken in the grain from the Feast of St Peter in Chains (August 1st) to the Nativity of the Blessed Mary (September 8th) under pain of 7d.

3. And that no sheep shall be allowed in the meadow at Wyldbrigg next to the meadow of the rector before the Feast of the Nativity of the Blessed Mary under pain each one of 4d.

4. And that each tenant of Wistow shall mend the road next to his land with stone before the Feast of St. Michael under pain each one of 12d.

5. And that no one shall mow or dig in the fen near the boundary ways by a width of three acres under pain each one of 40d.

6. And that no one shall glean in autumn who is able to earn 1d. a day and food under pain each one of 12d.

7. And that no one shall tether or pasture beasts in the wheat stubble this side the Feast of the Nativity of the Blessed Mary under pain each one of 12d. The jury of Wistow elect Robert Waryn, John Randolf, William Becker and Thomas ffraunces reeves of autumn and they were sworn.

8. Bylaws of Hitchin, 1471

1. It is ordained by the assent of the lord's council and of his tenants that none shall enter the sown field in autumn time to gather grain or spears[28] with rakes or by hand if they are capable of earning 2d. a day, under pain for each one doing contrary to this ordinance of 3s. 4d.

2. Those who are not capable of earning 2d. a day shall not enter or cross through the sown fields until the sheaves have been gathered, removed and carted from a space of four acres of land under the aforesaid pain.

3. And if they be boys and under age or someone's servants who are not able to satisfy the lord in respect of the aforesaid pain then their masters who have these persons in governance shall answer to the lord for the aforesaid pain.

27. **pain:** fine.

28. **spears:** stalks of grain.

Sources 9, 10, and 11 from Jules de Launay, Abstracts of Cranbrook Wills Proved in the Diocesan Courts of Canterbury *(Canterbury, England: Kent Records Collection, 1984), pp. 28–29; p. 30; p. 39.*

9. Will of John Jalander, Cranbrook, 1476

JALANDER, John
18 Apr 1476

To the High Altar of Cranbrook for tithes forgotten, 6d.
To the construction of the new chapel of the Blessed Mary, 6/8.
To my godson Nich. PEND, 6d.
To each each godchild, 4d.
To the repair of the way, where most needed, between the Cross of Hertle and Turneden, 40d.
To my wife Alice, my best cow.
To Rich. CRYSP, another cow.
To my son Robt., a cow & a calf.
RESIDUE of my goods, to my wife Alice and Rich. CRYSPE.
EXECS:[29] my wife Alice and Rich. CRYSPE.

WILL:
FEOFFEES:[30] Stph. CRAKREGE, Laur. TAYLOR, John KYTT, & John NETTAR son of Rich. NETTAR.
To my wife Alice, all my lands & tenements for life.
After her dec., my feoffees shall deliver to my son Robt. the sd. property in fee simple[31] on condition that the sd. Robt. my son pay his brother Wm. 18 marks within 6 yrs. after the death of my wife, at the rate of £2/yr.
To be sold to pay my debts and bequests: a garden with a passage to it, called Smythisfeld.
Should my son Robt. die before age 22 and without lawful issue, then I will that my dau. Alice CRYSPE have a croft of land called Loggecroft, in fee simple. And should my dau. Alice die without legitimate heirs of her body, then I will that the sd. croft be sold and the money be used for charitable works.
And if, as just said, my son Robt. should die before 22 without lawful issue, all my lands and tenements (except the croft bequeathed to Alice) shall be sold. The money therefrom shall be distributed as follows:
to my son Wm., 26/8;

29. **execs:** executors.

30. **feoffees:** trustees.

31. **in fee simple:** as a free holding, that is, with no labor obligations attached to it and able to be handed down to any of his own heirs.

to a suitable priest to celebrate in the church of Cranbrook for a year, for my soul and the souls of the faithful departed, 10 marks;

the remainder of the money shall be used to buy a chalice for the church of Cranbrook.

Robt. shall pay Mgt., the dau. of my dau. Alice 26/8 towards her marriage.

10. Will of Robert Lurker, Cranbrook, 1477

LURKER, Robert
30 Mch 1477.

To the High Altar of Cranbrook for tithes forgotten, 6d.
To the parish chaplain there, 2d.
To the parish clerk there, 1d.
To the Light of St. Christopher there, 4d.
To the repair of the foul ways from my mansion[32] to the messuage of Rich. BENETT, 12d.
To my wife Agnes, a bed and bedding, including a mattress and undercloth; also to her, a pan.
To my sons and daus., the RESIDUE of all my utensils, to be distributed among them at the discretion of my execs. and feoffees.
To my son Wm., all my instruments pertaining to his trade of wheelwright. I give to my son Wm. 800 felloes (felloe = the rim or part of the rim of a spoked wheel) and 1000 spokes.
RESIDUE of my goods, to Simon LYNCH & Wm. BASSOK, and they are my EXECS.

WILL:
FEOFFEE: Wm. BALDEN, enfeoffed in my lands in Cranbrook.
Wm. BALDEN shall deliver to my son Wm. in fee simple, my messuage in which I now dwell, and a garden thereto, & a croft called Blakland, on condition that my son Wm. pay my wife Agnes 40s within 2 yrs. after my dec.
My feoffees shall deliver to my son Alex., a piece of land called Derbers (?), (2 acres), to hold forever.
To my sons John and Simon, 2 pieces of arable[33] land and 3 pieces of grazing land called Stonerok, the Pucell, & the Wodes (27 acres), forever, on condition that John & Simon pay to the marriages of my daus. Margery, Petonille, & Agnes, 13/4 each.

32. **mansion:** house.
33. **arable:** farmable.

If my wife, who is pregnant, gives birth to a son, then this son shall share the 2 pieces of arable land and 3 pieces of grazing land with his brothers John & Simon.
My wife shall have her quarters in my messuage, and a solar, and a fire in the hall, and her easement there, and the use of the bakehouse, for 8 years.

11. Will of Thomas Herenden, Cranbrook, 1483

HERENDEN, Thomas
6 Jul 1483

To the High Altar of Cranbrook for tithes forgotten, 12d.
To the Light of the Blessed Mary, 4d.
To the chaplain of Holy Trinity of Milkhouse in the parish of Cranbrook, 2s, of which 12d immediately after my dec. and 12d later.
To my wife Eleanor, all the utensils now in my house.
EXEC: my son John HERENDEN, and to him the RESIDUE of my goods. . . .

WILL:
My son John shall have my messuage lying in the parish of Cranbrook upon the den of Hesilldenwode, with my lands, except 2 pieces of land with a garden called le Graunge, forever.
To my son Jas. (Jacobus), the 2 pieces of land with the garden called le Graunge, forever, he releasing and acquiting[34] the property of the feudal lord for 6/8.
My son John shall pay my wife Eleanor 16s.
I will that after the death of my wife, my son Jas. shall have 2 pieces of land called le Joyfeld and Bachell, he acquiting this land of the feudal lord for 3/4.
To my dau. Joan BARGH, after the dec. of my wife, 6/8, out of these last 2 pieces.
My wife Eleanor shall have a room in the southern part of my messuage, for life. Also to her, fire, a cow with its pasturage on my son John's land summer and winter.
My sons John and James (Jacobus) shall pay 13/4 for my funeral expenses and 13/4 for my month's mind.[35]

34. **releasing and acquiting:** paying the fees necessary to the lord to inherit the property.
35. **month's mind:** memorial service held one month after an individual's death.

Sources 12 and 13 from Zvi Razi, Life, Marriage and Death in a Medieval Parish: Economy, Society and Demography in Halesowen 1270–1400 *(Cambridge, England: Cambridge University Press, 1980), p. 142; p. 148. Reprinted with the permission of Cambridge University Press.*

12. Average Number of Offspring over the Age of Twelve in Halesowen Families, by Economic Status, 1350–1400

Economic Status	No. of families	Adjusted mean no. of offspring
Rich	60	3.0
Middling	89	2.0
Poor	81	1.4
Unidentified	23	—
Total	253	2.1

13. The Socioeconomic Status of Lessors, Lessees, Vendors, and Buyers of Land in Halesowen, 1350–1400

	No. of Leases (32)			No. of sales (81)		
	No. of lessors[36]	No. of lessees	Excess of lessees	No. of vendors	No. of buyers	Excess of buyers
Members of rich families	12	16	+4	17	25	+8
Members of middling families	11	8	–3	25	21	–4
Members of poor families	9	4	–5	30	9	–21
Total	32	28	–4	72	55	–17

36. **Lessors** leased or rented land to **lessees; vendors** sold land to buyers.

QUESTIONS TO CONSIDER

Though the two central questions for this chapter both center on the medieval family, you can see that the first one focuses on relationships between families and the second one on relationships within a family. The first is in some ways easier to answer because of the nature of our sources, since economic transactions and other interactions among members of the same family often left a historical record only if they were unusual or contested. The case referred to in Source 6, for example, would never have come to court if Henry Banard and Peter Parre had not both claimed the same piece of land; instead the land would have been transferred from generation to generation without much notice. The maintenance agreements found in Sources 3 and 4 probably were entered into the court rolls because there was some doubt that the younger people mentioned in them would actually support their elders; most such agreements were probably oral and never made it into the records. Court records thus offer a picture of familial relations that is skewed toward the negative and disputatious.

To answer the first question, you will need to gather your evidence about specific actions. Look again at Source 2, item 14. What is Thomas Tyler fined for doing? How would you compare his fine with those set for other types of infractions? What might account for the difference? Look at Source 5, item 4: What is Thomas Hatt fined for? Keeping these actions in mind, look at the bylaws in Source 7, especially items 2, 3, 5, and 7. How would you generalize about people's attempts to improve their economic position based on these sources? Why might the fines be so high? What do your calculations regarding Source 13 tell you about additional ways in which families improved their positions?

Go back to the charts you made tracking certain individuals in Source 2. What did William Wayte and William Clerk do to improve their own positions? How might their actions have helped their whole families? How might some of their actions have hurt their families? How might the nonfarming activities of various men and women mentioned in items 36 through 50 have strengthened their families' economic position? What other nonfarming activities are mentioned in the sources, and how might these have shaped a family's social and economic positions? (Be sure to think about activities that would have worsened a family's position as well as those that would have strengthened it.) How were a family's opportunities for improving its position shaped by the amount of wealth or land the family already held?

To answer the second question, you will again need to bring together information from many sources. What evidence have you found about relationships between spouses? Between siblings? Between parents and children? What differences do you see between daughters and sons, and between older sons and younger sons? Do the sources present a uniform picture, or are there contradictions in them? What might be some of the reasons for these contradictions? Have you found many references to an extended family or kin group, such as references to cousins, nieces and nephews, or uncles and aunts? What does this indicate about the way people conceptualized their family? (Here the legal case in Source 6 and the wills in Sources 9, 10, and 11 provide the most information.)

One of the central issues debated among historians of the pre-modern family is the depth of people's loyalty to family interests as compared to their loyalty to their own interests, usually termed *individualism.* Based on the sources you have read for this chapter, do loyalties to a family come first, that is, are there signs of people doing things that are against their own interests for the good of the family? Do people appear to be more individualistic when relating to their own family members, or to villagers who are not related? Based on the sources, how would you assess the relative importance of economic need and emotional ties in holding medieval families together? Do other sorts of factors help in this as well?

You are now ready to answer the central questions for this chapter: How did common people in medieval England seek to strengthen the economic and social positions of their families? How did they define "family" and relate to those they saw as members of this group?

EPILOGUE

The medieval families we have observed in this chapter might strike you as rather cold, as we have been able to see only their reflection in official legal documents. The private sources such as letters or diaries that flesh out our picture of family relationships in later periods simply don't exist for villagers in medieval England. Added to this is the problem that court records from any period reveal only things that are perceived as a problem. (You can imagine what a future historian's view of twentieth-century American families would be like if all he or she had to go on were divorce court proceedings.)

When used carefully, however, official legal documents can often reveal intimacies of normal family life as well as extraordinary cases. One medieval historian, Barbara Hanawalt, has used English records of coroners' inquests into accidental deaths to trace where children and adults were in their daily round of chores and activities. She finds, for example, that even at a very young age girls were more likely to die accidentally in the house and boys outside, and that the holes in the road, dung-heaps, and uncleared ditches that our sources in this chapter complain of so constantly could be very dangerous for people, especially those who were very old, very young, or drunk. Other historians have used the language of wills—of which we have a small sampling here—to trace the way men felt about the intelligence and competence of their wives, which no doubt had some bearing on day-to-day life in the household. Doing this kind of digging is hard, but the results are often fascinating, providing surprising insights into the lives of ordinary people. (We might think, for example, that rules about building a tennis court on one's property were a result of modern zoning restrictions, but our sources here have demonstrated that this was a concern more than five hundred years ago.)

Though in this chapter we have investigated family relationships and activities in only one time and place, when we combine our findings with those from other cultures and periods we can begin to make comparisons and trace changes. We could do this with cultures not too far removed (say, England before the Black Death, the period immediately preceding the one we have studied here), or far removed (say, Spanish villages in an era before urbanization and industrialization), or even farther removed (say, the contemporary family in Stockholm). Each of these comparisons will reveal different areas of similarity and difference, but the most important result of any of them may be an affirmation of the historical nature of the family, and the recognition that the family's structure and function (and the very meaning of the word "family") have changed many times in the past.

CHAPTER TEN

CRAFT GUILDS: ECONOMIC CHANGE AND SOCIAL CONFLICT

THE PROBLEM

The Commercial Revolution of the eleventh and twelfth centuries, with its reinvigoration of trade and development of a strong merchant class, came with, and was one of the causes for, a rebirth of town life. Especially in Italy and the Low Countries, but in many other parts of Europe as well, towns began to spring up around cathedrals, monasteries, and castles or at locations favorable for trade, such as ports or major crossroads. Some were totally new cities, but many developed on the sites of former Roman towns or Roman border camps.

As a town grew, its merchants and traders often joined together to form a guild that prohibited nonmembers from trading in the town. These same merchants often made up the earliest town government, serving as mayors and members of the city council, so that a town's economic policies were determined by its merchants' self-interests. Acting through the city council, the merchants' guilds determined the hours that markets would be open, decided which coins would be accepted as currency, and set prices on imported and local goods. Foreign affairs were also guided by the merchants, who chose as their allies either good trading partners or those who could prove useful against a competitor city. In many cities and towns, the merchants' guild was to all intents the city government, despite the official distinction between the two institutions.

Though the initial impetus to establish a town often came from trade and commerce, towns quickly became centers of production as well. A growing population attracted food and clothing producers; the wealth of the merchants drew producers of luxury goods. Merchants often imported raw materials such as wool or metals and supported the development of industries that manufactured products such as cloth and weaponry from these materials, then exported the finished products to other areas. Certain cities became known for their fine woolens or silks, their rugged arms and armor, or their elegant gold and silver work.

Like merchants, producers recognized the benefits of organization, and the twelfth century witnessed the birth of craft guilds that regulated most aspects of production. Each guild set standards of quality for its products and regulated the size of workshops, the training period required to become a member, and the conduct of members. In most cities individual guilds, such as those of the shoemakers or blacksmiths, achieved a monopoly on the production and sales of one product, forbidding nonmembers to work at their trade. In some towns each craft formed its own guild; by the thirteenth and fourteenth centuries more than one hundred separate craft guilds had been formed in many cities throughout Europe. In other towns related crafts were combined within larger guilds.

Each guild set the pattern by which its members were trained. To become a shoemaker, for instance, it was necessary to spend about seven years as an apprentice and then at least that long as a journeyman working in the shop of a master shoemaker. At the end of that period the journeyman was entitled to make his *masterpiece.* If the masterpiece was approved by the other master shoemakers and if they thought the market for shoes in their town was large enough to accommodate another shoemaker, the journeyman became a master and opened his own shop. Though the time that had to be spent as an apprentice and a journeyman varied slightly from guild to guild, all guilds followed this same three-stage process. Apprentices and journeymen usually lived with the master and his family and were often forbidden to marry. Conversely, most guilds required that masters be married, as they believed that a wife was absolutely essential to the running of the shop and household and, moreover, that married men were likely to be more stable and dependable.

The master's wife assisted in running the shop, often selling the goods her husband had produced. Their children, both male and female, worked alongside the apprentices and journeymen; sons were sometimes formally apprenticed but daughters were not, because most guilds limited formal membership to males. Most guilds did allow a master's widow to continue operating a shop for a set period of time after her husband's death, for they recognized that she had the necessary skills and experience. Such widows paid all the required guild dues but did not vote or hold office in the guilds because they were not considered full members. The fact that women were not formally guild members did not mean that they did not work in guild shops, however; along with the master's wife and daughters, female domestic servants often performed the tasks requiring less skill. In addition, a few all-female guilds were formed in several European cities, particularly Cologne and Paris, in which girls were formally apprenticed in the same way boys were in regular craft guilds.

Practitioners of a craft or trade required the permission of the city council to form a guild. Once this permission was granted, the guild could write its own ordinances and regulations. At first these ordinances were usually very brief, but over the centuries they were expanded as new problems arose or the guild tried to clear up ambiguities. The guild often set up a court to hear disputes between members, though a town's municipal court established by the city council remained the final arbiter; this municipal court also handled disputes between two guilds or between a guild and a nonmember. Guilds were jealous of their rights and privileges and were quick to complain when they felt someone was infringing on their monopoly. They were also careful to maintain the quality of their products by appointing several members to be inspectors; these inspectors visited workshops frequently, confiscating or destroying any product not up to standard. Guilds discouraged competition between masters by limiting the amount of raw materials each master could own and the size of the workshops, thus assuring each master that his household-workshop would be able to support itself.

Guilds were not simply economic organizations but also systems of social support. Though hostile to outsiders, they were protective and supportive of their own. They supported elderly masters who could no longer work, as well as widows and orphans. Guilds maintained an altar at a city church and paid for the funerals of members and the baptisms of their children. Guild members marched together in city parades, reinforcing their feelings of solidarity by special ceremonies and distinctive dress.

As craft guilds grew in economic power, they began to demand a share of the political power in their city and thus came into conflict with the city councils, which were dominated by merchants. After its first emergence in the fourteenth century, this conflict was to continue for centuries in many cities. In some cities, particularly in the Low Countries, the guilds triumphed, taking over control of the city's political as well as its economic life. In others, the merchants triumphed and excluded all craftsmen from political power. In still others, a compromise was reached whereby the guilds were allowed some members on the council and the council some power over the guilds.

During periods of high growth in their towns and times of economic prosperity, the guilds welcomed new members and the establishment of more and larger workshops. These workshops provided an important means of education and socialization for young people, placing them together with others their age who were learning the same skills. Apprentices and journeymen identified both with their peer group of young people at the same level of training and with the masters in their craft, whom they sought to emulate. Guilds also facilitated the mobility of labor, for a journeyman carrying a letter of apprenticeship could travel from town to town in search of the best opportunity for opening up a shop; theoretically, at least, he was entitled to be taken on by any master.

During periods of economic depression, the guilds were not so successful. At these times they generally tried to limit membership so that the supply of their product would not exceed demand. Only sons who inherited a shop from their fathers, or men who married masters' widows or daughters, were allowed to become masters. This meant that journeymen might remain journeymen their entire lives and never become masters. Journeymen who had been deprived of full guild membership in this way lost their sense of solidarity with the masters in their craft. In some cities they formed separate journeymen's guilds to defend their interests against those of the masters and demanded changes in their conditions of employment, including the right to marry and live in their own households as well as the right to determine who would work in the shop. To ensure workplaces for themselves, the journeymen tried to exclude anyone who was not an apprentice or a journeyman. In some cases they even tried to prevent the master's wife and children from working, though they were rarely successful in this effort. These conflicts within guilds were accompanied by increasing conflicts between guilds and the city council, for councils felt that the guilds' restrictive policies did not work to the economic advantage of the town as a whole.

Though in every town some production—especially of simple items such as soap, candles, and wooden dishes—remained free of guild control, the craft guilds were the most important institutions shaping patterns of employment and daily life in medieval towns. Often the majority of a town's population worked in guild shops and lived in households headed by master craftsmen. Guild records consequently provide information not only about the guilds themselves but also about many other economic and social issues. In particular, they highlight the varying responses of different groups of people to conflicts and problems in late medieval urban life. Your task in this chapter will be to use guild records to explore economic and social change in late medieval cities. What sorts of changes did the guilds view as problems, and how did they respond? What do their reactions tell us about the attitudes of this group of what we might term "middle-class" people?

SOURCES AND METHOD

We can find information about medieval craft guilds in a huge variety of sources, because record keeping was an important facet of guild activity. In general these sources can be divided into two basic types, a division that holds equally for sources from many other historical periods, as we have seen in Chapter 6. The first type is prescriptive—laws, regulations, and ordinances describing how the guild was supposed to operate and how the masters who wrote the ordinances hoped things would be. These documents do not simply describe an ideal, however; they were generally written in response to events that were already taking place, so they can tell us about real problems and the attitudes of the guild masters toward these problems. What they cannot tell us is if any of the proposed solutions worked, or what problems the solutions themselves caused. For this we have to turn to the second type of primary evidence, descriptive documents such as court records, city-council minutes, and petitions and supplications submitted by individuals. Through these records we can observe how the guilds attempted to enforce their regulations and how these regulations were circumvented or ignored. As you read the guild records, then, the first question you must ask yourself is whether a given document is prescriptive or descriptive, for confusing the two types of evidence can give a very skewed view of what life in a medieval city was like. (This kind of discrimination must be applied to any historical source, of course, and is not always an easy task. Sometimes even prominent historians have built a whole pyramid of erroneous theories about the past by assuming that prescriptive sources accurately described reality.)

The first eight selections are all taken from guild ordinances: Sources 1 and 2 from fourteenth-century England, Source 3 from thirteenth-century Paris, Sources 4 through 8 from sixteenth-century Germany. Read each carefully, both for the problems that are discussed explicitly and for the underlying concerns and attitudes of the masters writing these ordinances. At this point you may want to begin a three-column list or chart, one column for explicitly stated problems, a second for the solutions proposed in the documents, and a third for your speculations about the reasons that certain events were seen as problems or that a given solution was suggested. The regulations also provide a great deal of general information on conditions of apprenticeship, maximum size of the workshop, length of the workday, and noneconomic functions of the guild, such as religious activities and support of impoverished members.

Though all these selections are guild ordinances, some differences exist among them that may shape your conclusions. Source 3 concerns a women's guild, the silk spinners of Paris; all the others pertain to the more common men's guilds. Do you see any gender-related features in the regulations of the all-female guild? How would you describe the work of women in the other guilds? Sources 4 through 8 all come from the sixteenth century, a time when many guilds felt threatened and grew increasingly restrictive. What specific measures did the guilds take to reduce competition? Were these steps completely new, or did they follow a pattern that had been set by earlier ordinances as represented by the first and second documents?

Documents 9 through 11 are supplications or petitions. Source 9 is addressed to the English Parliament by the silk women of London; and Sources 10 and 11 to the city council of Frankfurt, Germany, by two widows. What problems were they seeking redress for? What solutions did they propose? Documents 10 and 11 discuss actions already taken by a guild. How do these actions reflect the guild's aims? What sorts of regulations was the guild trying to enforce?

The sources you have read so far have given you some impression not only of the guild masters and their aims and attitudes, but also of the relationship between the guilds and the city council. Before proceeding to the last group of sources, look at your list, or reread the previous documents, to assess the role of the town's political authorities. When did they become involved in the enforcement of guild regulations? How do the regulations and supplications refer to these authorities? When did individuals go to the city council or other authorities for assistance?

Now read the last four sources, which describe decisions or actions by a city council that relate to guild matters. Sources 12 and 13 come from fourteenth-century Flanders; Sources 14 and 15 from sixteenth-century Germany. These documents also bring up problems, propose solutions, and reflect attitudes, and so can be added to your list, though of course they reflect the opinions of the city council, not of the guild masters. Compare the information on your list from these sources with that from the earlier selections. Which problems did both groups consider important? How did the solutions proposed by the city council differ from those proposed by the guilds? What does this divergence tell you about the underlying attitudes of the two groups and about possible sources of conflict within the city?

THE EVIDENCE

Source 1 from James Harvey Robinson, editor and translator, Readings in European History, *vol. 1 (Boston: Ginn, 1904), pp. 409–411.*

1. Ordinance of the Spurriers' [Spurmakers'] Guild of London, 1345

Be it remembered, that on Tuesday, the morrow of St. Peter's bonds, in the nineteenth year of the reign of King Edward III, the articles underwritten were read before John Hammond, mayor, Roger de Depham, recorder, and the other aldermen; and seeing that the same were deemed befitting, they were accepted and enrolled in these words.

In the first place, that no one of the trade of spurriers shall work longer than from the beginning of the day until curfew rings out at the church of St. Sepulcher, without Newgate;[1] by reason that no man can work so neatly by night as by day. And many persons of the said trade, who compass[2] how to practice deception in their work, desire to work by night rather than by day; and then they introduce false iron, and iron that has been cracked, for tin, and also they put gilt on false copper, and cracked.

And further, many of the said trade are wandering about all day, without working at all at their trade; and then, when they have become drunk and frantic, they take to their work, to the annoyance of the sick and all their neighbor-

1. **without Newgate:** just outside the gate to the city called Newgate.
2. **compass:** know.

hood as well, by reason of the broils[3] that arise between them and the strange folk who are dwelling among them. And then they blow up their fires so vigorously, that their forges begin all at once to blaze, to the great peril of themselves and of all the neighborhood around. And then, too, all the neighbors are much in dread of the sparks, which so vigorously issue forth in all directions from the mouths of the chimneys in their forges.

By reason thereof it seems unto them that working by night should be put an end to, in order to avoid such false work and such perils; and therefore the mayor and the aldermen do will, by the assent of the good folk of the said trade and for the common profit, that from henceforth such time for working, and such false work made in the trade, shall be forbidden. And if any person shall be found in the said trade to do the contrary hereof, let him be amerced,[4] the first time in forty pence,[5] one half to go to the use of the Chamber of the Guildhall of London, and the other half to the use of the said trade; the second time, in half a mark;[5] and the third time, in ten shillings,[5] to the use of the same Chamber and trade; and the fourth time, let him forswear the trade forever.

Also, that no one of the said trade shall hang his spurs out on Sundays, or on any other days that are double feasts; but only a sign indicating his business; and such spurs as they shall so sell, they are to show and sell within their shops, without exposing them without or opening the doors or windows of their shops, on the pain aforesaid.

Also, that no one of the said trade shall keep a house or shop to carry on his business, unless he is free of the city;[6] and that no one shall cause to be sold, or exposed for sale, any manner of old spurs for new ones, or shall garnish them or change them for new ones.

Also, that no one of the said trade shall take an apprentice for a less term than seven years, and such apprentice shall be enrolled according to the usages of the said city.

Also, that if any one of the said trade, who is not a freeman, shall take an apprentice for a term of years, he shall be amerced as aforesaid.

Also, that no one of the said trade shall receive the apprentice, serving man, or journeyman of another in the same trade, during the term agreed upon between his master and him, on the pain aforesaid.

Also, that no alien of another country, or foreigner of this country, shall follow or use the said trade, unless he is enfranchised before the mayor, aldermen, and chamberlain; and that, by witness and surety[7] of the good folk of the said trade, who will go surety for him, as to his loyalty and his good behavior.

3. **broil:** fight.
4. **amerced:** fined.
5. **pence:** small silver coins; 12 pence = 1 shilling; 160 pence = 1 mark.
6. **free of the city:** a citizen.
7. **surety:** guarantee.

Also, that no one of the said trade shall work on Saturdays, after *nones*[8] has been rung out in the city; and not from that hour until the Monday morning following.

Source 2 from Edward P. Cheney, editor and translator, Translations and Reprints from the Original Sources of European History, *vol. 2, no. 1 (Philadelphia: University of Pennsylvania Press, no date), pp. 23–25.*

2. Ordinance of the White-Tawyers'[9] Guild of London, 1346

In honor of God, of Our Lady, and of All Saints, and for the nurture of tranquillity and peace among the good folks the megucers, called white-tawyers, the folks of the same trade have, by assent of Richard Lacer, mayor, and of the aldermen, ordained the points under-written.

In the first place, they have ordained that they will find a wax candle, to burn before our Lady in the church of Allhallows, near London wall.

Also, that each person of the said trade shall put in the box such sum as he shall think fit, in aid of maintaining the said candle.

Also, if by chance any one of the said trade shall fall into poverty, whether through old age or because he cannot labor or work, and have nothing with which to keep himself, he shall have every week from the said box 7d. for his support, if he be a man of good repute. And after his decease, if he have a wife, a woman of good repute, she shall have weekly for her support 7d. from the said box, so long as she shall behave herself well and keep single.

And that no stranger shall work in the said trade, or keep house for the same in the city, if he be not an apprentice, or a man admitted to the franchise of the said city.

And that no one shall take the serving-man of another to work with him, during his term, unless it be with the permission of his master.

And if any one of the said trade shall have work in his house that he cannot complete, or if for want of assistance such work shall be in danger of being lost, those of the said trade shall aid him, that so the said work be not lost.

And if any one of the said trade shall depart this life, and have not wherewithal to be buried, he shall be buried at the expense of their common box. And when any one of the said trade shall die, all those of the said trade shall go to the vigil, and make offering on the morrow.

8. **nones:** about 3 P.M.

9. **white-tawyer:** a person who dressed leather with salt, alum, and other substances, giving it a white surface.

And if any serving-man shall conduct himself in any other manner than properly towards his master, and act rebelliously toward him, no one of the said trade shall set him to work, until he shall have made amends before the mayor and aldermen; and before them such misprision[10] shall be redressed.

Also,—that the good folks of the same trade shall once in the year be assembled in a certain place, convenient thereto, there to choose two men of the most loyal and benefitting of the same trade, to be overseers of work and all other things touching the trade for that year; which persons shall be presented to the mayor and aldermen for the time being, and sworn before them diligently to inquire and make search, and loyally to present to the said mayor and aldermen such defaults as they shall find touching the said trade without sparing anyone for friendship or for hatred, or in any other manner. And if any one of the said trade shall be found rebellious against the said overseers, so as not to let them properly make their search and assay, as they ought to do; or if he shall absent himself from the meeting aforesaid, without reasonable cause, after due warning by the said overseers, he shall pay to the Chamber, upon the first default, 40d.; and on the second like default, half a mark; and on the third one mark; and on the fourth, 20s., and shall forswear the trade forever.

Also, that if the overseers shall be found lax and negligent about their duty, or partial to any person for gift or for friendship, maintaining him or voluntarily permitting him to continue in his default, and shall not present him to the mayor and aldermen, as before stated, they are to incur the penalty foresaid.

Also, that each year, at such assemblies of the good folks of the said trade, there shall be chosen overseers, as before stated, And if it be found that through laxity or negligence of the said governors such assemblies are not held, each of the said overseers is to incur the said penalty.

Also, that all skins falsely and deceitfully wrought in their trade which the said overseers shall find on sale in the hands of any person, citizen or foreigner, within the franchise shall be forfeited to the said chamber, and the worker thereof amerced in manner aforesaid.

Also, that no one who has not been an apprentice, and has not finished his term of apprenticeship in the said trade, shall be made free of the same trade; unless it be attested by the overseers for the time being, or by four persons of the said trade, that such person is able and sufficiently skilled to be made free of the same.

10. **misprision:** misconduct.

Source 3 from Julia O'Faolain and Lauro Martines, editors, Not in God's Image: Women in History from the Greeks to the Victorians *(New York: Harper & Row, 1973), pp. 137–139. Reprinted by permission of HarperCollins Publishers, Inc.*

3. Ordinance of the Silk Spinsters in Paris, 1254–1271

Any woman who wishes to be a silk spinster on large spindles in the city of Paris—i.e., reeling, spinning, doubling and retwisting—may freely do so, provided she observe the following customs and usages of the craft:

No spinster on large spindles may have more than three apprentices, unless they be her own or her husband's children born in true wedlock; nor may she contract with them for an apprenticeship of less than seven years or for a fee of less than 20 Parisian sols[11] to be paid to her, their mistress. The apprenticeship shall be for eight years if there is no fee, but she may accept more years and money if she can get them. . . .

No woman of the said craft may hire an apprentice or workgirl who has not completed her years of service with the mistress to whom she was apprenticed. If a spinster has assumed an apprentice, she may not take on another before the first has completed her seven years unless the apprentice die or forswear the craft forever.[12] If an apprentice spinster buy her freedom before serving the said seven years, she may not herself take on an apprentice until she has practiced the craft for seven years. If any spinster sell her apprentice, she shall owe six deniers to the guardians appointed in the King's name to guard the [standards of the] craft. The buyer shall also owe six deniers. . . .

If a working woman comes from outside Paris and wishes to practice the said craft in the city, she must swear before two guardians of the craft that she will practice it well and loyally and conform to its customs and usages.

If anyone give a woman of the said craft silk to be spun and the woman pawn it and the owner complain, the fine shall be 5 sols.

No workwoman shall farm out another's silk to be worked upon outside her own house.

The said craft has as guardians two men of integrity sworn in the King's name but appointed and changed at the will of the provost of Paris. Taking an oath in the provost's presence, they shall swear to guard the craft truly, loyally, and to their utmost, and to inform him or his agents of all malpractices discovered therein.

11. **sol, denier:** silver coins minted in France. In general, 12 deniers = 1 sol.

12. This appears to conflict with the first sentence in the second paragraph, but can be explained if we understand that **apprentice** in this paragraph is shorthand for **apprentice-spinster,** or what in other guilds would be called **journeyman** (there is no female equivalent in French for journeyman). Thus a girl would be an apprentice for seven or eight years (as stated in the second paragraph), an apprentice-spinster for another seven years, and finally a spinster.

Any spinster who shall infringe any of the above rules shall pay the King a fine of 5 sols for each offense . . . [from which the craft guardians deduct their own expenses].

Source 4 from Merry E. Wiesner, translator, unpublished ordinance in Memmingen Stadtarchiv, Zünfte, 471–1.

4. Tailors' Ordinance from Memmingen (Germany), 1543

Concerning seamstresses: All seamstresses who are not citizens here are to be sent away and forbidden to do any work as seamstresses in this city.

For those who are citizens, it is ordered that no one shall serve an apprenticeship of less than one year, and after this a period as a journeyman for at least one year, before she is allowed to become a master. She is also never to do anything which is limited to members of the tailors' or furriers' guild, and is to pay the guild five shillings [when she is taken on as a master]. She is to obey all regulations and ordinances. A woman who wants to become master is to appear before the sworn overseers,[13] who will test her on what she knows and explain the ordinances, which she will be expected to follow from that point on.

Those who do not follow the above regulations on one or more points are to be appropriately corrected and punished by the sworn overseers.

Sources 5 through 8 from Merry E. Wiesner, translator, unpublished ordinances in Nuremberg Stadtarchiv, Quellen zur Nürnbergische Geschichte, Rep. F5, no. 68/II, fol. 663; no. 68/I, fol. 441; no. 68/I, fol. 29; no. 68/I, fol. 115.

5. Ringmakers' Guild Ordinance, Nuremberg (Germany), 16th century

No one is to make use of any domestic servant to do any work in this craft from now on. This includes any and all work or assistance, with a fine of four pounds for each infraction.

Some journeymen are now marrying before they become masters, and using their wives to assist them in the craft, which has led to disputes. Therefore this ordinance is expanded: Because it is forbidden for female domestic servants to do anything associated with the craft, those women whose husbands are not yet

13. **overseer:** official in charge of the guild, who swore an oath to enforce its rules.

masters are also forbidden to work. Masters' daughters who are not yet married are allowed to work for their fathers as long as they live in their fathers' household, but those who have hired themselves out to another master as a maid can only do the work of a domestic servant, and nothing in the craft.

6. Needlemakers' Guild Ordinance, Nuremberg, 16th century

No master in this craft [needlemakers] is to teach or make use of a female domestic servant in place of a journeyman or apprentice for any type of work, under penalty of one pound per day. They can still teach their own children, however.

7. Ordinance for All Guilds in Nuremberg, 1543

To prevent further errors in regard to apprentices, it is ordered that from now on no widow in any craft is to take on a new apprentice, on the grounds that he will not be able to get a letter of apprenticeship from her as there was never a master in the shop. If, when the master dies, there is already an apprentice in the shop, he can complete his training with the widow.

8. Goldsmiths' Guild Ordinance, Nuremberg, 1535

If, when a goldsmith dies, there is no son who wants to inherit the shop or continue on in the craft, or none who is skilled or old enough to make the masterpiece at that time, his widow will be allowed to continue the shop (if she wants) three years after the death of her husband and no longer, unless she marries someone who is a master goldsmith or who makes his masterpiece during this time. Every widow who is continuing a shop will have to obey all the guild ordinances and bring her work to be inspected, and be liable to the same fines as a master if she breaks any regulations.

Source 9 from Julia O'Faolain and Lauro Martines, Not in God's Image: Women in History from the Greeks to the Victorians *(New York: Harper & Row, 1973), pp. 159–160.*

9. Petition from the Silk Women of London to Parliament, 1455

[Petition from] the silk women and throwsters[14] of the crafts and occupation of silk work within the city of London . . . [hitherto, thanks to the silk industry] many a woman lived full honorably, and therewith many households kept, and many gentlewomen and others in great number like as there now be more than a thousand, have been drawn under them in learning the same crafts and occupation. . . . [But] lately divers Lombards [Italians] and other alien strangers imagining to destroy the same crafts and all such virtuous occupations for women within this land, to the intent to enrich themselves and put such occupations to other lands, bring now daily into this land wrought silk, thrown ribbons, and laces falsely and deceivably wrought, and no silk unwrought, to the great hurt of all such as shall wear or occupy the same and the utter destruction of all the same crafts and occupations: The sufferance whereof hath caused and is like to cause great idleness amongst gentlewomen and other women of worship. . . . In reformation whereof [they ask Parliament to get the King to ban all finished silk from coming into] this land from beyond the sea.

Sources 10 and 11 from Merry E. Wiesner, translator, unpublished supplications in Frankfurt Stadtarchiv, Zünfte, Ugb. C-50, Ss, no. 4; Ugb. C-32, R, no. 1.

10. Widow's Supplication to the Frankfurt City Council, late 16th century

Distinguished and honorable sirs, I, a poor and distressed widow, wish to respectfully report in what manner earlier this year I spun some pounds of yarn, 57 to be exact, for the use of my own household. I wanted to take the yarn to be woven into cloth, but didn't know whom I should give it to so that I could get it worked into cloth the quickest and earliest.

Therefore I was talking to some farm women from Bornheim, who were sell-

14. **throwster:** a woman who twists silk fibers into silk thread.

ing their produce in front of the shoemakers' guild house, and they told me about a weaver that they had in Bornheim who made good cloth and could also make it quickly. I let him know—through the farmers' wives—that I wanted him to make my cloth. I got the yarn together and sent my children to carry it to him; as they were on their way, the weavers here grabbed the yarn forcefully from my children, and took it to their guild house. They said they had ordinances which forbade taking yarn to foreigners to weave, and told me they would not return it unless I paid a fine.

I then went to the lord mayors, asking them about this ordinance that would let people confiscate things without warning from the public streets. They said they didn't know about any such ordinance, and that my yarn should have long been returned to me. I then went to the overseer of the guild, master Adlaff Zimmermann who lives by the Eschenheimer tower, who answered me with rough, harsh words that they would in no way return my yarn to me, and that the guild did have such an ordinance.

Therefore I respectfully request, if they do have such an ordinance, I didn't know anything about it, and so ask you humbly and in God's name to tell the weavers to return my yarn. If, according to this ordinance, I am supposed to pay a fine, they should take it from the yarn, and give the rest back. I ask this of your honorable sirs, as the protectors of widows and orphans, and pray that you will help me.

Your humble servant, Agatha, the widow of the late Conrad Gaingen.

11. Widow's Supplication to the Frankfurt City Council, late 16th century

Most honorable and merciful gentlemen, you certainly know what a heavy and hard cross God has laid on me, and in what a miserable situation I find myself, after the much too early death of my late husband, with my young children, all of them still minors and some still nursing. This unfortunate situation is well known everywhere.

Although in consideration of my misfortune most Christian hearts would have gladly let me continue in my craft and occupation, and allowed me to earn a little piece of bread, instead the overseers of the woolweavers' guild came to me as soon as my husband had died, in my sorrow and even in my own house. Against all Christian charity, they began to order changes in my workshop with very harsh and menacing words. They specifically ordered that my apprentice, whom I had raised and trained at great cost and who had just come to be of use to me in the craft, leave me and go to them, which would be to their great advantage but my greater disadvantage. They ordered this on the pretense that there was no longer a master here so he could not finish his training.

Honorable sirs, I then humbly put myself under the protection of the lord mayors here, and asked that the two journeymen and the apprentice be allowed to continue on in their work as they had before unimpeded until a final judgment was reached in the matter. Despite this, one of the weavers began to shout at my journeymen whenever he saw them, especially if there were other people on the street. In his unhindered and unwarranted boldness, he yelled that my workshop was not honorable, and all journeymen who worked there were thieves and rascals. After doing this for several days, he and several others came into my workshop on a Saturday, and, bitter and jealous, pushed my journeymen out. They began to write to all places where this craft is practiced to tell other masters not to accept anyone who had worked in my workshop.

I now humbly beg you, my honorable and gracious sirs, protect me and my hungry children from such abuse, shame, and insult. Help my journeymen, who were so undeservedly insulted, to regain their honor. I beg you, as the protector of humble widows, to let my apprentice stay with me, as apprentices are allowed to stay in the workshops of widows throughout the entire Holy Roman Empire, as long as there are journeymen, whether or not there is a master present. Protect me from any further insults of the woolweavers' guild, which does nothing to increase the honor of our city, which you, honorable sirs, are charged to uphold. I plead with you to grant me my request, and allow me to continue my workshop.

Sources 12 and 13 from Carolly Erickson, The Records of Medieval Europe *(Garden City, New York: Anchor, 1971), p. 238. Translated by Carolly Erickson.*

12. Judgment Against a Draper[15] in Flanders, mid-14th century

When Jacquemars des Mares, a draper, brought one of his cloths to the great cloth hall of Arras and sold it, the aforesaid cloth was examined by the *espincheurs*[16] as is customary, and at the time they had it weighed, it was half a pound over the legal weight. Then, because of certain suspicions which arose, they had the cloth dried, and when it was dry, it weighed a half pound less than the legal weight. The *espincheur* brought the misdeed to the attention of the Twenty;[17] Jacquemars was fined 100 shillings.

15. **draper:** a person who made woolen cloth.
16. **espincheur:** cloth inspector.
17. **Twenty:** court of twenty men, made up of members of the city council.

13. Dispute Between Master Fullers[18] and Their Apprentices in Flanders, 1345

A point of discussion was mooted between the apprentice fullers on the one hand, and the master fullers on the other. The apprentices held that, as they laid out in a letter, no one could have work done in his house without taking apprentices. . . . For they complained of fulling masters who had their children work in their houses, without standing [for jobs] in the public square like the other apprentices, and they begged that their letter be answered. The fulling masters stated certain arguments to the contrary. The aldermen sent for both parties and for the Twenty also and asked the masters if indeed they kept their children as apprentices; each master said he did. It was declared by the aldermen that every apprentice must remain in the public square, as reason demanded.

Done in the year of 1344 [1345], in the month of February, and through a full sitting of the aldermen.

Sources 14 and 15 from Merry E. Wiesner, translator, unpublished decisions in Nuremberg Stadtarchiv, Quellen zur Nürnbergische Geschichte, Rep. F5, no. 68/I, fol.58 (1577); fol. 99 (1581).

14. Decision by the Nuremberg City Council, 1577

The honorable city council has decided to deny the request of Barbara Hansmesser that she be allowed to dye wool because the blanketweavers' guild has so adamantly opposed it. Because her husband is not a citizen, they are both ordered to get out of the city and find work in some other place, with the warning that if they are found in the vicinity of this city, and are doing any work here, work will be taken from them and the yarn cut to pieces. They can count on this.

15. Decision by the Nuremberg City Council, 1581

Anna Pentzin, a widow and citizen, is to be allowed to make tin boxes as she has requested, despite the objections of the tinsmiths' guild, until she has remarried or has begun to earn her living in another way. Regarding her children: she is not to have her son help her in any way, but her daughter can help her occasionally. Once her mother marries, or they move apart from each other, the daughter is not to have anything more to do with the craft of tinsmithing.

18. **fuller:** a person who beat finished cloth with sticks in order to clean and thicken it.

QUESTIONS TO CONSIDER

The records you have read have shed some light on a wide variety of issues in the medieval city. Along with learning about the guilds themselves, you have also found out about economic development, political conflicts, urban social structure, and family relationships. To draw some general conclusions and answer the questions for this chapter, you will need to divide the information from your sources according to these topical categories. This is exactly what historians who use such records do, especially if they are interested in more general questions such as economic or social change and are using guild records as only one of their sources. Investigating specific historical issues involves not only uncovering sources that deal with your problem directly but also extracting small bits of information from sources that cover a great many other areas. This is especially the case in the area of social change, for the effects of such changes can often be detected in many different facets of everyday life.

The easiest way to approach broad historical questions is by starting with the narrowest and most specific category of information, in this case material about the guilds themselves. Looking at your list, which problems were solely internal guild affairs? How did the guilds enforce their solutions to these problems? What impact did their solutions have on people who were not members of the guild? How did the guild regulate relations between master, journeymen, and apprentices? What noneconomic functions of the guild were regarded as important and worthy of regulating?

Now move to more general economic issues. What changes did the guilds regard as threatening? What actions did they take to deal with these threats? Do their actions and fears seem justified in all cases? Political conflicts were very often combined with these economic concerns, as we would expect in societies like these, in which the two areas are so closely linked. How would you describe the relations between the guilds and the city councils? How did individuals use the town's political conflicts to their own advantage? (The best examples here are the supplications: To whom did individuals turn for help, and why? What sort of language did they use to persuade authorities to help them?) The guild records provide information about not only internal city politics but external affairs as well. What was the general attitude toward foreigners, whom people in the Middle Ages regarded as anyone who did not live in their own town?

Next, turn to issues of social change and social structure. How would you describe the relations between masters and servants after reading these sources? How would you characterize the atmosphere in most shops—collegial and friendly or divided and somewhat hostile? What about relations between men and women in the shops? How were these relations affected by whether the man was a master or a journeyman, and the woman a widow or a domestic servant? What was the attitude of the political authorities toward women working within the guild structure? What was the attitude of the guilds toward elderly or suffering workers? Do you see changes over time?

As you have no doubt noticed, guilds did not regulate simply individual workers, but regulated their families as well. What special privileges were given to members of the master's family? Who objected to these privileges, and why? What measures did the guilds take in regard to the wives and children of other workers? How did the guilds treat widows of their members? Would you regard the guilds as helpful to families generally or only to certain types of families?

You are now ready to suggest some answers to the questions posed by this chapter: What economic and social changes did medieval guilds consider to be problems? What solutions did they propose? How did their attitudes toward men and women of different social classes shape their solutions? How did guild actions both reflect and affect the political structure of medieval cities?

EPILOGUE

Despite frequent conflicts with city councils and other political authorities, the craft guilds of most European cities were able to maintain their monopoly on production throughout the sixteenth century. Though in the short run this was beneficial to the guild masters, in the long run the restrictions imposed by the guilds contributed to economic and social problems that eventually worked to the detriment of both the guilds and the cities.

Limitations on workshop size and hours of production as well as strict regulations on product quality prevented individuals from experimenting with new and faster processes that required more workers or that produced lower-quality and therefore cheaper goods. Prohibitions against the use of machinery saved skilled jobs but also kept guild shops from expanding their output or making their products cheaper. Restrictions on the number of workshops not only led to conflicts between masters and journeymen, but also increased the number of people in the cities who had no opportunity to enter the guild system at all and who therefore had no sympathy with the aims of the guild masters. City councils recognized that these people needed employment and that their employment would have to come from outside the guild system.

To escape guild restrictions, people who wanted to make products on a larger scale than the guilds would set up workshops in the country or in small villages, often hiring many households with each household performing only one step of the process. This production process is called *cottage industry* or the *putting-out system,* and by the fifteenth and sixteenth centuries it was in open competition with urban guild production in some areas, especially the manufacture of cloth. These new industries could produce goods much more inexpensively than the guilds, and those who set them up were able to persuade cities to allow their cheaper products to be sold, a practice that undercut local guild production. Some city councils also recognized that these new industries could provide jobs for the increasingly large portion of the urban population that could not be absorbed into the guild system. They took away guild monopolies on production and allowed new industries to be established within the cities themselves, so that part of the late medieval urban economy also came to be organized as a putting-out system.

Though most guilds fought this trend, more enterprising or wealthier masters recognized the benefits of the putting-out system and began to hire other households to work for them, promoting a greater division within the guild between wealthier masters and the poorer masters and journeymen they hired. Some masters became so wealthy that they no longer had to work in a shop themselves, nor did their wives and family members.

The individuals who established these new industries invested their money in the same way the merchants and traders we examined in Chapter 6 did, so these cottage industries are also regarded as capitalist. Economic historians see capitalism in the West as developing through several stages. In the first stage, *mercantile capitalism,* capital was primarily invested in trade and commerce. In the second stage, investors put their money into production as well as trade; this period, beginning with the putting-out system, is often termed *proto-industrial capitalism.* Whereas the master craftsman in guild shops both worked with and owned the tools and raw materials, the investor in capitalist production did not perform any of the actual labor himself but simply provided the raw materials—and, in some cases, the tools—and paid households for their work. This division between labor and investment is seen, particularly by labor historians, as the hallmark of proto-industrial capitalism. During the eighteenth century, capitalism entered a third stage, known as *industrial capitalism,* in which workers were gathered in factories instead of working in their own homes and were paid as individuals rather than as families. By this time work and family were increasingly separated in a way they had not been in proto-industrial capitalism.

The rise of capitalist production did not bring an immediate end to the guilds, however. Guilds were still to be found in some industries and in some parts of Europe as late as the nineteenth century, though their power was much less than it had been in the Middle Ages. The political function of guilds was largely assumed by the new centralized states, which also regulated the economy. Their social functions, such as educating young people and caring for the elderly, were taken over by the schools and the relief agencies set up by the national governments. The guilds' decline in power paralleled that of the cities, which largely enjoyed independence in many parts of Europe during the Middle Ages but by the seventeenth century were controlled by larger regional governments or by dynastic states.

CHAPTER ELEVEN

LAY PIETY AND HERESY IN THE LATE MIDDLE AGES

THE PROBLEM

During the late Middle Ages, the Christian church went through a period of turmoil and disunity, with corruption and abuse evident at all levels of its hierarchy. Though the Church was officially an independent institution, many of its officials, such as bishops and archbishops, were actually chosen by secular nobles and rulers, who picked their own relatives or others who would do as they were told. Officials who were elected or appointed from within the Church itself were often selected for their administrative and legal skills, not for their piety, high moral standards, or religious devotion. These problems extended all the way to the papacy, which for much of the fourteenth century was located not in Rome but in Avignon in southern France, where it was dominated by the French monarchy. During this time the papacy lost its stature as an international power and had difficulty raising revenue from many parts of Europe, especially from the English, who rightly suspected that money sent to the pope might end up in the coffers of the French king, with whom they were at war. The Avignon popes had ever-increasing needs for revenue because they had to hire mercenaries to keep the Papal States in Italy under control, build palaces and churches in Avignon that reflected the power and prestige of the papacy, and pay the salaries of a growing corps of lawyers and bureaucrats who administered the papal empire.

The papacy devised a number of ways to meet its increasing need for money. Though the outright selling of Church offices, termed *simony,* was strictly forbidden, the popes required all candidates to pay for the privilege of taking over a vacant office, then hand over a large share of their first year's revenues directly to the papacy. Official prohibitions, such as those against priests having concubines or giving Church land to family members, could be ignored if the cleric paid the pope for a special dispensation. The papacy also collected money directly from laypeople, charging fees for clerical services such as marriage or baptism and for dispensations that legitimized children born out of wedlock.

The most lucrative source of income for the papacy proved to be the granting of *indulgences.* Indulgences were based on three doctrines developed by the medieval Church—the sacrament of penance, the concept of Purgatory, and the Treasury of Merit. To partake of the sacrament of penance, a believer was to confess all sins to a priest and be truly sorry, or contrite, for them, after which the priest absolved the believer, often requiring him or her to carry out certain acts as penance for these sins, such as saying prayers or going on pilgrimages. According to Church doctrine, penance did not end with death but might be extended into Purgatory, where Christians spent time atoning for the sins for which they had not done earthly penance. Only after a set time in Purgatory could most Christians be admitted to heaven. (Those who were going to hell, on the other hand, went directly there.)

Along with the doctrines of penance and Purgatory, the Church also developed the idea of the Treasury of Merit. This treasury was seen as a collection of all the superlative good deeds and meritorious acts that the apostles, saints, and other good people had done during their lives, which the pope as head of the Church could dispense as he wished through the granting of indulgences. The recipient of an indulgence received a share in the Treasury of Merit that took the place of having to do individual penance. Originally granted to people who performed special services for the Church, such as participating in crusades, indulgences gradually came to be exchanged for cash contributions. Though official theology taught that priestly absolution and true contrition were still necessary, unscrupulous indulgence peddlers often sold indulgences outright as easy substitutes for penance. Indulgences also began to be granted to relieve people of time in Purgatory and even to allow believers to shorten deceased relatives' time in Purgatory. To many people, it seemed that the Church was teaching that one could buy one's way into heaven, though this was not actually so.

Because Church officials at all levels were often chosen for their family connections or their legal and financial skills, they also bent official doctrines and saw their posts primarily in terms of income rather than spiritual duties. Bishops spent much of their time at the papal court trying to win the pope's favor and squeezed all possible revenues out of their dioceses in order to pay for their offices. These absentee officials, who left the affairs of the diocese in the hands of substitutes, often had very little idea about the needs or problems of their territory. Those who were successful in gaining papal backing might be appointed to many different offices simultaneously; they collected the income from all their posts, appointed badly paid proxies to carry out their duties, and might actually never even visit the diocese over which they were bishop.

With so little supervision, parish priests and monks were sometimes lax in their standards of morality and spiritual observance. Frequently parish priests were poor and badly educated, for most of the Church's wealth stayed in the hands of higher officials, who provided no opportunity for priests to gain an education; some priests did not even know Latin, but simply recited the Mass by rote without understanding what they were saying. During the week they farmed just as their parishioners did, for the income from tithes was not sufficient to support them. Some of the monasteries and convents maintained high standards, but others, caught in the squeeze for revenue, admitted any applicant who would pay the entrance fee, without determining if the person was fit for the monastic life.

With the Church embroiled in these problems, we might expect that people would turn away from religion to concentrate on other aspects of life, but this was not the case. Religion continued to dominate the lives of people in the late Middle Ages, which was in fact perhaps the most religious period in all of European history. What did change, however, was how people expressed and experienced their Christian faith. Not surprisingly, they turned away somewhat from the institutional Church and sought more direct paths to God through individual actions.

Much of this lay piety was supported by the Church hierarchy because it did not question basic theological doctrines such as life after death; the importance of the sacraments of baptism, communion, and penance; the honor owed to saints and their relics; and the right of the pope to grant indulgences, collect taxes, and determine correct doctrine. Pious laypeople also made frequent donations, which swelled the Church's revenue. Some individuals and groups went beyond personal piety, however, to question the Church's wealth and many of its central doctrines. The Church declared such people heretics and set up inquisitorial courts to investigate, try, and condemn them.

Your task in this chapter will be to examine late medieval lay piety and religious practices, both those approved by the institutional Church and those condemned as heresy. How did common people in the Middle Ages experience and express their religious faith? How did the Church as an institution respond to laypeople's ideas and actions?

SOURCES AND METHOD

Medieval Christianity, multifaceted in nature, may be explored from a number of angles. Christianity was a faith shared by most people living in Europe, whether they were highly educated or uneducated, wealthy or poor. We can find information about how educated men understood and interpreted Christianity fairly easily by reading theological treatises and official Church decisions, but these may not accurately reflect the religious views of the majority. For this perspective, we must turn to a much smaller group of sources that throw light on the religious beliefs of the common people.

Learning about and reconstructing the ideas of common people in the premodern period is extremely difficult, for such people were by and large illiterate. The surviving written records of their thoughts and actions thus all come through the filter of literate observers, whose perspective on and understanding of events might differ radically from the participants'. This is especially a problem when we are examining religious ideas, for in the Middle Ages most people who could read and write were clerics and thus part of the institutional Church. It was often hard for such observers to be objective about criticism directed against the Church, or even to comprehend how uneducated people interpreted and understood theological concepts.

Because of these problems, we must ask several questions about any written source concerning popular religious belief. Who actually wrote the document? Was the writer recording the words of an illiterate person or simply describing actions he or she had observed? Why was the piece written? If the writer is recording the words of someone else, did he or she clearly understand the language being spoken, or might there be some problems because of dialect? Is the writer translating a vernacular language such as English or French into Latin, and so possibly mistranslating religious ideas? Why were this person's thoughts recorded—did that person wish it or did the authorities, as was the case with trial records?

Artistic evidence might seem more direct, for people who could not read or write sculpted, painted, and made stained-glass windows. They did not always choose their own subject matter or sign their works, however, so medieval art does not directly express the individual personality and concerns of the artist in the way that modern art does. What it does reveal, however, is how common people learned about religion from windows and statues depicting biblical and other Christian scenes. We can also use frequently recurring images as a rough guide to popular religious sentiments, for individuals and groups commissioned art that reflected their own concerns. The dominance of certain images shifted throughout the Middle Ages as people's attitudes toward the Church and the right way to approach God changed.

Using artistic evidence as a source of information about popular belief requires a different set of initial questions from those needed for written evidence. Where and when was the piece probably made? Can we learn anything about the artist or patron, such as his or her identity? Where was the piece originally displayed? Are the materials simple enough that the piece could have been ordered or purchased by someone who was not wealthy? Is the image common or unusual?

Keeping in mind the limitations we have noted, turn now to the written sources. The first two are *sermon stories,* tales of miracles that learned preachers used in their public sermons; later they were collected by many different preachers and used widely in sermons all over Europe. These stories are consequently written not *by* laypeople but *for* them and reflect official Church doctrines. They do not present sophisticated theology, however, but show us how common people learned about Christianity. As you read, note the kinds of people who appear as main characters. Why would preachers use characters like these?

In the first sermon, to whom does the woman turn for assistance? When her prayers are not answered immediately, what does she do? Why would the preacher condone such a dramatic action? (To answer this question, think about the impact this story would have on the female members of the audience; Mary may not have responded instantly to prayer, but, like most mothers, she did so immediately once her child was taken from her.) What qualities of Mary does this story emphasize?

The second sermon discusses an important element in lay piety, the belief in saints and relics. Does the author support or condemn these beliefs? Is it the relics themselves or faith in them that is important? Why would the author, himself a priest, describe the priest in the story as "wily" and "wicked"? (Again, keep in mind the audience. Given the problems most people recognized in the Church, how would a lay audience respond to a story in which the hero is also a layperson?)

Though most laypeople in the Middle Ages could not read, some of them could, and one of the most popular types of reading material was stories about the lives of saints, termed *hagiography.* Like sermon stories, hagiography often presented quite ordinary people whose lives were touched by God and who could serve as an inspiration. Source 3 comes from the best-known collection of saints' lives, *The Golden Legend,* first composed in the late thirteenth century by an Italian bishop, and then translated and recopied throughout Europe during the late Middle Ages. It describes events from the life of St. Nicholas (the original Santa Claus) and miracles attributed to him after his death; these would have been familiar even to those who could not read because they would have heard this story from those who could. What type of people does Nicholas assist? What sort of problems does he solve for them?

Taking these three sources together, what types of actions do you think preachers and writers of hagiography were trying to encourage in people? What traits of lay piety did they praise?

The remaining written sources directly record the thoughts and actions of laypeople, some of whom the Church supported and some of whom it condemned. None of these people could read or write Latin, and so they qualified as unlearned by medieval standards, though some could read their own vernacular language. Source 4 is taken from the *Revelations* of Bridget of Sweden, a noblewoman who lived from 1303 to 1373. After her husband's death, Bridget traveled to Rome, where she began to see visions and give advice based on these visions to both laypeople and Church officials. Because she could not speak Latin, she wrote or dictated her visions in Swedish; these were later translated by her confessors and eventually were published in Latin. At the end of her life, Bridget made a pilgrimage to Jerusalem, where she had the visions reprinted here. How would you describe these visions? How did the fact that she was a woman shape her religious experience?

Source 5 is drawn from the first autobiography ever written in English, that of Margery Kempe, who was probably born in 1373, the same year Bridget died. Kempe, a middle-class woman from the town of King's Lynn, was illiterate in English as well as Latin. Although she was married and had fourteen children, she began to see visions in which Christ demanded that she set herself apart from most women. At the end of her most unusual life, she dictated her autobiography to several male scribes, who wrote it down in English. As you read, note how Kempe describes her actions and behavior. What made her most open to criticism? How does she defend her actions? She refers to herself, always in the third person, as "this creature." What does this practice indicate about her self-consciousness? Do her actions reflect this self-image? What aspects of Christianity most inspire or disturb her? How was the official reaction to her influenced by the fact that she was a woman?

The last two written sources come from trial records. Source 6 contains six testimonies from the Inquisition carried out between 1318 and 1325 by Jacques Fournier, bishop of Pamiers in southern France. All six accused were illiterate peasants who spoke Occitan, a regional dialect; their words were translated into Latin by scribes. Fournier launched the Inquisition because he suspected that large numbers of people in his district were *Albigensians* (also called Cathars), followers of a heretical movement that rejected many basic Church doctrines. Albigensians regarded the material world as evil and not made by God and did not believe in the possibility of eternal life. They denied the power of many Church ceremonies and rituals and urged that any Church leader, including the pope, should not be obeyed if he did not live up to rigorous moral standards.

As you read the testimonies, note which specific Christian beliefs were being challenged. Given their statements, would you call the peasants who were being questioned Christians? How might problems of translation have affected the records? How might the fact that this was a trial have affected what the individuals said?

Source 7 comes from a heresy trial of sixty people suspected of Lollard beliefs, conducted in the diocese of Norwich, England, between 1428 and 1431. Lollards followed the ideas of John Wyclif, an English scholar who lived in the fourteenth century; the selection itself presents all of the basic Lollard beliefs. Most of the trial record is in Latin because the trial was conducted by ecclesiastical authorities and recorded by clerics, but a few of the confessions were written down in English. The selection here is one of those, with the spelling modernized. What does the accused admit to having believed? The list of unacceptable beliefs in many heresy trials reflects not only the ideas of the person confessing but also those that the inquisitors thought were especially dangerous and in need of suppression. What did the inquisitors in this case appear particularly concerned about? How would this emphasis have shaped the confession? How was the accused to prove he had given up his heresy? Given his beliefs, would you call the person under questioning a Christian?

Now examine the two visual sources. Both are wooden statues carved in the fourteenth or fifteenth century by unknown artists and originally placed in churches in southern Germany. They are examples of the two most common religious images of the late Middle Ages. What aspects of popular belief that you have identified from the written sources do they reflect? Mary is shown wearing a crown and holding an orb, a sphere representing the world that normally was carried by monarchs. What qualities are emphasized through this depiction? Christ is shown in a dramatic pose of suffering. What does this attitude emphasize about his nature? Given what you now know about how common people understood Christianity, why would these two subjects be the most popular? Why do you think there is no depiction of God the Father?

THE EVIDENCE

Source 1 from C. C. S. Bland, editor and translator, Miracles of the Blessed Virgin Mary *(London: Routledge, 1928), p. 118.*

1. A Sermon Story About the Virgin Mary, 13th century

A certain woman of simple and upright life used to worship the Holy Mary, Mother of God, often strewing flowers and herbs before her image.

Now it chanced that the woman's only son was taken prisoner. And the mother weeping for him would not be comforted, and prayed with all her heart to the Blessed Virgin Mary for her son's deliverance. But seeing it was all in vain, she entered the church and thus addressed the image of the Blessed Virgin, "O Blessed Virgin Mary, often have I asked thee for the deliverance of my son and thou hast not heard me. Therefore, as my son was taken from me, so will I take away thine and will put him in durance as hostage for mine."

And taking the image of the Child from the bosom of Mary, she went home, wrapped him up in a clean cloth, and shut him up carefully in a chest. And, behold, the following night the Blessed Mary appeared to the captive youth bidding him to go forth and said to him: "Tell your mother to give me my Son." And he coming to his mother, described how he had been set free. But she with great rejoicing carried back the image of Jesus to Mary and gave her thanks.

Source 2 from Dana Carleton Munro, editor and translator, Translations and Reprints from the Original Sources of European History, *vol. 2, no. 4 (Philadelphia: University of Pennsylvania Press, no date), p. 14.*

2. A Sermon Story About Relics, 13th century

A certain knight loved most ardently the above-mentioned martyr, St. Thomas of Canterbury,[1] and sought everywhere to obtain some relic of him. When a certain wily priest, in whose house he was staying, heard of this he said to him, "I have by me a bridle which St. Thomas used for a long time, and I have often experienced its virtues." When the knight heard this, and believed it, he joyfully paid the priest the money which the latter demanded and received the bridle with great devotion.

God truly, to whom nothing is impossible, wishing to reward the faith of the knight and for the honor of his martyr, deigned to work many miracles through the same bridle. The knight seeing this founded a church in honor of the martyr and in it he placed as a relic the bridle of that most wicked priest.

Source 3 from Iacobus de Voragine, The Golden Legend, *included in* Lives of the Saints, *translated by William Caxton and selected and edited by George V. O'Neill, S.J. (Cambridge: Cambridge University Press, 1914), pp. 62–71.*

3. Extracts from the Life of St. Nicholas, *The Golden Legend,* ca 1270

Nicholas, citizen of the city of Patras, was born of rich and holy kin, and his father was Epiphanes and his mother Johane. In his young age he eschewed the plays and japes[2] of other young children. He used and haunted gladly holy Church; and all that he might understand of holy Scripture he executed it in deed and work after his power. And when his father and mother were departed out of this life, he began to think how he might distribute his riches, and not to the praising of the world but to the honor and glory of God. And it was so that one, his neighbor, had then three daughters, virgins, and he was a nobleman: but for the poverty of them together, they were constrained and in very purpose to abandon them to sin. And when the holy man Nicholas knew hereof he had

1. **St. Thomas of Canterbury:** Thomas Becket, the Archbishop of Canterbury who was murdered on the steps of the cathedral on the orders of Henry II for opposing the king's wishes. He was quickly made a saint, and Canterbury became the most popular pilgrimage site in England.
2. **japes:** toys.

great horror of this, and threw by night secretly into the house of the man a mass of gold wrapped in a cloth. And when the man arose in the morning, he found this mass of gold, and rendered to God therefor great thankings, and therewith he married his oldest daughter. And a little while after this holy servant of God threw in another mass of gold; which the man found, and thanked God, and purposed to wake for to know him that so had aided him in his poverty. And after a few days Nicholas doubled the mass of gold, and cast it into the house of this man. He awoke by the sound of the gold, and followed Nicholas, which fled from him, and he said to him: "Sir, flee not away so but that I may see and know thee." Then he ran after him more hastily, and knew that it was Nicholas; and anon he kneeled down, and would have kissed his feet, but the holy man would not, but required him not to tell nor discover this thing as long as he lived.

It is read in a chronicle that the blessed Nicholas was at the Council of Nice; and on a day, as a ship with mariners were in perishing on the sea, they prayed and required devoutly Nicholas, servant of God, saying: "If those things that we have heard of thee said to be true, prove them now." And anon a man appeared in his likeness, and said: "Lo! see ye me not? ye called me"; and then he began to help them in their exploit of the sea, and anon the tempest ceased. And when they were come to his church, they knew him without any man to show him to them, and yet they had never seen him. And then they thanked God and him of their deliverance. And he bade them to attribute it to the mercy of God and to their belief, and nothing to his merits.

It was so on a time that all the province of S. Nicholas suffered great famine, in such wise that vitaille[3] failed. And then this holy man heard say that certain ships laden with wheat were arrived in the haven. And anon he went thither and prayed the mariners that they would succor the perished at least with an hundred muyes of wheat of every ship. And they said: "Father, we dare not, for it is meted and measured, and we must give reckoning thereof in the garners[4] of the emperor in Alexandria." And the holy man said to them: "Do this that I have said to you, and I promise, in the truth of God, that it shall not be lessed or minished when ye shall come to the garners." And when they had delivered so much out of every ship, they came into Alexandria and delivered the measure that they had received. And then they recounted the miracle to the ministers of the emperor, and worshipped and praised strongly God and his servant Nicholas. Then this holy man distributed the wheat to every man after that he had need, in such wise that it sufficed for two years, not only for to sell but also to sow. . . .

And when it pleased Our Lord to have him depart out this world, he prayed Our Lord that he would send him his angels; and inclining his head he saw the

3. **vitaille:** food.

4. **garners:** storehouses for grain.

angels come to him, whereby he knew well that he should depart, and began this holy Psalm: "In te domine speravi," unto "in manus tuas," and so saying: "Lord, into thine hands I commend my spirit," he rendered up his soul and died, the year of Our Lord three hundred and forty-three. . . .

There was a Jew that saw the virtuous miracles of S. Nicholas, and did do make an image of the saint, and set it in his house, and commanded him that he should keep well his house when he went out, and that he should keep well all his goods, saying to him: "Nicholas, lo! here be all my goods, I charge thee to keep them, and if thou keep them not well, I shall avenge me on thee in beating and tormenting thee." And on a time, when the Jew was out, thieves came and robbed all his goods, and left unborne away only the image. And when the Jew came home he found him robbed of all his goods. He areasoned the image, saying these words: "Sir Nicholas, I had set you in my house for to keep my goods from thieves, wherefore have ye not kept them? Ye shall receive sorrow and torments, and shall have pain for the thieves. I shall avenge my loss and refrain my woodness in beating thee." And then took the Jew the image, and beat it, and tormented it cruelly. Then happed a great marvel, for when the thieves departed the goods, the holy saint, like as he had been in his array, appeared to the thieves, and said to them: "Wherefore have I been beaten so cruelly for you and have so many torments? See how my body is hewed and broken; see how that the red blood runneth down by my body; go ye fast and restore it again, or else the ire of God Almighty shall make you as to be one out of his wit, and that all men shall know your felony, and that each of you shall be hanged." And they said: "Who art thou that sayest to us such things?" And he said to them: "I am Nicholas the servant of Jesu Christ, whom the Jew hath so cruelly beaten for his goods that ye bare away." Then they were afeared, and came to the Jew, and heard what he had done to the image, and they told him the miracle, and delivered to him again all his goods. And thus came the thieves to the way of truth, and the Jew to the way of Jesu Christ.

A man, for the love of his son, that went to school for to learn, hallowed,[5] every year, the feast of S. Nicholas much solemnly. On a time it happed that the father had to make ready the dinner, and called many clerks to this dinner. And the devil came to the gate in the habit of a pilgrim for to demand alms; and the father anon commanded his son that he should give alms to the pilgrim. He followed him as he went for to give to him alms, and when he came to the quarfox[6] the devil caught the child and strangled him. And when the father heard this he sorrowed much strongly and wept, and bare the body into his chamber, and began to cry for sorrow, and say: "Bright sweet son, how is it with thee? S. Nicholas, is this the guerdon[7] that ye have done to me because I have so long

5. **hallowed:** honored.

6. **quarfox:** crossroads.

7. **guerdon:** reward.

served you?" And as he said these words, and other semblable,[8] the child opened his eyes, and awoke like as he had been asleep, and arose up tofore all, and was raised from death to life.

Source 4 from Katharina M. Wilson, editor, Medieval Women Writers *(Athens: University of Georgia Press, 1984), p. 245. Selection translated by Barbara Obrist.*

4. Two Visions of Bridget of Sweden, 1370s

After this the Virgin Mary appeared again to me, in the same place, and said: it has been a long time since in Rome I promised you that I would show you here in Bethlehem how my offspring had been born. And although in Naples I showed you something of it, that is to say the way I was standing when I gave birth to my son, you still should know for sure that I stood and gave birth such as you have seen it now—my knees were bent and I was alone in the stable, praying; I gave birth to him with such exultation and joy of my soul that I had no difficulties when he got out of my body or any pain. Then I wrapped him in swaddling clothes that I had prepared long ago. When Joseph saw this he was astonished and full of joy and happiness, because I had given birth without any help.

At the same place where the Virgin Mary and Joseph were adoring the boy in the cradle, I also saw the shepherds, who had been watching their flocks, coming so that they could look at the child and adore it. When they saw the child, they first wanted to find out whether it was a male or a female, for angels had announced to them that the savior of the world had been born, and they had not said that it was a savioress. Then the Virgin Mary showed to them the nature and the male sex of the child. At once they adored him with great awe and joy. Afterward they returned, praising and glorifying God for all they had heard and seen.

Source 5 from W. Butler-Bowdon, editor, The Book of Margery Kempe *(London: Oxford University Press, 1936), pp. 41–42, 86–88, 161–165, 167–168. Reprinted by permission of Oxford University Press.*

5. From the Autobiography of Margery Kempe, ca 1430

This creature, when Our Lord had forgiven her her sin, as has been written before, had a desire to see those places where He was born, and where He suffered

8. **semblable:** similar ones.

His Passion,[9] and where He died, with other holy places where He was in His life, and also after His resurrection.

As she was in these desires, Our Lord bade her, in her mind, two years ere she went, that she should go to Rome, to Jerusalem and to Saint James,[10] and she would fain have gone but she had no money.

And then she said to Our Lord:—"Where shall I get money to go with to these Holy Places?"

Our Lord answered to her:—"I shall send thee friends enough in divers countries of England to help thee. And, daughter, I shall go with thee in every country and provide for thee, I shall lead thee thither, and bring thee back again in safety. And no Englishman shall die in the ship that thou art in. I shall keep thee from all wicked men's power. And, daughter, I say to thee that I will that thou wearest clothes of white and no other colour, for thou shalt be arrayed after My will."

"Ah! Dear Lord, if I go arrayed in other manner than other chaste women do, I dread the people will slander me. They will say I am a hypocrite and wonder at me."

"Yea, daughter, the more ridicule that thou hast for My love, the more thou pleasest Me."

Then this creature durst not otherwise do than she was commanded in her soul. . . .

So they went forth into the Holy Land till they could see Jerusalem. And when this creature saw Jerusalem, riding on an ass, she thanked God with all her heart, praying Him for His mercy that, as He had brought her to see His earthly city of Jerusalem, He would grant her grace to see the blissful city of Jerusalem above, the city of Heaven. Our Lord Jesus Christ, answering her thought, granted her to have her desire.

Then for the joy she had, and the sweetness she felt in the dalliance with Our Lord, she was on the point of falling off her ass, for she could not bear the sweetness and grace that God wrought in her soul. Then two pilgrims, Duchemen, went to her, and kept her from falling; one of whom was a priest, and he put spices in her mouth to comfort her, thinking she had been sick. And so they helped her on to Jerusalem, and when she came there, she said:—

"Sirs, I pray you be not displeased though I weep sore in this holy place where Our Lord Jesus Christ was quick and dead."

Then went they to the temple in Jerusalem and they were let in on the same day at evensong time, and abode there till the next day at evensong time. Then the friars lifted up a cross and led the pilgrims about from one place to another where Our Lord suffered His[11] . . . and His Passion, every man and woman bearing a wax candle in one hand. And the friars always, as they went about, told them what Our Lord suffered in every place. The aforesaid creature wept

9. **Passion:** the crucifixion.

10. **St. James of Compostella:** a cathedral in northwestern Spain.

11. Word missing in manuscript.

and sobbed as plenteously as though she had seen Our Lord with her bodily eye, suffering His Passion at that time. Before her in her soul she saw Him verily by contemplation, and that caused her to have compassion. And when they came up on to the Mount of Calvary,[12] she fell down because she could not stand or kneel, and rolled and wrested with her body, spreading her arms abroad, and cried with a loud voice as though her heart would have burst asunder; for, in the city of her soul, she saw verily and clearly how Our Lord was crucified. Before her face, she heard and saw, in her ghostly sight, the mourning of Our Lady, of Saint John, and Mary Magdalene and of many others that loved Our Lord.

And she had such great compassion and such great pain, at seeing Our Lord's pain that she could not keep herself from crying and roaring though she should have died for it. And this was the first cry[13] that ever she cried in any contemplation. And this manner of crying endured many years after this time, for aught any man might do, and therefore, suffered she much despite and much reproof. The crying was so loud and so wonderful that it made the people astounded unless they had heard it before, or unless they knew the cause of the crying. And she had them so often that they made her right weak in her bodily might, and especially if she heard of Our Lord's Passion. . . .

[*She returned to England, where her crying upset many people and she was called to appear before the Archbishop of York.*]

On the next day she was brought into the Archbishop's Chapel, and there came many of the Archbishop's retinue, despising her, calling her "Lollard" and "heretic" and swearing many a horrible oath that she should be burnt.

And she, through the strength of Jesus, spoke back to them:—

"Sirs, I dread ye shall be burnt in Hell without end, unless ye amend in your swearing of oaths, for ye keep not the Commandments of God. I would not swear as ye do for all the money in this world."

Then they went away, as if they had been shamed. She then, making her prayer in her mind, asked grace so to be demeaned that day as was most pleasure to God, and profit to her own soul, and good example to her fellow Christians.

Our Lord, answering her, said it should be right well. At the last, the said Archbishop came into the chapel with his clerks, and sharply he said to her:—

"Why goest thou in white? Art thou a maiden?"

She kneeling on her knees before him, said:—

"Nay, sir, I am no maiden. I am a wife."

12. **Calvary:** where Jesus is believed to have been crucified.

13. **cry:** outcry, scream.

He commanded his retinue to fetch a pair of fetters and said she should be fettered, for she was a false heretic.

Then she said:—"I am no heretic, nor shall ye prove me one."

The Archbishop went away and left her standing alone. Then she made her prayers to Our Lord God Almighty to help her and succour her against all her enemies, ghostly and bodily, a long while, and her flesh trembled and quaked wonderfully, so that she was fain to put her hands under her clothes, so that it should not be espied.

Afterwards the Archbishop came again into the Chapel with many clerks, amongst whom was the same doctor who had examined her before, and the monk that had preached against her a little time before in York. Some of the people asked whether she were a Christian woman or a Jew; some said she was a good woman; some said "Nay."

Then the Archbishop took his seat and his clerks also, each of them in his degree, many people being present.

And during the time while the people were gathering together and the Archbishop taking his seat, the said creature stood all behind, making her prayers for help and succour against her enemies with high devotion, so long that she melted all into tears.

And at the last she cried aloud therewith, so that the Archbishop and his clerks and many people had great wonder of her, for they had not heard such crying before. When her crying was passed, she came before the Archbishop and fell down on her knees, the Archbishop saying full boisterously unto her:—

"Why weepest thou, woman?"

She, answering, said:—"Sir, ye shall wish some day that ye had wept as sore as I."

Then anon, the Archbishop put to her the Articles of our Faith,[14] to which God gave her grace to answer well and truly and readily without any great study, so that he might not blame her. Then he said to the clerks:—

"She knoweth her Faith well enough. What shall I do with her?"

The clerks said:—"We know well that she can say the Articles of Faith, but we will not suffer her to dwell amongst us, for the people hath great faith in her dalliance, and, peradventure, she might pervert some of them." . . .

Then said the Archbishop to her:—"Thou shalt swear that thou wilt neither teach nor challenge the people in my diocese."

"Nay, sir, I shall not swear," she said, "for I shall speak of God, and rebuke those that swear great oaths wheresoever I go, unto the time that the Pope and Holy Church hath ordained that no man shall be so bold as to speak of God, for God Almighty forbiddeth not, sir, that we shall speak of Him. And also the Gospel maketh mention that, when the woman had heard Our Lord preach, she

14. **Articles of Faith:** a standard series of questions, in which a person suspected of heresy was asked if he or she believed in the central doctrines of Christianity—the Trinity, the Virgin Birth, the efficacy of the sacraments, heaven and hell, the power of the Pope.

came before Him with a loud voice and said:—'Blessed be the womb that bore Thee, and the teats that gave Thee suck.' Then Our Lord again said to her, 'Forsooth, so are they blessed that hear the word of God and keep it.' And therefore, sir, methinketh that the Gospel giveth me leave to speak of God."

"Ah! Sir," said the clerks, "here wot we well that she hath a devil within her, for she speaketh of the Gospel."

As quickly as possible, a great clerk brought forth a book and laid Saint Paul, for his part, against her, that no woman should preach.[15]

She answering thereto said:—"I preach not, sir; I come into no pulpit, I use but communication and good words, and that I will do while I live." . . .

She, kneeling down on her knees, asked his blessing. He, praying her to pray for him, blessed her and let her go.

Then she, going again to York, was received by many people and full worthy clerks, who rejoiced in Our Lord, Who had given her, unlettered, wit and wisdom to answer so many learned men without disgrace or blame, thanks be to God.

Source 6 from Heresy and Authority in Medieval Europe: Documents in Translation, *edited and with an introduction by Edward Peters. (Philadelphia: University of Pennsylvania Press, 1980), pp. 259–261. Selection translated by Steven Sargent. Reprinted with permission of the publisher.*

6. Testimony from the Inquisition Led by Jacques Fournier, Bishop of Pamiers, 1318–1325

Testimony of Arnaud de Savinhan

"He said that as long as he could remember, which might be about thirty years since he was then about forty-five years old, he had believed completely that God had not made the world, namely heaven, earth, and the elements, but that it had always been existing in and of itself, and was not made by God nor by anyone else. Nevertheless he always had believed that Adam was the first man and that God had made him, and thereafter there had been human generation. But before God had made Adam, the world had lasted infinitely into the past; and he [the witness] did not believe that the world had had a beginning.

"He also said that he had believed for all that time up to the beginning of May in the present year that the world had never had a beginning, and thus that it would never end, and that the world would go on in the same way in the future

15. The first letter to Timothy in the New Testament, which until recently was believed to have been written by the apostle Paul, orders women to keep silent in church.

as it did now; and that just as men were generated now and as they had been generated from Adam onward, there would always be in the future the generation of men, and of vines, and of the other plants, and of all animals; nor would that generation ever end. He believed that there was no other world except the present one."

Testimony of Raimond de l'Aire, of Tignac

An older man told him that a mule has a soul as good as a man's "and from this belief he had by himself deduced that his own soul and those of other men are nothing but blood, because when a person's blood is taken away, he dies. He also believed that a dead person's soul and body both die, and that after death nothing human remains, because he didn't see anything leave the mouth of a person when he dies. From this he believed that the human soul after death has neither good nor evil, and that there is no hell or paradise in another world where human souls are rewarded or punished."

Testimony of Guillemette Benet

"Asked if, since she believed that human souls died with the bodies, she also believed that men would be resurrected and would live again after death, she answered that she did not believe that the resurrecting of the human body would happen, since she believed that as the dead body was buried, the soul was buried with the body; and since she saw that the body putrefied, she believed that it would never be resurrected. . . .

"Asked if she believed that the soul of Jesus Christ, who died on the cross, had died with his body, she answered yes, because although God is not able to die, nevertheless Jesus Christ died and therefore, even though she believed that God always existed, nevertheless she did not believe that Christ's soul lived and existed. . . .

"Asked if she believed that Christ was resurrected, she said yes and that God had done this."

Testimony of Arnaud Gelis, of Pamiers

Arnaud's beliefs	*Roman Catholic orthodoxy*
1. The souls of dead people do not do any other penance except to wander from church to church, some faster, some slower according to their sinfulness.	1. All souls of dead people go to purgatory, where they do the penance they had not completed on earth. And when this is done they go to the heavenly paradise where Christ, Mary, the angels, and the saints reside.

2. After they are finished going around to churches through the streets, the souls go to the place of rest, which is on this earth. They stay there until the judgment day.	2. When their penance is done, the souls of the dead go to the joy of the celestial paradise, which is no place of rest on earth, but rather in heaven.
3. No soul of any man except the most saintly goes directly to heaven or the heavenly kingdom. Souls do this on the day of judgment.	3. All souls of the dead, when their penance is done in purgatory (if they had need of it), enter the heavenly kingdom.
4. Souls of children who died before baptism go to an obscure place until the judgment day. There they feel neither pain nor pleasure. After the judgment day they enter paradise.	4. The souls of unbaptized children will never be saved or enter the kingdom of heaven.
5. No soul of a dead person, no matter how evil, has entered or will enter hell.	5. The souls of all evil persons—i.e., those who perpetrate great crimes that they do not confess or do penance for—go immediately after death to hell, where they stay and are punished for their sins.
6. At the last judgment God will have mercy on all who held the Christian faith and no one will be damned, no matter how evil he was.	6. All souls that held the Christian faith and accepted its sacraments and obeyed its commandments will be saved; but those who, even though holding the faith and accepting the sacraments, did not live according to the commandments will be damned.
7. Christ will have mercy on the souls of all heretics, Jews, and pagans; therefore none of them will be damned.	7. All souls of heretics, pagans, and Jews, who did not want to believe in Christ, will be damned. They will be punished eternally in hell.
8. Human souls, both before the body's death and after, have their own bodily form just like their external body. And the souls have distinct members like hands, eyes, feet, and the rest.	8. Human souls, both while in the body and after its death, because they are spirits, are not corporeal, nor do they have corporeal members, nor do they eat or drink, nor do they suffer such corporeal necessities.
9. Hell is a place only for demons.	9. Hell is a place for demons and for wicked people, where each is punished eternally as he deserves.

Disbelief in Indulgences: Testimony of Guillelme Cornelhano

"He also said that about two years before around the feast of Pentecost . . . a seller of indulgences passed by [him and Guillelma Vilara, wife of Arnald Cuculli] who had with him many indulgences. And after he had left them, Guillelma said, "Do you believe that any man is able to indulge or absolve anyone of his sins? Don't believe it, because no one can absolve anyone except God." And when he himself said that the pope and all priests could absolve man from sins, Guillelma answered that it was not so, only God could [do that]."

Testimony of Peter Sabatier

"When questioned, Peter said and confessed willingly that about three years ago on a certain day in the village of Varillis . . . when he returned from the church [to his house], he said that whatever things the priests and clerics were chanting and singing in the church were lies and tricks; but he never doubted, rather always believed, that the sacraments of the church and its articles of faith were true."

He persisted in this belief "for about a year, and believed out of silliness that priests and clerics, in singing and chanting those things in the church while performing the divine offices, sang and chanted in order to have the contributions, and that there was no good effect wrought by those divine offices."

Source 7 from Norman P. Tanner, editor, Heresy Trials in the Diocese of Norwich, 1428–1431, *Camden Fourth Series, vol. 20 (London: Royal Historical Society, 1977), pp. 111–113. Spelling modernized by Merry E. Wiesner.*

7. A Norwich Heresy Trial, 1428–1431

In the name of God, before you, the worshipful father in Christ, William, by the grace of God bishop of Norwich, I, John Reve, a glover from Beccles in your diocese, your subject, feeling and understanding that I have held, believed, and affirmed errors and heresies which be counted in this confession, that is to say:

That I have held, believed, and affirmed that the sacrament of baptism done in water in the form customary to the church is of no avail and not to be demanded if the father and mother of the child are christened and of Christian beliefs.

Also that the sacrament of confirmation done by a bishop is not profitable or necessary to man's salvation.

Also that confession ought not to be made to any priest, but only to God, for no priest has the power to forgive a man of sin.

Also that I have held, believed and affirmed that no priest has the power to make God's body in the sacrament of the altar, and that after the sacramental words said by a priest at mass nothing remains except a loaf of material bread.

Also that only consent of love in Jesus Christ between a man and woman of Christian beliefs is sufficient for the sacrament of matrimony, without any contract of words or solemnizing in church.

Also that I have held, believed and affirmed that only God has power to make the sacraments, and no other creature.

Also that I have held, believed and affirmed that no creature of Christian belief is required to fast in Lent, on the Umber Days, Fridays, vigils of saints nor any other times which the Church commands should be fasted, but it is lawful for people of Christian beliefs to eat meat at all such times and days. And in affirming this opinion I have eaten meat on Fridays and the other aforementioned days.

Also I have held, believed and affirmed that it is lawful for all Christ's people to do all bodily work on Sundays and all other days which the Church has commanded to be held holy, if people keep themselves from other sins at such days and times.

Also I have held, believed and affirmed that every man may lawfully and without sin withhold and withdraw his tithes and offerings from churches and curates, if it is done prudently.

Also I have held, believed and affirmed that it is lawful for God's people to act contrary to the precepts of the Church.

Also that censures of the Church and sentences of cursing whether from bishops, prelates, or other ordinaries are not to be taken into account or dreaded, for as soon as such bishops or ordinaries curse any man, Christ himself assails him.

Also that I have believed, held, and affirmed that no manner of worship ought to be done to any images of the crucifix, of Our Lady or of any other saints.

Also that no manner of pilgrimages ought to be done to any places of saints, but only to poor people.

Also that I have held and believed that it is not lawful to swear in any case.

Also that I have held, believed, and affirmed that the pope of Rome is the Antichrist and has no power in the Holy Church as St. Peter had unless he follows in the steps of Peter in his manner of living.

Also that all bishops, prelates and priests of the Church are the Antichrist's disciples.

Also that I have held, believed and affirmed that it is as meritorious and as profitable to all Christ's people to be buried in meadows or in wild fields as it is to be buried in churches or churchyards.

Because of which and many other errors and heresies which I have held, believed, and affirmed within your diocese, I am called before you, worshipful father, who has the cure of my soul. And you are fully informed that the said my holding, believing, and affirming are judged errors and heresies and contrary to the Church of Rome, wherefore I willingly follow the doctrine of holy Church and depart from all manner of heresy and error and turn with good heart and will to the unity of the Church. Considering that holy Church will not spare her bosom to him that will return nor God will the death of a sinner but rather that he be returned and live, with a pure heart I confess, detest and despise my said errors and heresies, and the said opinions I confess as heretical and erroneous and repugnant to the faith of the Church at Rome and all universal holy Church. And for as much as I showed myself corrupt and unfaithful through the said things that I so held, believed, and affirmed, from henceforth I will show myself uncorrupt and faithful, and I promise to keep the faith and doctrine of the holy Church truly. And I abjure and forswear all manner of error and heresy, doctrine and opinion against the holy Church and the determination of the Church of Rome—namely the opinions listed before—and swear by these holy gospels which I am bodily touching that from henceforth I shall never hold error nor heresy nor false doctrine against the faith of holy Church and the determination of the Church of Rome. No such things shall I obstinately defend. I shall defend no person holding or teaching such things openly or privately. I shall never after this time be an assistor, counselor, or defender of heretics or of any person suspected of heresy. I shall never ally myself with them. I shall not wittingly show fellowship to them, nor give them counsel, gifts, succor, favor, or comfort. If I know any heretics or any persons suspected of heresy, or people who counsel, assist or defend them, or any persons holding private conventicles or meetings, or holding any singular opinions different from the common doctrine of the Church, I shall let you, worshipful father, or your vicar general in your absence or the diocesans of such persons know soon and immediately. So help me God at holy doom and these holy gospels.

In witness of which things I subscribe here with my own hand a cross—X. And to this part intended to remain in your register I set my sign. And that other part I receive with your seal to keep with me until my life's end. Given at Norwich in the chapel of your palace, xviii day of the month of April in the year of our Lord one thousand four hundred and thirty.

Source 8 from Bavarian National Museum, Munich.

8. Madonna, Germany, ca 1430

9. Crucifix, Germany, 14th century

QUESTIONS TO CONSIDER

The written sources and the religious statues have provided you with evidence for the two central questions of this chapter. Looking again at those questions, you can see that the first concerns the religious beliefs and practices of laypeople, and the second the official Church reaction to those beliefs and practices. You now need to sort through the sources to separate the information you have gained about each question.

Look first at lay piety itself. Which Christian beliefs were numbers of people attracted to? Why were these beliefs especially appealing? Why might it have been difficult for most people to respond to more esoteric points of theology such as the Trinity? Many of the sources have described or depicted the extremely important role of the Virgin Mary in lay piety. Why do you think people turned to her, rather than to God the Father, in their prayers and devotions? In official Christian theology, Mary is not a goddess but completely human, and believers were urged to honor but not to worship her. From the sources, do you think most laypeople understood this distinction? Looking at the first sermon story, which relates beliefs and practices approved of by the Church, was this distinction always made clear to laypeople?

You have seen that for most people, religion was not simply a matter of belief but also involved real-world practices and acts. What practices were most popular? How did people see these as contributing to their spiritual lives? One of the sermon stories, the life of St. Nicholas, and the works of Bridget and Margery Kempe refer matter-of-factly to visions and miracles. What does this imply about the divisions between the natural and the supernatural in most people's minds?

The two heresy trials record beliefs that deviated from those that were officially accepted. Do you find evidence of similar beliefs, though perhaps not carried so far, in any of the other sources? For example, what religious beliefs and practices of Margery Kempe opened her to the accusation of heresy? How would you compare the two heresies from the sources reprinted here? Does either appear to deviate further from official Church teachings than the other? Which teachings do both dispute? Can you make any generalizations about late medieval heresy from these examples, or are the differences between them more striking than the similarities?

Now turn to the second question. Official Church reaction to lay piety was both positive and negative. Positive reactions included attempts by preachers and priests to shape popular belief and to encourage certain actions that they felt strengthened the Church. Judging by the sermon stories and the life of St. Nicholas, what beliefs and practices were preachers and hagiographers trying to encourage? Did the religious statuary encourage similar ideas? How did the archbishop try to influence Margery Kempe? Negative reactions included the Church's attempts to eradicate unacceptable beliefs and behavior, with sanctions ranging from mild scoldings to execution for heresy. Judging from the heresy trials and Margery Kempe's autobiography, what kinds of beliefs were Church officials especially worried about? Did they appear to be more concerned with beliefs or with behavior?

Many of those charged with heresy or with suspect beliefs in the late Middle Ages were women, and the Church hierarchy was of course totally male. Thinking particularly of the experience of Margery Kempe, do you find evidence of gender differences in official attitudes toward lay piety? Even women whose ideas were initially accepted could later be judged heretical. For example, Bridget of Sweden was made a saint less than twenty years after her death, but only forty years later the authenticity of her visions was questioned and she was dismissed by some Church officials as a chatterbox deluded by the devil. Do you find anything in the visions printed here that might have been disturbing to the all-male clerical establishment?

Both lay piety and the official reaction to it were shaped by political and economic factors as well as by theology and doctrine. From your sources, which beliefs and practices encouraged or condemned by the Church would have had economic repercussions? Especially in the Norwich heresy trial, which ideas did the Church view as a political threat? Why would the ideas expressed in that trial have been seen as more dangerous than those of Margery Kempe? Reread the discussion in your text of the political and economic changes that late medieval Europe experienced. How was the Church involved in these changes? Do your sources provide evidence for any of the developments described in your text?

You are now ready to answer the two central questions of this chapter: How did common people in the Middle Ages experience and express their religious faith? How did the Church as an institution respond to laypeople's beliefs and practices? Are your answers more complex or less complex than you expected?

EPILOGUE

Most of the strong lay piety in the late Middle Ages remained inside the boundaries judged acceptable by the Church. Groups branded as heretics were usually small, and they were quite successfully wiped out by intensive inquisitions and campaigns of persecution such as those carried out against the Albigensians and Lollards.

Persecution did not put an end to dissatisfaction with the institutional Church, however, nor were preachers and priests ever able to exert total control over the beliefs or activities of common people. Indeed, the more historians study the beliefs of "unlearned" people, the more they discover that people do not passively absorb what they are told but add their own ideas to it. Illiteracy does not preclude imagination or intelligence, and influence between the learned elite and the common people runs in both directions.

Though lay dissatisfaction persisted, it did not cause the institutional Church to change or initiate reforms during the late Middle Ages. In 1377, the papacy returned to Rome, and when the pope died the following year the Roman people forced the college of cardinals, the body of church officials that chooses the pope, to elect an Italian pope. This pope, Urban VI, tried to institute reforms aimed at some of the Church's problems, but he did so in such a belligerent way that he set most of the college of cardinals against him. They responded by declaring that the pope's election was invalid because they had been put under duress and, calling for his resignation, elected another pope. Urban did not step down, however, and a forty-year power split began in which two and later three popes simultaneously excommunicated the others, collected taxes, made appointments, and granted indulgences. The Great Schism, as this period is called, was probably the low point in the history of organized Christianity in the West, but the eventual reunification of the Church in 1417 did not resolve all problems. For the next century, the popes concentrated their energies on artistic patronage and expansion of their political power in Italy. Despite several major attempts at reform and increasing recognition of internal problems by many Church officials and scholars throughout Europe, low standards of discipline and morality, and high levels of corruption, persisted.

Martin Luther's break with the Catholic church in the early sixteenth century began as yet another attempt at reform but quickly grew into a revolution that split Western Christianity from that time on. The swift and widespread acceptance of Luther's ideas gave vivid testimony to the depth of popular dissatisfaction with the Church. At the very beginning, at least, common people in many parts of Germany saw the Protestant Reformation as the change they had been looking for, a movement that emphasized personal piety and played down the priest's role in the individual's salvation. However, while they supported Luther initially, they quickly realized that he was not the leader they had hoped for and that he was attacking many of the practices, such as pilgrimages or the veneration of Mary, that were dearest to them. Thus the strong lay piety movement of the late Middle Ages is an important factor in understanding not just medieval Christianity in all its complexity but the roots of the Reformation as well.